MANAGERIAL CONTROL OF BUSINESS

MANAGERIAL CONTROL OF BUSINESS

Editor-in-Chief
George T. Trundle, Jr.

Associate Editor
S. A. Peck

Contributing Editors

W. E. Savage

R. C. Trundle

R. P. Brooks

H. L. Wood

C. A. Hyre

C. O. Malpas

A. Dangler, Jr.

JOHN WILEY & SONS, INC., NEW YORK
CHAPMAN & HALL, LTD., LONDON

FOREWORD

M any years of service to and contact with the managements of American industry and business have convinced us of the urgent need for an organized explanation of the manner in which techniques of management are developed and applied to an enterprise.

The material presented in the following pages is based on an extensive and practical experience covering 29 years of management engineering service to every type and size of enterprise.

This book will bring to executives generally the management practices that have made many enterprises enduring and profitable. In writing it we have had in mind particularly the average-sized company which, owing to its limited size, cannot permanently employ the specialized staff talents for management and industrial engineering in its plant.

It is important today that the average-sized company know and apply the correct tools of control and the proper principles of management to its own operation. It is our hope that this book will enable such companies to adapt these well-established and proved practices and principles to their own use; and so we have endeavored in this text to discuss every phase of management from the viewpoint of its importance to the typical manufacturing operation.

Many general subjects of sociological significance in the field of human relations and much voluminous technical detail usually supplied in handbooks have been purposely omitted from the text. This has been done in order to outline and discuss in detail the approaches to and solutions of the many operating and financial problems which a company faces in today's complex economy. For the same reason only a very few case examples are used to amplify the text, in spite of their apparent desirability to emphasize the points made or the results achieved.

The text is divided into five sections. The first section, "Analyzing the Company Operation," deals in a condensed form with the over-all study to determine the kind and degree of existing problems. This analysis is necessary, in whole or in part, because a problem that is not defined is usually a problem that cannot be solved. No improvements can be made and no economies can be effected unless this first step is taken.

Later sections cover in more detail the solutions of problems uncovered by the study outlined in Section 1, and, as is noted in Section 1, are cross-indexed by chapter to the specific chapters in this section.

In Section 4, particularly, the chapters on maintenance, production control, and labor control spell out in detail their application to a manufacturing enterprise. Owing to their importance in any plant producing goods for sale to the American consumer, the treatment of these subjects has been as specific and explicit as it is possible to be on such matters.

I am greatly indebted to my many associates for their untiring effort and unstinted attention to the task of bringing this book to the point of publication, particularly S. A. Peck, W. E. Savage, R. C. Trundle, R. P. Brooks, Jr., H. L. Wood, C. A. Hyre, C. O. Malpas, and A. Dangler, Jr. To these men fell the task of collecting and preparing the material, drawn from the experience of our entire staff, used in the book.

I also wish to acknowledge the kind permission of McGraw-Hill Book Company, to include, in the first part of Chapter 29, Section 4, a condensation of our chapter on Production Control originally written and published in Donald's *Handbook of Business Administration* in 1931.

GEORGE T. TRUNDLE, JR.

C O N T E N T S

SECTION 5   INDUSTRIAL RELATIONS

THE ECONOMICS
OF BUSINESS

•

Only when man's genius for profits went into partnership with engineering—in research, invention and manufacture—were men and materials, the raw stuff of nature, converted into civilization.—Geo. T. Trundle, Jr.

FUNDAMENTAL PRINCIPLE

The economic purpose of any enterprise engaged in the production of goods for sale is to make a profit (pay wages) for the venture capital that created and supports that enterprise.

The enterprise may have other purposes, social or political, and the profit may not necessarily be in money; *but a profit there must be,* whether the enterprise is a factory, a club, or a philharmonic orchestra. Otherwise it will eventually wither away.

This is the fundamental principle of the American economy. Without this *profit motive* American industry could not have attained world leadership. Our entire economy is based on this principle of free enterprise, as it is frequently called. It is a heritage handed down to present-day management by the founding fathers of our system of democratic society.

There have been many contributing factors to this principle: a virgin country rich in raw material resources; a vigorous growing people impatient of Old World restraints; and an ingenuity and a capacity for industrial genius that seems to have been inherent in Americans, and particular to the industrial environment of the United States.

An enterprise may fall into any one of three classifications. It may be a *business* engaged in commerce, trade, or service, such as public transportation, a retail store, or a laundry. It may be an *industry* engaged in the manufacture of goods, or conversion of materials. It may be a *farming* operation devoted solely to the growing of foodstuffs or other materials for eventual human consumption or use.

For the purposes of this introduction, however, the term *business* is used in its more general meaning as applying to all human busyness in any profit-making activities that concern our economy.

In later sections of this book *industry* has been considered the basic type of enterprise, because there *is no business* without industry. It is evident from the most casual analysis that at least three jobs are created (in transportation, selling, and service) for every job that industry creates for itself. This is the miracle of our economy; the more we produce, the more jobs are created and the higher becomes our standard of living.

COMPLEXITIES OF MODERN BUSINESS

Years ago, when our national economy was less complex than it is today, the economics of a business involved but a simple pattern. Labor was closely integrated into the community and industry; its wants were simple and easily satisfied. Materials were readily available because mass production had not yet been born. Modern specialized industrial requirements had not yet been developed. The problems of organization and distribution were easily met because of the local character of all business in that era.

Today the effects of a national labor ideology on the delicate merchandising balance of a fully integrated economic system, closely knit by modern methods of communication and transportation, make the problem of keeping a business secure and profitable one of grave import to every manager.

In addition, as an aftermath of global war, American industry faces two other factors which gravely affect its future well-being: (1) an enlarged capacity for production, the potential limits of which are not really appreciated, and (2) a revision and development of industrial technology that has largely started on its way.

None of these problems of labor, materials, merchandising, production capacity, or technological advance tends to simplify the administration of an enterprise. On the contrary, they merely add to the difficulties that have beset management since American industry emerged from the handicraft stage. Yet in spite of all these problems, American industry has been and can be as profitable as management's ability permits it to be. But only if management applies the same genius to control that it has applied to engineering and manufacturing.

Profits and Volume

Essential to the control of a business is a thorough knowledge of its profits and volume relationship. This includes the point of volume at which the company "breaks even" with neither profit nor loss; its cost of being in business, that is, the stand-by or fixed expense; and the rate of profit on sales volume above the break-even point.

These relatively simple relationships are basic in the economics of a business. Without an understanding of them, management has made and can make unwise decisions affecting every phase of the company's operation. Prices may be set and details of operation established that merely intensify the difficulties or losses it is currently experiencing.

Full cognizance of their meaning and importance, on the other hand, places management in a position of positive assurance that its decisions and actions have been properly guided and correctly applied.

The implications of the profit–volume relationship are manifold. Every action in manufacturing, administration, and merchandising contributes to and is affected by this relationship. The manager who violates the fundamental precepts contained in it has entered on his ledger of accomplishment a debit that will not be balanced off easily.

THE ECONOMIC ELEMENTS

Generally speaking, there are six economic elements that require the careful consideration of the management of every business. They are:

1. Products—without which there is no enterprise.
2. Markets—where the product is sold and the profit is realized.
3. Organization—which includes every employee from the president down to the janitor, and embraces all human effort in the enterprise.
4. Facilities—the means of production, including everything which contributes to the placing of the product on the shipping dock—the buildings and machinery, as well as the office equipment.
5. Materials—out of which the products are made or which contribute to their manufacture, including not only raw materials, but also supplies, paper forms, etc.
6. Finances—the venture capital which makes the enterprise a going institution, and provides the blood stream necessary to its life.

1. Products

Americans are a peculiar people, as we have often been told. We buy what we *want,* not what we *need.* Perhaps that is why our standard of living is the highest in the world; we have gratified our desires and have not been content with merely satisfying our needs.

The problem of gratifying these desires has been met by the inventive genius and resourcefulness typical of American industry. Products have been developed, and sold, *and bought,* starting an endless spiral of production and buying power whose potential limits are only subject to our inefficiencies.

As the principal element in the economics of a business, the product necessarily deserves first consideration in determining the direction, scope, and stability of an enterprise. The first attention must be given to two fundamental factors: the type of income market to be reached (that is, low-, medium-, or high-priced), and the proper and complete engineering of the product itself.

This means that facilities for manufacture take a lower place in the sequence of consideration than is frequently allotted this question. To buy a plant before a product is finally decided on and fully engineered, because it is cheap or quickly available, or because it would be a possible monument to manager or owners of the enterprise, is as inconsistent with sound business practice as buying a suit of clothes for a man without knowing his size, taste, and personality.

Because products and markets go hand in hand, the two must be considered together, before too much detailed attention is given to the other four economic elements. It is logical, therefore, to consider the market next.

2. Markets

There is no profit until the product is sold. The marketing of a product, if it is presumed that the price is correct and the necessary facilities for distribution are adequate, requires people who want to buy it: customers, in a word. If the product is something people want, the available market takes into consideration only two elements: the number of people who are potential customers, and the number and strength of competitors.

Outside of certain special situations, all markets are expressible in terms of their population and their occupational and geographical character, that is, agricultural, industrial, urban, southern zone, and so on.

Reaching the market involves three important factors:

1. An acceptable product.
2. A satisfactory price—to both seller and buyer.
3. Adequate methods of selling and distribution.

All three of these factors reach back into the internal operation of a business.

A product acceptable to the consumer presumes good functional design and easy servicing—both matters of sound engineering practice for field applications as well as for manufacture.

A satisfactory price presumes good manufacturing methods, low costs, proper control of quality and quantity, and a realistic conception of the enterprise's function—to earn a profit.

Adequate selling methods presume a good sales organization; adequate sales controls; and an intimate knowledge of the buying habits, purchasing power, volume potentiality, and competition of the area being exploited.

3. Organization

Andrew Carnegie once said, "Take away my mills, but leave me my organization and I will be back in business in a year." Until the breath of human attention and effort is blown on inanimate equipment, it produces nothing, no matter how perfectly it may be adapted to the purposes of production. Conversely, equipment, no matter how inadequate, can, with human care and sufficient human effort, be made productive to a degree that may or may not be profitable.

Organization, which is the aggregate sum of all the people in the business, is therefore the next important element in the economics of a business. It is the nervous system of an enterprise, controlling the muscles of production, the flow of the blood of finance, and the physical effort of the entire body of the company itself. Organization is the *vital* element that animates the entire operation and determines its destiny in the economic system of which it is a part.

Third only to the product itself, organization is of primary importance, therefore, in the internal aspects of a business. From this viewpoint it must be seriously reckoned with in computing the end result—profitable operation.

4. Facilities

A business structure without proprietorship of its plant and equipment subjects itself to the hazard of eviction from the economic system. Certain types of business can and do operate with very meager facilities. This is true even of certain types of manufacturing operation, although to a lesser extent. Such enterprises, although profitable to their entrepreneurs, can hardly claim to add to the productive wealth of the American economy. Certainly they lack the permanency associated with truly productive enterprise.

If it is assumed then that physical facilities are an essential element, their degree of effectiveness becomes a measure of their profitableness. Money invested in the brick walls of a factory is completely sterile beyond a certain point of building obsolescence. This is also true, to a certain extent, of machinery and other productive and nonproductive equipment.

The point at which this obsolescence occurs is most important. Many industries get along very well with what they have in buildings and equipment, provided technological advance has not been too rapid and a reasonable degree of improvement on existing facilities has been made. On the other hand, barring inflationary or speculative values placed on facilities desired, there is no reason why an enterprise should handicap itself with inadequate structures and machinery when modern low-cost units can be acquired at a satisfactory price.

Although facilities, the means of production, are the fourth element in the economics of a business, that is not necessarily their position of importance in relation to the other elements involved. Their importance must be measured by the external factors that affect the enterprise. These include volume, selling prices, technological advance in processes and equipment, and the profitableness of the enterprise itself.

5. Materials

We have been a prodigal nation in the use of our natural resources and now find ourselves fearful of seeing the bottom of the barrel. The global war accelerated the consumption of many of our basic materials. The natural growth of the country, requiring wider use of the materials with which nature so bountifully supplied us, has made this problem a matter of deep concern to our whole economic system.

The old saying that it is an ill wind that blows no good finds fitting application here. Dire necessity, born of the war, has been instrumental in bringing forth new materials and new applications to take the place of those so rapidly squandered. These new materials and new applications have presented and continue to present an ever-widening opportunity in the fields of product research and development.

World War II caused many years of normal development to

be telescoped into the few years of the war's duration, under the spur of national self-preservation. Today science has furnished industry with a cornucopia that is pouring out materials undreamt of a generation ago. Industry now has some assurance that no enterprise will be completely hobbled by vanishing resources of materials and can safely chart its course for continued stable and profitable operation.

Raw materials alone are not all the substances required by industry. There are many other materials contributory to the manufacture of the basic product. Their availability also enters largely into the company picture and makes it necessary to view the problem of materials as a total of many things rather than a single itemization.

Except in rare instances, materials are the largest element of cost in the sales dollar and deserve the fullest attention of management in projecting or controlling operation. It must be borne in mind that the raw material of one company is the finished product of its vendor, back through every phase of its transformation. In the last analysis the cost of products of American industry is composed largely of labor. Therefore, consideration of material in the economics of a business must also take into account the labor content in the material itself. The company's course of action necessarily will be influenced by this fact in its long-term projections.

6. Finances

Last but not least, consideration must be given to the life blood of business—money. There are two phases to this aspect of an enterprise:

1. The venture capital that starts the business.
2. The working capital that provides for its continuing operation.

Every business starts with venture capital—the money put into it. Sometimes the investment is very small at the start and remains so if the business is successful and prospers moderately. If the business expands beyond its ability to finance itself out of earnings, or is not sufficiently profitable, additional venture capital must be furnished until adequate working capital is available.

Working capital has two sources. Part of it may and should come from the money put into the enterprise as a venture investment, and part of it should come from the profits secured through the actual operation of the enterprise. In all successful companies, the working capital must turn frequently. This is merely another way of saying that the current assets should be extremely liquid at all times.

CONCLUSION

It is apparent from the brief discussion of these subjects that the economics of business involve something more than merely marking up cost to provide a desired margin of income. The mark-up is very necessary, but it can only yield a profit if all six economic elements have been properly considered and integrated into an effective pattern of accomplishment. Such accomplishment can result only if there is a keen awareness on the part of management of the necessity for promptly translating good judgment into decisive action.

Finally, the entire structure of elements requires a careful bonding for successful integration. Like the mortar that binds the bricks into a wall, *control* binds the elements of an enterprise into a going profitable operation. Control is therefore an essential method of management and consists of four major steps:

1. Defining the objective, or, as more commonly phrased, setting the standard.
2. Comparing actual performance with the standard set.
3. Analyzing the difference, or determining the cause for the variances.
4. Applying corrective action.

A management alert to the advantages which present-day control techniques afford need have little fear of results if these techniques are intelligently applied and vigorously executed. And it will also find that the economics of business are easily turned to the advantage of the enterprise for which it is responsible.

1

*Analyzing the
Company Operation*

CHAPTER 1

PROFIT–VOLUME
RELATIONSHIPS

•

GENERAL CONSIDERATION

The fundamental problem of any business enterprise is to determine whether or not it is operating profitably; and, if not, why not.

The chief executive of a company must have this consideration constantly in mind, if he wishes to operate his company with the proper financial advantage to his stockholders and to his entire organization, and to insure continuity of operation to his employees and service to his customers.

To arm himself with these facts requires a close and factual knowledge of every phase of the operation. This is best gained by an organized study of all of the factors that enter into the operation.

It is the purpose of this section of the manual to outline briefly the various steps and procedures necessary to attain this knowledge. To assist the reader in correlating this section with the remainder of the text, the following chart will be helpful in relating each of its chapters with the corresponding solution chapters:

ANALYSIS		SOLUTION	
Section No.	Chapter No.	Section No.	Chapter Nos.
1	1. Profit–Volume Relationships	2 3	15, 17 20
1	2. Product	3	20
1	3. Sales Volume	2 3	12 20, 21, 24
1	4. Organization	2 4	12, 13, 14 25
1	5. Financial Controls	2 4	15, 16, 17, 18 30, 33
1	6. Selling	3	21, 22, 23, 24
1	7. Manufacturing	2 4	13, 14 25–32 incl.
1	8. Engineering and Research	3	20
1	9. Compensation and Incentives	2 3 4 5	19 23 31 35
1	10. Costing and Pricing Methods	2 3 4	15, 17 22 31, 33
1	11. Industrial Relations	5	34, 35, 36

Naturally the very first thing any manager or owner is interested in is the profit–volume relationship of his company, that is, the relation of his profits and losses, if any, to the variations in volume which his company experiences.

ACCOUNT ANALYSIS

This information may be gained either by study of the over-all figures or by a detailed analysis of the various income and expense amounts that enter into the books of account. The latter method is so superior and so essential to the attainment of real control over the company operation that no other method should be attempted.

This over-all analysis starts with the general books of account, to determine, over any selected period of years or months, the *income* from sales, investments, and the like in their respective categories. The *outgo* figures must then be broken down into separate accounts, if not already provided for by the accounting system.

Each account requires analysis to determine how it has been influenced by the activity of the business during the periods under consideration. It is evident that certain accounts like depreciation and taxes are not affected by the degree of business activity. Others, like direct labor and factory supplies, are completely dependent on production activity. To determine which expenses are fixed with relation to the activity that creates them and which are variable, use a combination of visual and graphical analysis.

Accounts that show minor or no fluctuation, regardless of sales or production activities, may be set aside as fixed expense accounts. Those that range between noticeable limits as business activity varies are probably variable or a combination of fixed and variable. Because this relationship is important, it must be determined as precisely as possible. This is best done by the graphical method described in Section 2, Chapters 15 and 17.

FIXED AND VARIABLE EXPENSE

After this relationship has been completed, the operating statement will then appear as follows for each month or other period chosen:

Total income from sales		$xxxxx
Total costs	Fixed	Variable
Labor (direct)		$xxxxx
Material (direct)		$xxxxx
Factory overhead	$xxxxx	$xxxxx
Admin. expense	$xxxxx	
Selling expense	$xxxxx	$xxxxx
Other expense	$xxxxx	$xxxxx
Total	$xxxxx	$xxxxx

The next step is to reduce the variable costs to percentages of the sales dollar. The statement then becomes as follows:

Total income from sales		100.00%
Variable costs only:		
Labor	15%	
Material	30%	
Factory overhead	15%	
Admin. expense	4%	
Sell. expense	10%	
Other	1%	
Total	75%........	75.00%
Difference		25.00%

MARGINAL INCOME

It is apparent that there is a spread (termed marginal income) between the sales dollar and the sum of all the variable expenses of 25 per cent. Only out of this margin can the fixed expenses and the net profit be paid.

If the fixed expenses shown in blank amount above are assumed to be $10,000 and the total sales to be $50,000, the important profit–volume relationships are then determinable:

(a) The break-even point of volume at which no profit or loss is shown is the fixed expense, $10,000, divided by the marginal income, 25 per cent; or $40,000.

(b) The net profit is $50,000, less fixed expense ($10,000), less variable expense (75 per cent × $50,000 = $37,500), or $2,500, which is 5 per cent.

(*c*) The break-even point, $40,000, is at 80 per cent of the sales volume of $50,000.

BREAK-EVEN POINT

These relationships are illustrated in more detail in Section 2. They may also be determined directly from the monthly state-

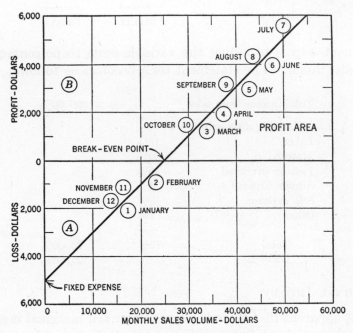

FIG. 1.   Profit–Volume Chart

ment by plotting or charting each month's profit against the month's sales for a period of 10 to 12 months, as illustrated in Figure 1 (a typical marginal income chart).

PRODUCT ANALYSIS

After this relationship is found for the over-all operation, the same procedure should be carried through for each line of products, providing the bookkeeping records permit such determinations.

It has been found that the following ratios represent the limiting ranges for good operation:

(a) Marginal income should never be less than 15 per cent or more than 35 per cent; 25 per cent is a normal amount.

(b) The break-even point should represent 50 to 60 per cent of the average and normal volume.

After these analyses have been made, products with low marginal incomes should be segregated and examined as to their costs, pricing policies, and design. Steps may then be taken to correct whichever appears to be primarily responsible for the low marginal income and the consequent low net profit.

CHAPTER 2

PRODUCT

•

Market Acceptability

Frequently, analysis of the profit–volume relationship is not conclusive as to the causes for low profit operation. But, even if such an analysis is quite definitive, a study should still be made of the product or products to determine the market acceptability of the line.

Quality

The determination as to quality can be made by statistical research and actual studies in the field, to determine if the product is acceptable to the trade and if the pricing of the entire line is suitable to the market in which it is being offered. Such points as reputation, need, and performance should be carefully investigated.

Pricing

Quality usually speaks for itself in the returns and allowances which must be made to customers. To determine if the pricing is right two factors must be considered:

1. The price must be sufficiently high to permit reasonable profit at the volume actually attained.
2. The price must be sufficiently low to secure consumer acceptance.

Design and Styling

It is not easy to attain this happy balance between price and quality. Market study may show that the design, styling, and packaging are detrimental to full acceptance. The study should therefore query the mass consumer or manufacturer consumer on these points and endeavor to learn how the product should be designed to meet the purpose intended. At the same time the inquiry should be pointed toward the possibility for new products that might fit the consumer's requirement as well as the production and marketing facilities of the company.

COMPETITION

The next and equally important question to consider in conducting the product market study is that of competition. A good deal of this work can be conducted in the home office. It chiefly involves a comparison of prices and products and an examination of the patent situation affecting the company's products and those of competitors. This information can also be secured in the field, but it is not always reliable and certainly not always complete. A careful program to secure these data through the auspices of the company's own office will ordinarily supply the required information.

PRODUCT LINES

The final step in completing the product market study consists of assembling the information thus far secured and determining from it the completeness of the company's line of products, with respect to both its present products and the new or related products discovered to be suitable. Although many attractive possibilities may have been uncovered, great care should be exercised so that the company should not become committed to additional products that do not fit naturally into its facilities. They may require radical new conceptions as to organization and distribution, unless they can be developed as a part of a well-co-ordinated plan to expand the company's activities.

CHAPTER 3

SALES VOLUME

.

Sales Trends

The direction of a company's operation is usually revealed by an analysis of its volume trends. Although an inspection of the sales records is revealing over a period of years and months, a more conclusive method is to chart such information as shown in Figures 2 and 3.

Figure 2 illustrates the cyclical trend of sales volume over the years and indicates the effect of economic and technological factors on a company's operation as a whole. Similar charts made up for each product will indicate the detailed effect of such influences and serve to guide future merchandising and manufacturing policies.

Figure 3 illustrates the method of determining the seasonal trend of the company operation. The superimposition of several years on the same chart will indicate the consistency of such effects. This procedure should be carried through for each line of products or for each product as may be required.

Potentials

The determination of volume potential follows, more or less easily, by the cyclical trend being projected into the future. Such projections, however, must be carefully qualified by the following limiting conditions:

1. The potential saturation point of the market.
2. The degree and permanency of competition.

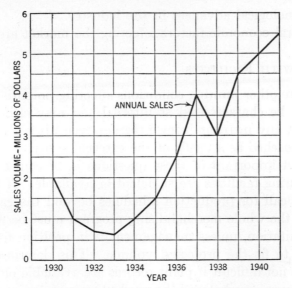

FIG. 2.   Cyclical Trend of Sales Volume

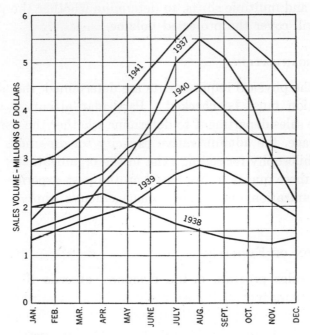

FIG. 3.   Seasonal Trend of Sales Volume

3. Technological advances in the industry.

4. General economic factors affecting the market area.

BALANCE WITH FACILITIES

There are other limiting conditions affecting potential volume. They may be characterized as internal and may either expand or contract any merchandising program even after a conclusion has been reached as a result of the external study.

The most important of these questions is, of course, whether manufacturing facilities are sufficient or available. If projected operations call for production schedules beyond the capacity of the plant, the whole merchandising program must be reoriented to this limitation, unless management is in position to consider expansion to fit the projected volume. This determination of capacity is not difficult if plant records are available on tonnage, machine-hours, or whatever the production measure of the plant may be. Schedules can be drawn up from these data, on a basis of single and multiple shifts, to determine whether the potential output will cover the projected volume.

SALES ORGANIZATION

After the physical requirements are determined, the matter of organization must be checked. Particular attention must be given the sales department to determine whether the man power for coverage, the administrative capacity for direction, and the proper philosophy for selling exist in the organization. The answers to these questions are based on the past experience of the sales organization and general management's appraisal of the problem.

EXPANSION OF FACILITIES

If the sales program of the company exceeds the available facilities, management immediately faces an expansion problem that may have serious implications. If the desired expansion can take place, and *should* take place, at the present site, the problem is a financial one primarily. It can be handled as an internal operating problem.   If, however, the potential market involves volume and distribution on a scale that shipping rates, labor, and raw material resources cannot satisfy by local expansion, then the company is involved in a major problem.

When this is the case, the whole project must be reviewed. Further studies must be made of the economic and merchandising factors involved and a balance struck off that will give the optimum advantage to the decision reached.   Generally speaking, the major influence in this decision should be whether the distribution of the product will be best served by a local expansion or by the location of satellite plants in strategic marketing points.

CHAPTER 4

ORGANIZATION

•

Importance

The real strength of a company lies in its organization. It is important, therefore, that management take a close look at its organization structure, to make sure that its functional relationships are correctly spelled out and understood by its members.

Organization Charts

If no organization charts exist, they should be made. Organization charts express the lines of authority and responsibility as they currently exist among the technical, operating, and control functions of the company.

Figure 4 shows a typical form of organization chart and illustrates the general practice in organization relationships. Although there are several kinds of organization charts (see Section 2, Chapter 12) for this management purpose, the type of chart shown is sufficient. It delineates the extent of co-ordination between the line and staff functions.

Organization Manuals

Few companies have organization manuals which detail, in an orderly way, the position title, the function, the responsibilities, and the detail duties required of each executive. Management should have each position incumbent write up his job in this manner and then compare these write-ups with the organization

chart it has had prepared. The comparison will be revealing. It
will indicate where lack of understanding and confusion exist

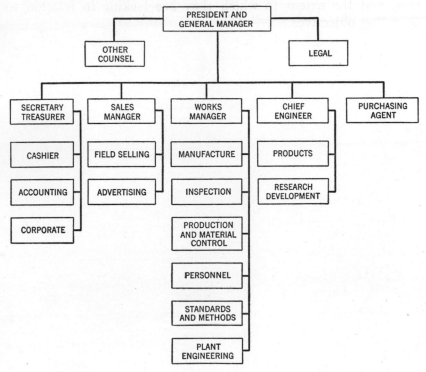

Fig. 4.   General Practice in Organization Relationship

with respect to functional responsibility and will point out the
obvious corrections that must be made to carry out the policies
of the company.

Policies

At this point management needs to look inwardly at its own
function. All companies operate under a code of policies. They
are seldom written out as such, but are reflected in instructions,
memoranda, rules, and the like, that have been issued as individual situations arose which required statements of management policy.

These should be collected and compiled in orderly form and examined with respect to their consistency, their effect on past operations, the effect they may have on the future of the business, and the extent to which they are lacking in relation to operating objectives.

CHAPTER 5

FINANCIAL CONTROLS

•

BUDGETS

The financial controls of a company lie in the financial and accounting functions of its operation.

The most important control and the one most frequently lacking is the budgetary control. If the company has none, the degree of financial control which management has been able to exercise can be ascertained by comparing its operating statements and balance sheets for the preceding years. Such comparisons merely reflect historical results and do not show performance against predetermined objectives. Conclusions thus derived are seldom valid.

When budgets have been established and validated over a period of years, their effectiveness and adequacy must be determined in the light of current operation. The following checks should be made:

1. Flexibility. Does the budget provide for self-adjustment to varying degrees of operation? If sales show an increase of 10 per cent over the forecast or objective, will the budgeted profit be automatically adjusted to this change?

2. Detail tie-in with selling, manufacturing, and accounting. Does the budget compare, in its detailed formulation, with the compilation of actual results in the books of account? Does it use as its basis of performance measure the actual results that have been thus recorded?

3. Promptness and accuracy of comparisons between perform-ance and standards. Does the budget accurately reflect the stand-ards periodically revised to match the conditions to which they apply? Can variances from the budget be traced to their source so that corrective action can be taken?

4. Method and promptness of presentation to executives. Does the budgetary control provide for a systematic form of reporting within a few days after the books of account are closed?

Negative answers to any of these questions will show manage-ment the need for the control necessary to profitable operation.

ACCOUNTING PROCEDURES

Following the budget closely and intimately related to it are the company's accounting procedures, particularly the matter of complete, prompt, and accurate entry of all transactions. If accounting procedures do not provide for daily or current entry, little control can be exercised. Management will have no cur-rent authentic information on which to base its decisions and actions.

The following detail checks should be made of the accounting procedures and conclusions drawn as to whether the system is operating satisfactorily and meeting afore-mentioned require-ments.

1. Trace the detail of all procedures on accounts payable and receivable through the registers, journal, and general ledger.

2. Determine if asset items are correctly reflected in condition and amount on the balance sheet, through the accounting proce-dures used.

3. Determine if the liquid assets are properly classified, par-ticularly inventory, as to service (repair), current, and obsoles-cent items, and if there is any apparent excess.

4. Determine if all accounts are clearly defined or if they con-tain unrelated items.

Much of the solution of this accounting problem depends on the type of auditing used. If public certified accounting audits are made of the company's books, there will usually be little to correct, except in the matter of handling all transactions promptly. If internal auditing is used, slackness may have developed in the procedural routines. The conclusions derived from the foregoing investigation will point the way to corrective measures.

Cost Procedures

Leading directly from the accounting procedures are those of costing. Frequently, cost procedures are quite independent of the general books. This should not be the case and represents a major fault in the business controls which should be corrected. If it is assumed that the cost system stems from and supplements the general books of account, it should be checked for the following major requirements:

1. Accuracy of compilation and recording of the cost of labor, material, and expenses.
2. Completeness and promptness of presentation of all cost data.
3. Simplicity and suitability of the system to the business.

Clerical Procedures

A great deal of the effectiveness of the accounting and cost system depends on the effectiveness of the clerical procedures in the other divisions of the company which process orders through the office and plant. This is naturally true; nearly all accounting and cost activity results from doing business with customers. Any laxity in handling orders has immediate repercussions in every other phase of the business.

To check the effectiveness of clerical procedures, a typical customer's order should be followed through the business, from its original receipt in the sales department to its final disposition in the billing department, including all manufacturing procedures that stem from it.

Points at which clerical operations are too slow, too complicated, or too inaccurate will be readily uncovered through this study of the order flow. Corrective measures can be devised and applied which will remedy such situations.

INVENTORIES AND INVENTORY POLICIES

No one thing is more important to the business health of a company than the condition of its inventory. Many factors enter into this condition, and each should be analyzed carefully to determine its bearing on the entire situation.

Accuracy

The most important consideration is, of course, the accuracy with which the inventory is reported. Physical checks, if no perpetual inventory record is used, should be made periodically.

If the inventory is large in quantity and number of items, such physical checks are time-taking and expensive. More conveniently operated are perpetual inventory systems, which lend themselves to continuous physical checking at a minimum of time and cost as part of the routine operation of stockkeeping. If large discrepancies are discovered by either method, careful investigation should be instantly launched to correct the error and its consequent effect on the profit and loss operation of the company.

Classification

Next in importance is the question of classification of the inventory, that is, whether the records show the quantity and number of items that are:

1. *Current,* being used on orders received for the regularly sold line of products.

2. *Slow-moving,* being used on orders that specify odd sizes or special models of the product.

3. *Obsolete,* being used on orders for products that are no longer made or catalogued, or on products for which there is no longer any active demand.

With this information before it, management can set sales and production policies that will eliminate excess in any of the three categories.

Valuation

Equally important is the method of inventory valuation. The cost at which the product is placed in the inventory should be carefully investigated. If standard costing is used, management must assure itself that variance charges are written off in the operating statement and not carried into inventory as an asset.

If actual costs are used (generally a less desirable method), provision must be made to identify the cost with each inventory lot. Withdrawals will then carry out of the inventory the same value that they carried into it.

Many complications develop under actual costing methods. The most meticulous bookkeeping is required in the inventory records to assure the elimination of residual inventory amount balances not represented by actual inventory goods. If such records are lacking, management must decide either to supply them or to engage in a major project of standard costing.

Turnover

The inventory usage, or turnover, has some very important financial aspects. First of all, it costs real money to carry inventory (see Section 4, Chapter 30). In addition, a static inventory ties up working capital in sterile investment and eventually involves a company in financial difficulties.

After the inventory classifications and amounts have been determined, the inventory turnover for each class should be computed on a basis of cost of sales. Depending on the character of the business, the turnover rate may vary from as high as 12 times a year to as low as twice a year.

The turnover rate at its best should equal the time required for production; at its worst it should not exceed twice the production cycle time, unless it is necessary to level out production for annual employment. If such is not the case, management should immediately investigate its purchasing policies, its production planning and scheduling, and its sales policies with regard to deliveries, to determine which of these conditions is responsible for the slow turnover rate. Corrective measures can then be devised.

Other Relationships

The relationship of the inventory to the production schedules is particularly important in this connection; the two are intimately involved with each other. If production schedules are not properly related to plant capacity or sales orders or both, it is inevitable that excessive and sometimes obsolete inventory will result.

The amount of inventory to be carried in raw material, work in process, and finished form should be in a predetermined and controlled ratio in each category. Management can set these on a basis of procurement time, manufacturing time, and delivery time, using whatever factor of safety quantity is considered most desirable.

CAPITAL EXPENDITURES

The final condition for satisfactory financial control lies in the regulation of capital expenditures. Money tied up in surplus buildings and equipment or in overelaborate facilities is completely sterile; once there it can never be recaptured in profits.

Management must first check to see what method of control has been used. Too frequently the control consists of keeping capital expenditures from depleting the cash balance of the company. If new investment capital is not available to the company, capital betterments should come from the earnings of the company only.

A conservative policy to follow is to limit capital expenditures each year to the amount set aside for depreciation. Balance sheet ratios should also be used to limit the total amount invested in fixed assets, so that the proper turnover of capital is maintained in the sales volume of the company.

CHAPTER 6

SELLING

•

TERRITORIAL COVERAGE

Certainly no one phase of business operation is more essential
to the life of a company than that of selling. Without sales
there can be no business, and for this reason alone all the selling functions of a company should receive the closest scrutiny
of management.

Because sales depend on consumers, who live densely or
sparsely in geographical areas, the territorial coverage secured
for the company rates first consideration. The kind, number,
and location of customers, both actual and potential, should be
carefully determined, carefully tabulated, and charted on an area
map. From the sales records of each salesman the method and
frequency of contacting them should be determined.

A correlation of these data will indicate the intensity of the
field selling effort and point out the profitable territory and the
nonprofitable territory. Physical limitations of distance, inaccessibility, and other causes will be revealed. Decisions as to
more extended or more limited exploitation may then be made.

CHANNELS OF DISTRIBUTION

Nearly every company maintains several channels of distribution, such as direct sales to consumer through the home office or
field salesmen, and indirect sales through manufacturer's agents,
jobbers, distributors, or retailers. Other outlets such as agents,
branches, and brokers may also be used.

Over a period of years some of these channels may become unsuitable, owing to technological changes in the physical methods of distribution or economic changes in the field of merchandising.

Regardless of how well they are known to management, the channels of distribution used by the company should be carefully checked to determine whether they are still proper to the product and the market. This may be discovered by analysis of the orders received from each channel of distribution in relation to the area served, the kind of products ordered, and the quantity ordered. Decisions as to the propriety of the distribution channel should take into account, however, applicable sales policies of the company, competitive methods, and any other considerations such as selling cost, which may be pertinent. A conclusion should be reached, as a result of this study, which will find expression in a well-ordered program of distribution.

SALES POLICIES

A consistent merchandising program must be founded on sound policies—policies which yield the maximum benefit to the company and the greatest service satisfaction to the customer.

These policies are concerned with prices, terms, allowances, and deliveries, and should be compiled, reduced to written form, and then checked for their effect on sales. Customer complaints are the measuring stick of a company's sales policies. Such complaints can be segregated from the general files, classified as to their content, and used as a means for the check.

QUOTAS

Many satisfactory merchandising programs are scuttled by ill-advised methods of establishing sales quotas. The sales quotas must be realistic and reasonably attainable. They should represent a measurable potential based on a carefully determined forecast.

Management should check the quotas set by its sales department to see that they measure up to these requirements and, if they do not, take immediate steps towards accomplishing this result.

SELLING COSTS

The vexing problem of selling costs includes three major items:

1. *Sales promotion,* which includes advertising of all kinds, samples, allowances or special discounts, and the direct selling effort required to establish an account.

2. *Compensation* for the field force, which includes salaries, commissions, and, in the case of indirect distribution channels, discounts.

3. *Expenses,* which includes sales office expenses as well as travel and field expenses of the salesmen.

All three should be checked for consistency and relation to the sales produced, both on a company over-all basis, and on an individual basis. Reducing these costs to a percentage of the sales dollar, collectively and individually, will enable management to correct or eliminate conditions that are unsatisfactory.

CHAPTER 7

MANUFACTURING

•

IMPORTANCE OF CONTROL

Of the two major controls exercised over a business—financial control and production control—the latter ranks in importance equally with the former. Financial control directs the fiscal destiny of a company. Production control establishes the effectiveness of the entire manufacturing process to the end that the enterprise will operate profitably, serve the customer adequately, and attain the objectives set by the financial control.

PRODUCTION CONTROL

Production control is defined as that system of records and direction which, extending over a long period of time, regulates the order of movement of the elements of a manufacturing program in relation to each other and to the whole (see Section 4, Chapter 29).

Procedures

The first step, therefore, in analyzing this control for its effectiveness and suitability is to review the entire procedure now being used, giving particular attention to:

1. Routines for ordering material.
2. Routines for scheduling material.
3. Routines for scheduling hours.
4. Routines for making delivery promises.

5. Record-keeping practices.
6. Routines for issuing orders.

Method

Next must be determined the type of manufacturing engaged in, whether production is for:

1. Stock orders.
2. Job orders.
3. Continuous lots.

and the method of inventory control being used to maintain production and delivery.

The results of such a study should clearly indicate, particularly in the relation of delivery promises to actual deliveries, how well the system is serving its purpose. This will be especially true if inventories prove to be accurate and of a minimum amount.

Stability of Operation

A final test of production control lies in the stability of operation actually secured. A quick and simple way for determining this correlation is to chart production, over a period of a year, in terms of shipments made and orders received, as shown in Figure 5.

Ironing out production peaks will bring remarkable results in the stabilization of employment and the securing of low costs. Figure 5 typifies the ideal setup for a seasonal type of operation with a stock production item, such as warm-air domestic furnaces. Although the plan introduces a temporarily large finished inventory for the few months prior to the peak shipping season, the manufacturing economies can be so worth while that the inventory cost and risk are negligible.

LABOR CONTROL

The problem of labor control deserves very close scrutiny. Many manufacturing enterprises are woefully weak in this regard and, as a result of unsatisfactory labor relations, find themselves in continual operating difficulties. This is one phase of company operation that requires a soul searching of self by man-

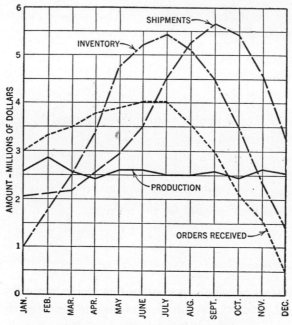

Fig. 5. Operation Stability Chart

agement, without bias and with minds open to the long-range social and economic trends in our national economy.

Policies

Such a study requires a critical review of past and present labor relations policies, set down in writing, followed by an honest appraisal of the actual situation resulting from that policy.

For example, the statement that it is the policy of the company to maintain safe working conditions for its employees, followed by the admission that the company has a very high accident rate, should indicate to management that its policy is not being carried out by the operating staff.

Or the policy that wages for the week will be paid the following Friday, compared with the fact that a large percentage of employees are receiving advances, should cause management to question the correctness of this position.

Closely allied to these situations are others concerned with the selection and employment of men, and the methods used to keep labor turnover low. The size of a company has a great deal to do with the type and size of the personnel department required. No company is too small to have this function systematically organized around one or more capable individuals, fitted by temperament and experience for this type of work.

Wages

Practically all major labor relations problems revolve around the question of wages. Low labor rates may enhance the individual fortune of the company's owner, but they are economically unsound and in the long run will eventually put a company out of business.

Wage policies are vital to any operation. Again management should set its policies down in written form and compare them with conditions that actually obtain in the industry, in the community, and in its own plant. Substandard wages are not compatible with successful operation. In reviewing its own wage policies, management should keep this fact always in mind.

Labor Cost

The final consideration in the problem of labor control is that of labor cost. Labor cost should not be confused with wages. Low wages do not mean low labor costs, and high wages do not mean high labor costs. Management's study of labor control should conclude with a detailed investigation of the cost of labor in terms of units produced. The answer will spell itself out.

QUALITY CONTROL

The results of production and labor control are reflected in the quality of the product produced by labor. Facilities and working conditions may be largely responsible for poor quality. But good quality, in the last analysis, depends on the personal equation—the desire of the workman to produce a product that measures up to the quality specified.

Cost and Cause

To determine the effectiveness of quality control over the operations, detail reports should be prepared, if not already available, to show the cost and quantity of work spoiled in the process of manufacturing.

These should be accompanied by a statement from the inspection department giving the cause of such spoilage. The completeness and accuracy of these records should likewise be checked, to make sure that all material and all production have been accounted for. Poor quality can result from only five causes:

1. *Poor workmanship or handling.*
2. *Defective material.*
3. *Defective tools or equipment.*
4. *Incorrect specifications.*
5. *Bad design.*

Inspection

It is the function of the inspection department to detect variations from the specifications and to report them to management. The inspection function does not create quality; the workman does that. Nor is it the function of the inspection department to determine quality standards; management does that through its engineering department.

The method of inspection should be considered in relationship to the other manufacturing functions and their proper integration. The high importance of product quality in merchandising gives added weight to the need for a most critical study of all these factors. Corrective measures should be devised if they are needed.

Methods and Standards

Modern industrial operation is based on the formal organization of manufacturing standards and methods. These set up the measures and means for economical and orderly manufacture.

The first step in determining whether such standards are truly serving their purpose is to follow a product through every operation, from the receipt of raw material to final shipment, recording all handlings, inspections, and operations. The results may logically take the form of a record, as shown in Figure 45, which is known as an operation or process sheet. If there is no standards or methods department to do this work, some one from the operating or engineering staff must be appointed to carry out this compilation.

Operation Flow

A time study, if not already available, should then be made for each operation. The labor cost established for it should be recorded on the operation sheet. This can then be compared with the cost on record and prescribed procedure.

The operation sheet should then be carefully checked, operation by operation, for possible improvements in methods of manufacture, or lowered costs of labor and material. Frequently it will be found that an operation involving complicated tooling and equipment can be done more cheaply and with better quality, by breaking it up into several operations. Or, conversely, a laborious hand operation may be improved and speeded up by a simple fixture or device used in connection with a power-driven machine. In either case the conclusive test will be whether better or equal quality is produced at a lower cost.

Such an analysis leads naturally to an investigation of tools, equipment, and methods used in performing an operation. The inspection, engineering, and operating staffs should be solicited for critical suggestions. A decision as to their adoption can then be based on the cost and quality factors involved.

Plant Layout

Satisfactory standards, methods, tools, and equipment will all fail in their purpose if their *total use* is not efficiently provided for. In other words, if the plant layout of equipment and space and material handling does not provide for their most efficient

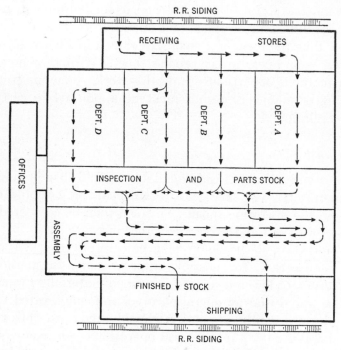

Fig. 6. Layout of Material Flow

utilization, maximum benefit will not result even with perfection in other details. The flow of material through the plant between departments, and over the equipment in each department, should be charted in detail as shown in Figure 6. Desirable rearrangements will automatically suggest themselves, but no moves should be made until their costs are determined and balanced against the economies anticipated.

Such an investigation may lead into a major betterment program, and it therefore deserves an unstinted use of organization time and talent. If a major rearrangement seems desirable but involves new equipment and buildings, competent outside counsel should be engaged to review these recommendations before any final action is taken.

FACILITIES

The study of the entire manufacturing operation should be concluded with a general survey of all the facilities, to determine:

1. *Their suitability and adequacy.* Are they of the right kind and quantity?
2. *Their normal and maximum capacity.* Will they satisfy the projected merchandising program?
3. *Their condition.* Are the housekeeping and maintenance at the required degree of appearance and care?

If the answers to these questions are satisfactory, management can proceed on its master plan with full assurance that all reasonable precautions have been taken to avoid costly errors of judgment.

CHAPTER 8

ENGINEERING
AND RESEARCH

•

PURPOSE

The company that lacks an organized program of engineering research on its product and processes eventually finds itself out of business. Such programs need not be elaborate, but they must be sufficient to keep the enterprise technologically up-to-date.

PRODUCT DESIGN

Product design must be in a continuous state of development, and the following assignment should be given the engineering department for investigation and report:

1. Determination of the materials used in the product, and comparisons in weight, construction, and functional suitability with that of competitors' models.

2. Recommendations for the possible substitution of better and cheaper materials, and designs for cheaper and better fabrication and assembly.

Tremendous strides have been made in recent years in the development of new materials and equipment for practically every industrial field. These afford an unlimited opportunity for application. The engineering department should be judged by its ability to apply them to its own product.

RESEARCH AND DEVELOPMENT

Product development can only follow, however, when it has been preceded by true research in the engineering fields that are applicable. This requires a scope beyond the four walls of the engineering department. The department must be supplied with all technical literature pertinent to the company's operation and to the end use of its products.

For example, the manufacturer of radio equipment must be constantly associated with the scientific research carried on in the field of electronics. The commercial advent of television will thus find him prepared to enter this market with a product acceptable in engineering concept and practical in manufacture.

PROJECT PROGRAMS

Such research should be organized through a series of related project programs, organized well in advance of use, and kept currently modified through knowledge of scientific and engineering developments in the company's field of activity.

The lack of such programs will indicate to management, immediately, the deficiencies of its engineering functions and point the way to corrective action in organization or facilities.

CHAPTER 9

COMPENSATION AND INCENTIVES

•

CONSISTENCY OF APPLICATION

The problem of compensation for labor was the subject of study in an earlier chapter (Section 1, Chapter 7). The whole problem of factory and office wages and salaries should be carefully investigated for consistency in their relationship to each other and their influence on the operation of the company.

A systematic approach is required in this matter, and there are many techniques available. Salaries and hourly rates should be submitted to the process of classification or evaluation to determine their equity within the company. In addition, they should be compared with going area and industry rates. Conclusive proof that the wage and salary structure is sound may be found from formalized job rating or evaluation techniques (see Section 5, Chapter 35).

With these results before it, management will be in a position to orient its policies in the direction of good industrial relations and satisfactory profits.

INCENTIVES

The attainment of satisfactory production performance in the plant cannot be left entirely to base compensation or wages of the employee. Man responds to incentives, either spiritual or material, depending on the nature of his life work. In the field of physical endeavor, monetary incentives provide the "something extra" that induces men to make the added effort that results in more profit for himself and for his employer.

These incentives take varied forms, depending on the character of the operation, the position of the employee, and the philosophy of management itself. They are, to mention the most common forms:

1. *Measured day work.*
2. *Piece work.*
3. *Premium work.*
4. *Bonuses.*
5. *Profit sharing.*

Management should determine whether any of these plans is applicable to its operation or, if any one of them is already in use, whether it has been correctly established, consistently applied, and equitably distributed (see Section 4, Chapter 31).

POLICIES

Emanating from this study should be a set of policies that will assure the healthful continuation of the compensation plan and its essential by-products—good industrial relations and profitable operation.

Such policies, when implemented through the proper organization function, will provide an organized system of wage and salary administration which will keep the company in harmony with general economic conditions.

CHAPTER 10

COSTING AND PRICING METHODS

•

EXPENSE RATIOS

No effective control over profits is possible unless costing and pricing methods are correctly pointed in this direction. Any analysis made of these matters must be critical in its approach and precise in its determinations.

The first avenue of investigation leads into the analysis of the fixed and variable expenses in each class of expense. This can be done most readily by the graphical method described in Section 2, Chapters 15 and 17. Once these amounts and ratios have been ascertained, the degree of control will be indicated by the variation of expenses as they follow an increasing or decreasing volume.

It will be found, usually, that, as volume decreases, expenses are not reduced proportionately. Management can then readily apply the necessary administrative direction required to accomplish the desired results. This analysis can be carried further into the problem by carrying the distribution to products, departments, and even down to the equipment itself, to determine whether accurate and proper allocations have been made.

PROFIT MARGINS

Once the total costs in these various categories have been determined, the sales income can then be allocated to them and the available profit margins discovered.

Usually, for purposes of analysis, it will be sufficient to carry this study down to the products only. The objective at this stage of investigation is the relation of costs to pricing rather than actual control of the costs themselves. From prior investigation (see Chapter 2, this section) the prices that the customer is willing to pay will have been determined, competition and other factors being taken into account. They should now be checked against actual results discovered by the foregoing analysis, to determine whether a consistent pricing formula has been used and where price changes are indicated in order to provide desired profit margins.

EFFECT OF VOLUME

It does not necessarily follow that every product must produce a uniform amount of profit. The effect of volume must be taken into consideration. It may be found highly desirable to take a modest profit on end sizes in order to maintain the price structure on popular sizes.

This is well illustrated in men's clothing and shoes, where the price structure is based on the popular sizes and applied to all the other sizes, regardless of the actual labor and material cost. In industrial products involving larger units, the price structure can range with the progression of size.

EFFECT OF ORDER QUANTITY

In certain lines the effect of order quantities may also be a factor in pricing, particularly if the product has special features for the customer's account. All these factors are to be considered in examining the relation of costs to prices. They will enable management, in concluding its study on this phase of operation, to decide how and where the price structure can be modified to yield greater profit.

CHAPTER 11

INDUSTRIAL RELATIONS

•

NEED

In view of modern sociological trends, the over-all survey of the operation should not be concluded without a thorough examination of the personnel activities of the company.

In the mechanized industrial economy of today, it is important that employees be carefully fitted to their jobs. The cost of training new members of the organization can reach prohibitive proportions if employment is not handled in an organized and scientific manner.

TESTING AND SELECTION

This process starts in the employment office itself. Inquiry should be made on the following matters:

1. Are applicants' qualifications adequately appraised by interview and tests?

2. What factors are considered in actually selecting persons for employment?

3. Are these factors pertinent to the nature of the job offered?

4. After selection, is the placement of the employee on a job followed up by a regular plan of introduction to the organization, the rules and regulations of the company, and the work itself?

5. After employment, is there a systematic procedure for up-grading personnel, based on periodic review and appraisal of the employee's work and inherent capabilities?

Training

After the employment process has been completed, the employee still remains raw material as far as many phases of the company operation are concerned. The actual fitting of the employee to his job should not be left to unorganized personnel procedure. The following requirements should be checked:

1. Does the new employee undergo an organized method of training for the work he is to do?
2. Is this training program correctly conceived for the job requirements?
3. Are properly qualified trainers used?
4. What further training programs are available to employees to fit them for more important or more responsible work?
5. Is this advanced training systematically organized and administered?

Policies

All these considerations of employment and training lead in to the question of personnel policies. All personnel actions are usually in accord with company policy, but frequently these policies are unwritten, incomplete, and do not currently reflect the industrial relations philosophy of the management. A written statement of personnel policies from the personnel department or function, charged with this responsibility, will reveal to management its own as well as the personnel department's deficiencies and point the way to better practices.

Procedures

Any organized program of good industrial relations requires tools and equipment, just as does manufacturing. The following points should be checked to determine if the industrial relations program has proper physical equipment:

1. Is the employment office adequate in its space requirements and location on the plant site?

2. Are all personnel records centered in it? Are they readily accessible, systematically arranged, and kept up-to-date?

3. Are the necessary reports on all personnel actions made up promptly and distributed to management?

4. Are welfare activities (lunchroom, medical, social, financial) efficiently administered and the necessary records and reports made?

If the answer to all these questions is not in the affirmative, management should not feel satisfied that it has placed its operation on a sound footing. No matter how well equipped a plant may be with machinery, buildings, and systems, it is not a living organism until it is peopled with satisfactory and contented workers. A sound industrial relations program is the readiest means to this end.

2

*General Management
Problems*

CHAPTER 12

ORGANIZATION

•

DEFINITIONS

Organization is the arrangement of men's activities in the performance of work, co-ordinated for harmonious attainment of a predetermined objective. It is a relationship between co-operating units. In a machine, it is the *linkage* by which power is transferred. In personnel, it is likewise the mechanism for applying power, to accomplish a definite objective in the business.

Every business, through design or by trial and error, has developed a form of organization that functions more or less satisfactorily. The perfect man-made organization does not and probably never will exist. Therefore any existing organization, theoretically, is subject to improvement. Repeated experience has demonstrated that a careful examination of an organization by a trained observer will reveal faults of form, personnel, or direction.

Different forms of organization have been tried and tested, the most important ones being functional, line, and line and staff.

The line and staff form of organization has withstood best the tests of time and experience and is considered most desirable and effective.

Line Functions

Line functions are repetitive in nature and pertain to the routine of operations. Included in line functions are: accumulating costs, supervising labor, controlling material, and directing labor and machine operations. Certain definite authority, within prescribed areas, is associated with these functions.

Staff Functions

Staff functions are nonrepetitive, or advisory, or consist of an analysis of some subject or the preparation and issuance of instructions, standards of performance, and similar activities. Included in staff functions are: setting labor standards, establishing budgets, analyzing markets, analyzing trends in products and costs, analyzing expenditures, revising routines of production planning, cost accounting, order handling, and many other activities of a similar nature. Delegated authority within very narrow limits is sometimes associated with some of these functions.

FUNDAMENTAL PRINCIPLES

Whether a new organization is to be designed or an existing one revised, the quality of the developed organization plan will depend on the degree of observance of certain fundamental principles. These include:

(a) *Management's Objective,* which may involve increase or decrease of production, expansion of plant, an exhaustive program of research, for product development, or the manufacture of new products.

(b) *Organization Form,* which affects the determination of departmental divisions, for economical operation.

(c) *Selection of Personnel,* which implies the disposition of forces of man power, for effective operation.

(*d*) *Administration,* which is the method whereby the various forces are directed for economical effective operation.

For effective operation of any organization all functions, lines of authority and responsibility must be clearly defined and maintained to avoid overlapping or gaps.

Illustrative of this problem is the question of whether or not to appoint a general manager to administer the purely operating functions of a business. Basically, the line of authority in an organization stems directly from the board of directors who by law are charged with the duty of managing the affairs of the corporation.

The execution of these duties is, by the company's regulations and by-laws, delegated to various officers of the company or committees of the board. These regulations usually provide that the president is the chief executive officer, having general power to manage and direct the business and affairs of the company. The authority and responsibility of other corporate officers of the company within their respective fields are also usually defined.

Frequently no provision is made for a general manager to function separately from the office of president. Thus, if the organization plan provides for a general manager other than the president, care should be exercised to obtain specific authority from the board of directors.

The appointment of a general manager ostensibly vests him with the full operating authority and responsibility. These powers, normally belonging to the president, should be relinquished by the president, to the extent that they are imposed on the general manager. The line of demarkation should be clearly drawn to avoid confusion.

A general manager, even though his duties and powers may not have been expressly defined, stands before the world as legal agent of the company in all actions taken in furtherance of the company's business. The laws of agency apply without exception, and the company is bound by his acts and actions.

For these reasons the appointment of a general manager other than the president requires the careful consideration of the company management in devising its organization plan.

If after such consideration, the directors or president deem a general manager separate from the president as desirable or necessary, he should be given organization rank second only to the president as shown in Figure 7 (alternate form). It is not advisable to appoint a general manager over only a part of the company's functions unless the title of the office descriptively limits and defines the job, such as general manager of blank division or general manager of sales.

Merely defining the functions of each position and specifying the lines of authority do not make a good organization. An organization is composed of individuals. Each individual has certain abilities and weaknesses; each has certain ambitions; each has his own likes, dislikes, temperament, and personal characteristics. All these must be considered in planning or developing an organization.

MULTIPLE MANAGEMENT

In an endeavor to pool abilities, an organization form known as multiple management is occasionally found in a company. This form of organization provides, in addition to the regular line and staff positions, a series of boards at the several organization levels. The functions of these are purely advisory, but they are extremely valuable in that they develop in the management group a more direct sense of responsibility for profitable operation.

The various boards established are:

1. *Senior Board,* usually consisting of the board of directors, which passes or acts upon the recommendations of the other boards.

2. *Junior Board,* usually consisting of most but not including at any one time all department heads of the office and manufacturing divisions.

3. *Sales Board,* composed of sales department heads.

4. *Factory Board,* composed of factory department heads.

The successful application of multiple management requires an accepted philosophy of industrial democracy in the top management of a company and a sincere conviction of its desirability.

To establish an effective organization, there must be:

(a) *A determination of the positions required* and a clear definition of the duties to be performed in each position.

(b) *The assignment of suitable personnel* to the various positions.

(c) *The establishment of proper supervision* and administration to insure performance of the functions and duties in the specified manner.

GENERAL CONSIDERATIONS

The positions required for the operation of the business depend on the size, the type of the company, and its policies as to development of products and expansion or contraction of operations. The positions to be filled may therefore vary greatly among different concerns, but the functions to be performed are common to most of them.

A large business creates many more specialized departments and positions than a small business. That is, a large company may require separate departments for the accounts receivable and the accounts payable, whereas a small business should have only one position for accounts payable, accounts receivable, and general accounting.

A major problem is that of grouping similar functions either into a single position or into a department. The basic principle that applies is: *Keep staff functions separate from line functions.*

A distinct separation of these two types of functions is an organization necessity, because work is performed by men and not by machines. A machine operator or a department foreman can seldom be expected to establish a proper standard of performance, a staff function. He will almost invariably provide allowances for delays, interruptions, and unforeseen contingencies and is placed in the position of both judge and jury.

Separation of line and staff functions is a positive necessity for purposes of analysis. Their placement in the organization requires the exercise of good judgment, with due consideration for the character of the business.

For a job shop or a small business, both line and staff functions may be placed under the direction of a superintendent or a plant manager. For a large manufacturing operation, certain staff functions, such as research engineering or industrial relations, and the line function of controlling material become important management problems. They may have to be treated as such under the direction of top management.

Material control presents a good example of this. Quite properly, material control is an important part of production control, which is a staff function. Material control itself, except for the maintenance of control records, is a line function, including as it does the receipt, storage, issuance, and internal transportation of material. These are all line functions, but experience has demonstrated the need for associating them with production control activities.

Engineering presents another illustration. For the small manufacturing plant, all engineering (including research, product development and design, drafting, methods, quality specifications, plant maintenance, and the determination of labor production standards) may be placed under the direction of a chief engineer, since it is a combination of line and staff functions.

For a large manufacturing plant, these functions may be placed under different directing heads. Research, which is purely staff, may be placed on a higher plane, under a research director or research engineer. Methods and labor production standards, which are also staff functions, may be combined under the direction of a methods engineer or treated as separate departments under different directing heads.

Line and staff functions exist and are necessary at various levels throughout the whole organization setup. The highly placed directing staff members are generally known, and their places in the organization are understood. Staff functions at lower levels are not so well known and recognized. It is very important, therefore, that these be established clearly, in connection with any organization plans, in order to avoid confusion of line and staff activities or friction in the exercise of authority.

In determining the required positions, the following steps should be taken:

(a) Combine like functions as much as possible into one position.

(*b*) Determine the necessary positions without consideration for personnel. After the position has been determined, select an individual with the necessary qualifications to fill that position.

(*c*) Provide for a minimum number of department heads or junior executives reporting to the senior executives.

(*d*) Plan senior executive positions free of routine functions, so that seniors can devote the major part of their time to planning or to the solution of unexpected difficulties.

(*e*) Properly balance the various positions and departments. If more positions are established in one department (accounting, for example) than in another (say the production planning department) merely to provide for a monthly peak of work, an unbalanced condition will exist, and excess costs will occur.

(*f*) Avoid duplication of positions. As an example: The payroll department may prepare a payroll distribution for factory use, and the accounting department another for accounting purposes; yet the only difference may be a slightly different grouping.

(*g*) Separate staff functions from line functions.

With recognition of the foregoing principles, an organization chart can be drawn and submitted to top management for approval.

ORGANIZATION CHARTS AND MANUALS

Four types of organization charts are shown herewith for purposes of information and comparison.

Figure 7 illustrates a purely functional form of organization. Responsibility for each major function of a business is placed with all individuals, each having an appropriate title but all being on the same plane and reporting to top management.

The theory supporting this type of organization is that responsibility in the hands of capable executives, each with full authority in his sphere, will result in maximum teamwork and effective performance. With few exceptions this form of organization, although theoretically attractive, has not functioned according to expectation, for several reasons.

Among the reasons for its failure are jealousy and hunger for power, human characteristics inherent in most men. Although given equal status, top men often develop the opinion that their functions are most important. Failure to obtain recognition and

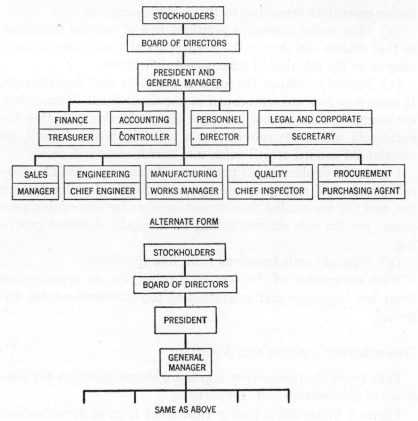

FIG. 7. Major Organization Functions

higher status can and does cause them to nurse grievances which lessen their interest and effectiveness and most certainly have an unfavorable effect on co-operative effort.

The greatest weakness, however, is that each top man establishes the standards which govern performance in his particular division. This arrangement violates the principle of separation of line and staff functions and places him in the highly impractical position of being both judge and jury.

This purely functional type of organization has not met the test of modern requirements, and few examples now exist in actual practice.

Figure 8 shows an example of line organization. This type of organization stresses those functions with direct lines of au-

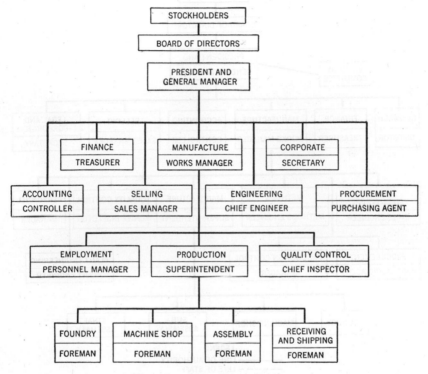

Fig. 8.   Line Organization

thority, ignoring staff functions as such or incorporating them with line functions.

Although many examples of this type of organization exist, it is not considered the best form or in line with the best organization principles. Better results are secured with clear separation of line and staff functions.

Figure 9 provides an example of line and staff organization, illustrating the separation of these functions. More and more the older forms of organization are being revised along these lines, with an increasing appreciation of the advantages of the arrangement.

Figure 10 represents what is generally referred to as a "functional organization chart." This is merely an endeavor to make

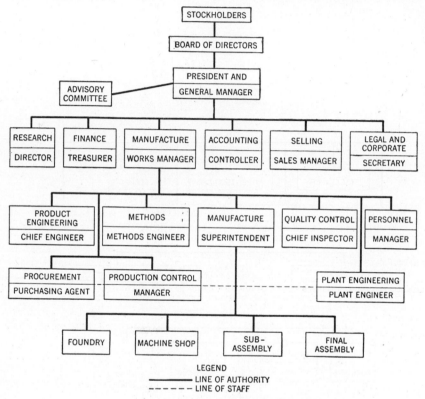

FIG. 9.   Line and Staff Organization

the organization chart convey the maximum amount of information by listing the most important functions in each area of responsibility. This type of chart is meeting increasing favor because of the greater information it conveys and because of its availability for quick reference when questions of responsibility arise.

Organization manuals are a necessary supplement to organization charts, in order to convey the organization plan adopted by management to all concerned.

It is the purpose of the organization manual to amplify the information given by the organization chart. Detailed instructions provide clear definitions of the responsibilities and duties of each important position, down to and including foremen of the various departments. Each instruction should be complete and

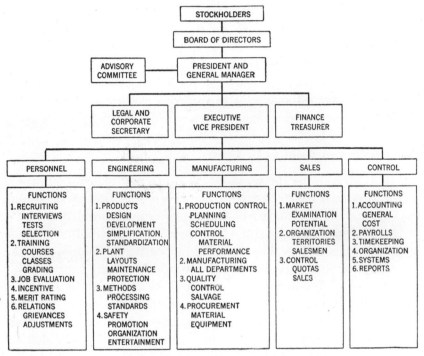

FIG. 10.   Functional Type of Organization Chart

in accordance with a formal arrangement. A widely used arrangement is illustrated by the following side headings:

Position.
Title.
Responsible to.
Duties and Responsibilities.

It is common and commendable to provide departmental organization charts, associated with the written instructions in the organization manual. These charts should be designed to show the departmental organization in greater detail than may be practical with the major organization chart. They should also show to whom the head of the department is responsible and should break down the department into its various functional divisions.

Manuals of standard practice instruction are also important. These are detailed instructions covering all important systematic procedures. They should be written in accordance with a pre-scribed format, each one being positively identified, preferably by title and number, and correctly indexed for ready reference. These manuals should, of course, be continually subject to change because of constant endeavor to improve routine procedures and to increase their effectiveness.

SELECTING AND ASSIGNING PERSONNEL

After determining the required positions and securing approval of the proposed chart of organization, the selection of personnel for some of the positions will present a difficult problem. Many of the positions may be filled by the present occupants of these or similar positions. The remaining positions will require the most careful consideration of all available talent.

Good policy dictates selection of individuals for these positions from existing personnel wherever possible. Resort to new em-ployees should be made only after a careful canvass of available talent has shown the necessity for such action. Clearly defined paths of promotion and regular promotion from the ranks are outstanding aids in the creation of the high morale so essential to the proper functioning of any organization.

Consideration of candidates should be free from prejudice. An individual may have made a mistake at some time or offended someone; this should not prevent an examination of his qualifi-cations nor his appointment if he qualifies otherwise. Quite fre-quently added responsibility causes men to reveal unsuspected qualities of leadership and administration.

An unwise selection may have sorry consequences, resulting in poor administration and, finally, the demotion and possible loss of the man selected. A good workman may make a poor foreman. A good foreman, given the opportunity, may prove to be an unsatisfactory superintendent. This is particularly true with foremen of departments where technical knowledge rather than administrative ability is the major requirement. Pattern shops, toolrooms, automatic machine departments and plating departments are good examples of such background.

A man may be an excellent engineer and yet be unable to qualify for the position of chief engineer. The very qualities of interest and concentration that enable him to do an outstanding job with one project may prevent his satisfactory administration of a number of varied projects. Instead of impartial furtherance of all projects in accordance with schedule, he is likely to concentrate his energy and forces on those which interest him most at the expense of others more important. Organization is the disposition of forces for the performance of work. Mistakes will be made even with the exercise of utmost discretion in the careful selection of men. When, after a fair trial of a new incumbent of a position, it is recognized that a mistake has been made, the condition should be remedied promptly by the appointment of another man better equipped to meet the responsibilities of the position.

Before assigning men to positions, their personal characteristics must be carefully considered. For example:

1. When a department is large (several hundred or more persons), it is more essential that the head of the department be an experienced executive than that he be experienced in the technical details of the work being performed.

2. The selection of men for subordinate executive positions should supplement the characteristics of the chief executives. A chief executive with great experience in merchandising and little experience in manufacturing should be supported by subordinate executives with more than ordinary manufacturing experience.

3. The selection of personnel is a difficult matter and cannot be left entirely to mechanical devices. Tests, merit rating plans, references, and other devices all have value, but judgment on the part of the employer must also play a part in the selection.

4. Compatibility between the employer and his subordinates is desirable but must not be carried to a point where individual initiative is killed.

Administering the Organization

In large measure the successful or otherwise performance of an organization is dependent on the character of the administrative direction given it by management. The direction and control of an organization necessitate a system of balances and checks for the information of management and the attainment of harmonious performance.

Policies

It is the function of management to enunciate and interpret established policies, to co-ordinate the various functions of the business, and to secure maximum co-operation from all levels of the organization.

Its policies should be written out and formally published as management's official philosophy of operation.

Co-ordinating the Functions

Clear precise written instructions, stating by whom authorized, are a first requirement. Standard practice instructions meet this requirement for repetitive routine procedures. Special instructions of similar character should be issued for all departures from established routines.

The necessity for such instructions is obvious. Without them individuality may manifest itself in cumbersome overlapping expensive procedures, with consequent friction and confusion. In addition to avoiding such consequences, written instructions are also valuable because they constitute a sound basis for reporting accomplishment and failures.

Unless management has such information currently, the exercise of judicious control is practically impossible. Without it, the direction of affairs must be based on incomplete or prejudiced information, or intuition, with more or less unsatisfactory results.

If the organization is to function as anticipated, instructions and reports are an imperative requirement. As a general rule, men respond with their best efforts when given recognition for extraordinary accomplishment. Equally, they resent unmerited censure, which is unwholesome, if frequently indulged, and can defeat the major purpose of organization: effective teamwork.

Securing Co-operation

The finest organization or group of individuals becomes ineffective when improperly directed. The normal individual has pride in his position and company and wants both to be well regarded by the public and the customer. It is management's function to direct the organization so that:

1. Proper co-ordination of the performance of various groups is obtained for common results.

2. The work to be done at each position is performed as promptly and effectively as possible.

3. The personnel devote all their time to the work assigned to their positions and do not become involved in work assigned to other positions.

4. Promotions are made when vacancies occur, wherever possible, in preference to the employment of outsiders.

5. Salaries and wages are established equitably, on a basis of the service rendered and the skill and ability required.

6. Provision is made for added compensation or other recognition of unusual performance.

7. A co-operative spirit, an attitude of loyalty, and a high degree of morale are developed and maintained.

RULES AND REGULATIONS

A set of employee rules and regulations is an essential requirement for any good organization. These are usually printed in the form of small booklets, a copy of which is issued to each employee. Contents include a list of rules affecting attendance and conduct, for the purpose of maintaining discipline, and also a statement of the company's policies as to benefits in the form of loans, insurance, or rewards for long satisfactory service.

Limiting Considerations

Certain limiting considerations must be kept in mind when compiling a book of rules and regulations. Each statement of a rule should be as brief and precise as possible. A rule should be established for each situation that may require exercise of disciplinary measures. The difficulty associated with this requirement is readily apparent. Statement of a rule may be phrased with utmost care and yet under extraordinary conditions be subject to other interpretation.

A statement of rules and regulations is an essential requirement. A further requirement is that their interpretation shall at all times be consistent.

SUMMARY

In order to establish proper organization definition and control, it is essential first to establish a standard. A standard can best be expressed in:

1. *An organization chart.*
2. *An organization manual.*
3. *A manual of standard practice instructions.*
4. *A system of reports to management.*
5. *A booklet of rules and regulations.*

The organization chart should show:

1. *The name of each department or the title of the executive or both.*
2. *The name of the executive in each department.*
3. *The function of the department, usually outlined in the name of the department or the title of the executive.*
4. *The lines denoting authority on policy problems as well as the lines for discipline,* for example, the methods engineer may report to the factory manager for discipline but to the president for determination of policies concerning wage rates.

Supplementing the organization chart should be an organization manual covering in detail the jobs charted. The manual will show a statement of:

1. *The position.*
2. *The title.*
3. *Responsible to.*
4. *Responsibility.*
5. *Duties.* Clearly defined.

Note: A detailed functional organization chart of the department is, in many instances, a desirable addition to the written instructions.

Further supplementing the organization chart should be a manual of standard practice instructions, covering in detail the various routine procedures. The manual will:

1. *Describe the work to be done.*
2. *Indicate who shall perform it.*
3. *Provide an exact, detailed statement of how the work shall be done.*

A system of reports is required to enable management to balance and check performance in the various departments and to co-ordinate all activity. These should be kept to the essential minimum and should show:

1. *The department identification.*
2. *The character of the work to be done.*
3. *The degree of performance of work, compared with a standard or a schedule.*

A booklet of rules and regulations is a further requirement. The booklet should contain:

1. *A rule for each situation affecting discipline.*
2. *Statement of policies affecting employer and employee relations, including attainable benefits and rewards.*

Organization is the backbone of a business. There is no limit for a company that has an effective, co-ordinated and co-operating organization. Without it no business can attain permanent success. Without it facilities, products, and money are useless. The need for good organization transcends all other requirements of a business, and "The Ten Commandments of Good Organization," published by M. C. Rorty years ago, are still fundamental in any enterprise:

"1. Definite and clean-cut responsibilities should be assigned to each executive.

"2. Responsibility should always be coupled with corresponding authority.

"3. No change in the scope or responsibilities of a position should be made without a definite understanding to that effect on the part of all persons concerned.

"4. No officer or employee, occupying a single position in the organization, should be subject to definite orders from more than one source.

"5. Orders should never be given to subordinates over the head of a responsible officer. Rather than do this, the officer in question should be supplanted.

"6. Criticisms of subordinates should, whenever possible, be made privately, and in no case should a subordinate be criticized in the presence of officers or employees of equal rank.

"7. No dispute or difference between officers or employees as to authority or responsibilities should be considered too trivial for prompt and careful adjudication.

"8. Promotions, wage changes, and disciplinary action should always be approved by the officer immediately superior to the one directly responsible.

"9. No officer or employee should ever be required or expected to be at the same time an assistant to and a critic of another.

"10. Any officer whose work is subject to regular inspection should, whenever practical, be given the assistance and facilities necessary for him to maintain an independent check of the quality of his work."

CHAPTER 13

MANAGEMENT PROGRAM

•

PURPOSE

A plan of operation is a basic requirement for the successful conduct of any business. Without a plan the control of operation of the business is limited or nonexistent. The purpose of the plan of operation is to provide a sound basis for control by establishing certain attainable objectives affecting all divisions of the business, to the end that a satisfactory profit will be made.

Such a plan is best reflected in the form of a management program which, obviously, should be written out and in such form that schedule dates for accomplishment can be set for each program item.

A typical management program follows. It was designed to convert an unprofitable operation into a profitable one and applies to a going enterprise, not to one in the process of organization.

The sample program is in a highly condensed form and in actual practice should be supported with sufficient details to outline clearly exactly how each of these steps is to be accomplished.

1. Management Policy

(a) Establish the current normal volume range between $3,500,000 per year and $5,000,000 per year.

(*b*) Establish a future normal volume range between $7,000,-000 and $9,000,000 per year.

(*c*) Reduce the fixed expenses from $700,000 per year to $600,000 per year for present conditions.

(*d*) Reduce the variable costs from 84 per cent of the sales dollar to 80 per cent of the sales dollar for present conditions.

(*e*) Establish the break-even volume at $3,000,000 per year for present conditions by accomplishing the afore-mentioned changes in fixed and variable expenses.

(*f*) Establish a policy to recapture the volume business.

2. Sales Policy

(*a*) Design the product to meet the volume business requirements so that they can be sold at competitive prices.

(*b*) Make a market study to determine whether all outlets for the product are being properly utilized.

(*c*) Establish an organized procedure for selecting and training salesmen.

(*d*) Analyze all territories for improved territorial divisions.

3. Organization

(*a*) Realign organization functions, and reduce personnel in accordance with the proposed organization chart as rapidly as procedure changes will permit.

(*b*) Establish stronger sales management that will permit the development of salesmen to greater effectiveness.

(*c*) Simplify the purchasing department procedure, and reduce the personnel in accordance with the organization chart.

(*d*) Establish a methods engineering department to concentrate exclusively on tooling and tool design and analyze all tooling to improve present operations.

(*e*) Transfer the time study functions from the production control department to the controller's department. Reduce the personnel of the time study group, and improve the quality of their work. Adopt a single standard for each operation, and revise the existing standard on that basis.

4. Controls

(a) Simplify the procedure in the cost and pay roll department, and provide for a single basis of standards for pay roll, accounting, and estimating purposes.

(b) Revise material, labor, and burden standards in accordance with the current level of prices and wages and taking into consideration the expected economies.

(c) Simplify the production control procedures which will provide for greater co-ordination between sales requirements and manufacturing.

(d) Establish limits on quantities of recurring items, and provide for approval by management of those limits to minimize repeat purchase orders for materials.

(e) Establish and enforce rigid budgetary control of all divisions of the business.

(f) Install the use of operation cost sheets to show all pertinent information for each part and unit, including the operations to be performed and the standard labor and material costs.

(g) Establish a uniform method of preparing estimates.

(h) Establish standard inspection cards and transfer the inspection department headquarters to the factory.

5. Reports to Management

Provide for the establishment of reports to management which will include:

(a) A daily report showing the financial condition of the company, including the cash on hand, the amount of the accounts receivable, the amount of the accounts payable, and the purchase commitments.

(b) A daily sales report, showing sales for the month to date and unfilled orders.

(c) A daily force count showing the number of employees.

(d) A daily labor report showing the labor performance.

(e) A daily production report showing the number of units produced and the number of units in process.

(f) A monthly profit and loss statement.

(*g*) A monthly report of the kind and locations of inventory.

(*h*) A monthly report showing open engineering projects, their estimated time of completion, and their cost.

6. Manufacturing Facilities

(*a*) Analyze all equipment carefully, and provide for a modernizing program to be executed as a part of the general fiscal policy. In the future, new installations should be planned with sufficient capacity for the whole plant's needs instead of for a single station.

7. Labor Control

(*a*) Revise the present wage payment plan to one that will be more simple to operate without sacrificing any of the incentive features.

Based on the preceding years' performance of volume, the following economies can be realized by the installation of the program just outlined.

SUMMARY OF ANNUAL SAVING

	Per Year
(*a*) Reduction in general overhead, through simplified procedure	$ 60,000
(*b*) Reduction of factory expense, through expense control	40,000
(*c*) Reduction in direct labor, through improved wage plan and labor control	35,000
(*d*) Reduction in indirect labor, through improved indirect labor control	40,000
(*e*) Reduction in direct material costs, through redesign of product	75,000
Total	$250,000

This program illustrates that, for the company in question, improvements in various activities are necessary. To effect only some of the improvements will, of course, result in economies and improved performance; but for the company to obtain its desired objective of operating normally, well above its break-even point and at a reasonable rate of profit, it is essential that all parts of the program be put into effect.

General Policies

A management program is a practical plan for realizing certain predetermined objectives.

In order to establish such a program, analysis of the company operation along the lines described in preceding chapters is a first requirement. With such analysis a sound basis is provided for the determination of managerial policies.

With complete knowledge of past and present conditions and prospective trends, sound general policies can be established. They will affect the volume of business to be secured, its probable cost, the extent of plant extension if necessary and its cost, and the expected profit.

Financial policies can then be established. With foreknowledge of financial requirements the sources from which financial aid may be secured can be determined and steps initiated to secure such aid in advance of need. This is highly important because failure to secure financial aid when needed can cause the failure of an otherwise well-developed program.

In view of the foregoing affecting volume and finances, it may be necessary to revise existing policies applying to the form and character of the organization, or the type of controls, or the number and kind of required reports. Also some changes in policy may be necessary concerning plant facilities in matters of additions, rearrangement of layouts, and maintenance.

In order to consummate the plan, some changes in labor policy may be necessary in the way of revision of production standards, changes in the method of wage payment, or other matters.

Sales Policies

Sales policies may require some adjustment, because, in order to secure the planned volume of business, it may be necessary to make changes in present products or add new ones or open up new territory and increase the sales force, possibly with consequent rearrangement of all territories. A change in the method of compensation is also a possibility.

INVENTORY POLICIES

Policies relating to the control of inventories also require examination and possible change. New standards may have to establish what inventories are to be carried, and where, and their amount. All of this, of course, is an important factor affecting financial policies.

Necessity for such a sweeping review of policies will be readily understood and recognized, particularly if the program involves a considerable expansion or contraction of operation.

ORGANIZATION

In connection with the organization, important changes may have to be made. Changes in departmental divisions may be necessary, dividing functions into separate departments in some cases, or combining functions for larger departments, in others. Changes in personnel for the direction of certain departments or the selection of personnel to direct new departments thus created may be necessary as a consequence of organization rearrangement.

CONTROLS

New controls may have to be established or the present controls changed for adequate administration of the program. In any case, the controls presently in use should be carefully reviewed for possible simplification or improved effectiveness. Since the successful administration of the adopted program depends on complete coverage of all important activities, the necessity for such review and possible revision will be recognized.

FACILITIES

Examination of all manufacturing facilities is an important part of the program. Facilities must be adequate for the requirements of the planned volume of business. If the plan involves increased volume, this is particularly true. A careful analysis of requirements in relation to existing facilities must be made in order to locate any possible limitations or bottlenecks. Additional facilities must then be planned for and procured, with care that they be sufficient, but not excessive.

New layouts of equipment may be necessary in order to promote the economical flow of material through process. These must necessarily make provision for the accumulation of material at certain places in process and may have to provide extension or rearrangement of existing storage places, stockrooms, or warehouses.

While the existing layout is being examined or a new one prepared, the most careful scrutiny of accepted practice should be made to find improved methods affecting either economy of performance or quality of product. Each possibility for improvement, particularly if additional facilities are involved, should be carefully considered, the advantage to be secured being weighed against its cost.

LABOR

In view of the important part of labor in the program, it is necessary to make a complete examination of labor relations and to determine what changes if any should be made to insure attainment of the planned objective.

New layouts and changes in methods necessitate revision of standards for those operations affected. A complete revision of all labor performance standards may be necessary, as a consequence of the whole study.

A different wage payment plan may be an essential requirement, for purposes of simplicity of administration, better control, or improved management and labor relations.

REPORTS

Administration of the program requires the exercise of control over all important activities. Adequate control is possible only on the basis of sufficient pertinent information immediately available at specified times. Therefore, the existing system of reports requires a careful review, to insure prompt availability of essential information, with the elimination of all that may be considered nonessential.

Practically every company or business enterprise finds itself in one of three classifications:

(*a*) The company may be experiencing a trend toward decreasing profits, or may have incurred losses for a sustained period of time to such an extent that working capital has been depleted, or may be losing its position in its industry because of the encroachment of competition.

(*b*) The company may desire to expand, either by adding additional products to its present line or by obtaining additional or new markets for its present products.

(*c*) The company may have passed through a period of expansion and now desires to consolidate its gains and hold its position by improving efficiency and thereby increasing its profit.

Every company has some objective. Regardless of the classification into which it falls, a program must be established in order to obtain the desired objective—at a minimum cost—in the shortest possible time—and with the least amount of confusion.

Such a program must indicate the results that are to be obtained and the manner with which they are to be accomplished.

In the preparation of a program, consideration must be given to all activities of the business. These activities necessarily include the subjects in the preceding paragraphs and may be classified into divisions, namely:

1. *The product.*
2. *The manufacturing facilities.*
3. *The merchandising methods.*
4. *The finances.*
5. *The administration including organization and controls.*

Unless consideration is given to all five divisions, it is quite possible that an unbalanced situation may result. That is, a company may find itself with an excellent product and effective merchandising methods, but lack the necessary finances to promote the product to its fullest extent.

Or a company may improve its cash position and improve its merchandising methods but neglect to develop its product properly. Or a company may develop a satisfactory product, improve its manufacturing facilities and merchandising methods to the utmost, and have sufficient finances available, but neglect to establish the proper administration over the various activities.

Therefore, a management program should be established only after a thorough analysis has been made of all activities of the business. Such an analysis has been described in preceding chapters devoted to the subject, "Analyzing the Company Operation." Survey will reveal the weaknesses in various divisions and permit the determination of steps toward their correction.

Every management program should include two statements:

1. *A projected profit and loss statement* for a low volume and a high volume, which will show the profit or loss under existing operating conditions. A second set of statements, also for the high and low volume, should then be prepared incorporating the savings, economies, or improvements contemplated, in order to show their effect on the profit and loss statement.

2. *A cash forecast,* again for the low and high volume contemplated, in order to show the borrowings necessary or the cash that will be available and the time when such borrowings are needed.

These two statements will show the results to be accomplished by the management program. Comparison should be made frequently (at least once a month) between actual performance and projected performance, in order to determine how well the program is being followed and what steps should be initiated for improvement when performance fails to conform with the plan.

It must be noted that every program is different, because it must be prepared for a different set of conditions in every instance, being based on the findings resulting from the business survey.

A great many well-conceived management programs fail in their accomplishment through lack of formal recording and publishing of the final decisions.

During the period of discussion, minutes should be kept of all conferences and periodically summarized and classified as to subject matter in accordance with the basic outline of the program.

Failure to put everything into writing is conducive to errors and inconsistencies in the final draft of the program. Frequently this nullifies the careful reasoning that may have gone into the discussion of each program subject.

CHAPTER 14

MANAGEMENT METHODS

·

DEFINITION

The term management is generally used to designate both administration and management of a business. A definite distinction should exist, however, and the duties and responsibilities of each be clearly defined.

The management consists of the directors of a company or, when the company is owned by one or two individuals, of these owners. It may consist of financial interests, such as banks or investment houses, operating through their own selected directors and the principal officers.

The duties of the management of any business are to establish over-all major policies and to make sure that they are carried out. The management must assume the responsibility for the result to the business, whether it be a profit or a loss.

The management *must establish the policies of the company.*

ADMINISTRATION

The administration may consist of an individual employed for this purpose or a committee group composed of various members of the organization. If an individual owns the business, it will consist of that owner, who also serves as the management.

The administration of a company is concerned with *execution,* the "carrying out" of orders, decisions, or policies. The duties of the administrators may be defined, therefore, as the control and direction of all activities of the business, in accordance with the *policies established by management*. Administrators necessarily include some of the lower levels of the organization, even minor department heads in frequent cases, who, because of the special characteristics of their departmental functions, are in effect implementing the policies of management.

EXECUTION

The policies of a business define the basic objectives and the procedures which guide its operation. They should be determined by management and executed by administration.

Policies are established and in effect in every business, but are not always recognized as such. They are seldom clearly defined and recorded, are frequently determined quickly, often without sound data, and often are made known to the organization by word of mouth or by hearsay. They frequently remain in effect for a long period of time without management realization that they no longer apply to current conditions.

Policies enter into all phases of a business. A few policy questions are suggested here:

1. Merchandising. Is it the policy of the company to develop its products and sales organization to reach all divisions of a particular market? Or to develop products for markets that may not even be related or that cannot be reached through established outlets?

2. Quality of Product. Is it the policy of the company to produce only the highest quality of product, regardless of sales volume or costs? Is it a policy of the company to back the quality of their product with a money-back guarantee? Or is it a company policy to maintain present quality until competition forces management to improve it or to engage in research in order to stay ahead of competition?

3. Expansion Desired in Manufacturing. Is it the policy of the company to expand manufacturing facilities from profits or to expand by means of outside financing?

4. Method of Dealing with Employees. Is it the policy of the company to promote from the ranks or to go outside for new talent when an opening occurs? Is it a company policy to have the president deal directly with employee representatives or only indirectly through the personnel director? Is it the policy to furnish new employees with a manual covering the rules of the company?

These are only a few of the policy questions which enter into every business. Their importance makes it self-evident why they should be properly recorded and currently reviewed by management. The method of recording is of little import so long as the administrators receive written memoranda covering the policy. Copies of all policies should be kept in one place, readily accessible to those who must carry them out.

Every company should bring its policies out into the light. If they are not recorded, it is the duty of management to set them down on paper, to analyze them, to see how many are being carried out as management intended and how many no longer apply to present conditions.

When this task has been completed, a revised set of policies should be drawn up. Administration will then know what management requires of it. Obsolete policies will be discontinued. Employees will have management's viewpoints on problems vital to them and to the business.

One of the most important policies is that relating to the method or type of administration. A small business frequently finds the owner also acting as active manager. A large business generally has its ownership divided among a large number of persons who must employ a manager.

The owner–manager will generally display more "drive" because his incentive includes not only his salary and his participation in the profits but also his pride in the continued operation of a business. The incentive for an employed manager lies largely in the continuation of his salary or in the security of his job.

An owner–manager may lack certain characteristics of a good manager but have the support of a strong board of directors or an advisory committee to balance his weaknesses. On the other hand, an employed manager may be a strong individual with all the "drive" of an owner–manager, and yet be unable to secure proper benefits to ownership because of a weak board of directors and no executive or advisory committee.

In the case of an owner–manager, invariably the time comes when ownership must be divided, either due to a desire for more funds, or because the owner–manager is no longer able to operate the business. Careful study of the administration to be substituted must then be made.

Some of the questions to be answered in determining the proper method of management and administration are:

1. Should there be a strong, active board of directors?

2. Is an employed manager to be a strong creative type of individual?

3. Should there be an executive, operating, or advisory committee—or all three?

4. Is the ownership to be transferred from a single individual to the public? If so, is the former owner still to be active in the affairs of the business?

5. Should an additional incentive be offered the proposed employed manager in the form of participation in ownership or profits?

SUMMARY

The effect of a clearly understood and applied management method is to tie the organization closely to the management program. Without a well-defined management method, the implementation of the program may easily fail in accomplishment, through the failure of individuals to recognize or to differentiate between their specific areas of responsibility and activity.

Sometimes it is even desirable to indicate on the organization chart itself the various functional levels at which management gives way to administration and administration gives way to performance.

In any case, a clear understanding of these several relationships, by the men and women who are the vital elements of an enterprise, is essential to the successful continuity of a business.

CHAPTER 15

BUDGETARY CONTROL

•

DEFINITIONS

In the operation of all companies there are certain fiscal data and ratios which serve to guide business toward profitable results. These statistical facts, if properly employed, constitute the working tools of management, just as machine tools and other factory equipment constitute the working tools of production.

These tools are called "controls," more specifically in this case, budgetary controls, simply because they are used for that purpose.

Budgetary control provides the basis for maintenance of proper relationship between the income and the expenses of a business. It is the master control of the enterprise. It must include sales, in order to determine the income, and all expenses (for labor, material, supplies, and overhead charges) as well as capital expenditures for development, research, and new equipment, in order to keep the total expenditures within the total income.

A *budget* is a measurement of what was accomplished against a predetermined standard.

A *flexible budget* is one that relates the budget standards directly to the actual performance, rather than to a predetermined activity. This calls for a distinction between a *budget* and a *forecast*. They are not the same, although many executives think of them synonymously.

A *forecast* is a "look forward"—a proposal—with objectives determined by projection or judgment or, in many cases, by wishful thinking.

It is sometimes difficult, when forecasting the next year's program for a business, to make this distinction mentally. It is an important distinction and must not be disregarded in management's thinking if flexibility of budgetary control is to be achieved.

To make flexible budgetary control a working governor in the business, three principles of timing must be observed. They are:

1. The control must cover current fiscal periods. These may be a day, a week, or a month. Any period greater than a month nullifies the effect of budgetary control.

2. The basis of measurement must be the current activity. This may be in sales, for measuring selling expense and direct labor for factory expense. Direct labor may be expressed in dollars, hours, tonnage, or quantity.

3. Results must be reported promptly. This means that, whether the fiscal period is a day or a week or a month, the record of budget efficiency must be in the hands of management promptly.

If a daily control is exercised, the results of each day must be on the desks of those responsible early the following day.

If monthly control is exercised, especially in smaller companies, good organization and planning of clerical work should place the budget statements in the hands of management within seven working days following the period's closing date.

Many companies close their budget statements earlier than this. If a longer time is taken, the statements lose their control value and become merely historical.

Preparation

Installation of flexible budgetary control requires the following major records:

1. Charts of accounts and their description.
2. Distribution of labor payroll to departments.
3. Analysis of payroll by account for each pay period.
4. Distribution of expense terms by account to each department.

5. Distribution of sales by products and units.
6. Distribution of other income.
7. Record of orders booked.
8. Labor standards per unit of production.
9. Material standards per unit of production.

The first step in preparing the budget is a study and charting of past expenditures by months, and the expression of all expenses as fixed, semifixed, or variable. A few simple techniques have been developed in recent years to make these determinations somewhat more of a science than an art.

The traditional accounting viewpoint considered an expenditure as *fixed,* only when the ledgers showed a uniform charge to an account over a continuous succession of fiscal periods. The modern viewpoint presumes that every expenditure has a fixed content when it does not vary directly and entirely with the activity that creates it.

Naturally depreciation, taxes, insurance, dues, and similar expenses are "fixed," because they are expense functions dependent entirely on *time,* and the necessity of "being in business." They may fluctuate by reason of changes in the basic structure of the business or of discretionary changes in management policy, but they do not *vary* ordinarily with changes in the business' activity. Exceptions to this rule, such as a usage application of depreciation, are too rare to be considered.

Accounts such as supervision; indirect labor; heat, light, and power; and office salaries may seem to be constant, and appear merely to fluctuate during various periods of operation. A great many of these are not really *constant* and, by a simple analysis explained later, show the very definite hybrid characteristic of being partly fixed and partly variable.

A variable expenditure, which may be either an expense or a direct cost, is one that varies *directly* with the activity causing it. For example, direct labor ordinarily is a true variable based on units produced, because at zero operation direct labor cost is zero, but it increases continuously and uniformly with production. Direct material is another true variable and varies directly with the direct labor input to the plant. The actual fact that it may not be merely reveals a bad operating condition (such as waste, requisition error, or faulty accounting control) or some rare exception in processing technique that is peculiar to the enterprise.

Some expenses are true variables also, such as indirect labor. And again a distinction must be drawn between indirect labor which serves direct labor (such as truckers and setup men) and nonproductive labor which serves the enterprise itself (such as watchmen, janitors, and millwrights).

Supplies and small tools are usually considered true variables, depending on their definition in the business requiring them.

The hybrid expenses mentioned earlier, those that are partly fixed and partly variable, require special consideration. They bulk large in any system of expense control and are the large concern of budgetary control. If we keep in mind the basic definitions, these semifixed expenses comprise two elements of measure, *time* and *activity*.

To illustrate this point, an account like purchased power will consist of a stand-by or connected load charge which is a monthly fixed expense based on a *time* interval, as well as a consumption charge based on kilowatts used, which is a variable expense dependent on activity. A domestic gas or light bill is a good illustration of a semifixed expense.

ANALYSIS OF EXPENSE

With these understandings in mind, the practical question arises as to how the characteristics of an expense can be determined. There are two ways: a trial-and-error method, which is a composite of experience, perception, and comparison; and a precise and scientific analysis of experience, which mathematically resolves the relationship.

There are two methods of making this analysis. One is purely mathematical, involving the cumbersome equation of least squares. The other, the graphical method, is just as accurate but much easier to understand and apply. The graphical method of expense analysis, being the most practicable, is described in detail in the following pages.

GRAPHICAL ANALYSIS

Figure 11 shows the basic graphical relationships between an expenditure and its parent activity.

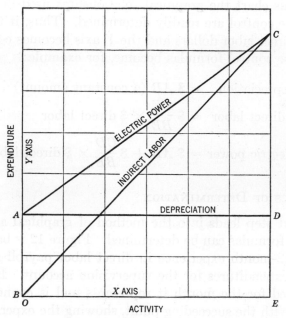

FIG. 11.   Expense–Activity Relationship Graph

The horizontal (or X axis) measures activity from zero to the right and can represent dollars, units, employees, or any other activity effort of a business.

The vertical (or Y axis) measures expenditure from zero upwards and, although usually in dollars, could just as well represent quantity or people, depending on the relationship being analyzed.

The lines AC and AD are the *relationship* lines between values for activity and expenditure. Thus, line *AD* shows that, no matter what value is selected in the activity range, the expenditure value is the same, as measured on the vertical scale. It is a *fixed expense,* but line *BC* uniformly increases from zero as activity increases, indicating a *variable* relationship between the two axes. Line *AC* shows a *semifixed* relationship, because at zero activity it shows a residual expenditure and thereafter increases proportionately as activity increases.

From this chart the graphical relationships used in establishing expense control are readily determined. Thus, if the *X* axis becomes direct labor dollars and the *Y* axis becomes cost dollars, the expense control formulas become, for example:

$$\text{Depreciation} \quad = \$\, AB \text{ (a constant amount)}$$

$$\text{Indirect labor} \, = \$\, \frac{CE}{BE} \times \$ \text{ direct labor}$$

$$\text{Electric power} = \$\, AB + \$\, \frac{CD}{BE} \times \$ \text{ direct labor}$$

Mechanics of Determination

The next step leads into the method of graphical analysis by which the formulas can be determined. Figure 12 is based on an assumed 12-month experience in direct labor payroll and corresponding expenditures for the supervision account. Each point is numbered for the month it represents and is connected by a light line with the succeeding point, showing the experience path the account has taken.

The problem, first, is to find the best line going through the pattern of points. The best line will, of course, be the one passing closest to all the points in the pattern and will naturally pass through a point which is the average of all the points. On the chart, this is shown by the point *M*.

Next the slope of the best line passing through the average point must be determined. This requires the use of a formula:

$$a = \frac{\Sigma xy}{\Sigma x^2}$$

in which a is the slope of the line, and x is the algebraic value of the distance of each point from the *average* point measured on the horizontal axis. y is then the algebraic value of the distance of each point from the average point measured on the vertical axis.

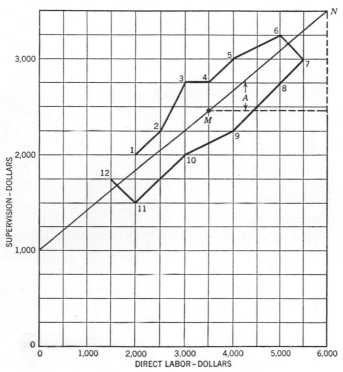

Fig. 12.   Graphical Analysis of an Expense

The "algebraic sum" is required because points to the left or below the average point or both will have a minus value in the formula. For example, if the significant numbers are used, point 1 has an x value of -3, and a y value of -2; point 3 an x value of -1 and a y value of $+1$; and point 5 an x value of $+1$ and a y value of $+2$.

The detail of this computation is as follows:

Point No.	x	y	x^2	xy
1	-3	-2	9	$+6$
2	-2	-1	4	$+2$
3	-1	$+1$	1	-1
4	0	$+1$	0	0
5	$+1$	$+2$	1	$+2$
6	$+3$	$+3$	9	$+9$
7	$+4$	$+2$	16	$+8$
8	$+3$	$+1$	9	$+3$
9	$+1$	-1	1	-1
10	-1	-2	1	$+2$
11	-3	-4	9	$+12$
12	-4	-3	16	$+12$
Total			76	54

$$a = \frac{\Sigma xy}{\Sigma x^2} = \frac{54}{76} = 0.71$$

On the chart shown, these calculations have been made, and the slope of the best line through M is found to be 0.71. The equation for a straight line is $y = ax$, in which a is its slope and has just been found to be 0.71. A value for x, say 5, is then assumed, and the equation $y = ax$ is then solved for y, which gives point N on the chart. A line is drawn through M and N, as shown on the chart, and the result is the "best line."

On the many budget installations where this method is used, the mechanics of the foregoing procedure were readily picked up by clerks with very inferior mathematical education after just a few minutes of practice. Using a year's experience for the analysis of each account, the average clerk can make five account analyses an hour. This means that, if there are 100 accounts in the accounting controls, a whole year's operation can be analyzed within three days (if it is assumed, of course, that the charts have been kept up during the year).

Why all this precise use of mathematics on figures that in themselves are frequently arbitrarily assigned to an account? The answer is: In flexible budgeting the formulas used must contain no errors of judgment. Otherwise, the budgetary control will not correctly measure performance against standard. The experience used may indeed be very bad, but that error must not be compounded by the addition of judgment error in analysis.

The question may also be raised as to why mathematics is used when the line could as easily be drawn by sight. In the example given, an ideal pattern of experience was purposely selected. On actual expense experience, patterns of points will be found that cannot be resolved by any other method than the one just described.

SELECTING THE FLEXIBLE BUDGET LINE

Figure 13 illustrates the practical application of the graphical analysis. Line AC is the one just determined by actual experi-

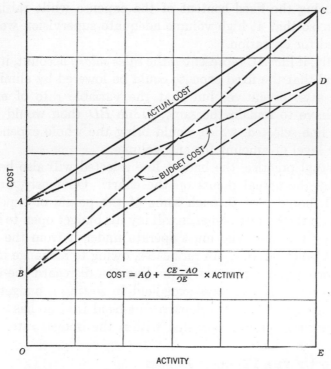

FIG. 13. Application of Graphical Analysis

ence in Figure 12. Where should the budget line be? Shall the line be made to come down faster from C to B, or should it merely be lowered to BD? In other words, shall the reduction be made in the fixed or variable part of the expense?

It all depends on the character of the expense. Assume that the line AC represented purchased electric power. Obviously, the stand-by or demand charge cannot be lowered (except by new contracts with the power company or changes in the plant layout and equipment), and so economies would have to be effected in the kilowatt consumption alone. Therefore, a budget line would be selected, as illustrated on the chart by AD, giving the same fixed rate but a lower rate of variable cost.

If line AC represented the supervision account, it might be decided that low volumes did not warrant the current elaborate salaried organization. The budget line would then be set as BC, by reducing the fixed content of the expense while raising the variable, so that at high volume adequate supervision would be provided for operation.

Finally, if line AC represented the *sales salary* account, it might be found that the fixed expense could be lowered by eliminating certain sales executives but that the variable rate of expense would have to remain the same. Line BD then would be the budget line selected, which would bring the whole expense into a lower level of amount for any volume.

In actual practice, the budget line selected will also be influenced by the actual points on the chart. Obviously, any line selected should pass through some of the points of experience. Otherwise the budget manager will lay his budget open to serious attack by the man who must operate under it from the standpoint of practicability. In rare cases, owing to a change in technique, or equipment, or rates, the line can disregard the experience entirely. It is always expedient in setting a budget, however, to be able to show a department head that he has at some previous time actually operated within the budget rate.

Setting Up the Flexible Budget

Figure 14 shows a highly simplified example of a flexible budget for an enterprise with high volume double its low volume. As may be noted, the factory expense budget is computed on direct labor and the general expenses on net sales.

To take up the first account, indirect labor, the budget is found by multiplying the direct labor $5,000 by the variable expense

BUDGET STATEMENT
GENERAL EXPENSE IS BASED ON NET SALES
FACTORY EXPENSE IS BASED ON DIRECT LABOR

MONTHLY LOW VOLUME

Acct. Name	Fixed	Budget Variable	Total	Actual Total	Variance Over	Variance Under
Direct Labor		10%		$ 5,000		
Net Sales		100		50,000		
Mfg. Expense						
Indir. Labor	$ 700	25	$1,950	1,900		$ 50
Indir. Mat.	300	15	1,050	1,000		50
Indir. Exp.	500	10	1,000	1,200	$200	
Total	1,500	50	4,000	4,100	100	
Gen. Expense						
Selling	500	4	2,500	2,600	100	
Admin.	1,000	1	1,500	1,400		100
Total	1,500	5	4,000	4,000		
Grand Total	$3,000		$8,000	$ 8,100	$100	

MONTHLY HIGH VOLUME

Acct. Name	Fixed	Budget Variable	Total	Actual Total	Variance Over	Variance Under
Direct Labor		10%		$ 10,000		
Net Sales		100		100,000		
Mfg. Expense						
Indir. Labor	$ 700	25	$ 3,200	2,900		$300
Indir. Mat.	300	15	1,800	1,900	$100	
Indir. Exp.	500	10	1,500	1,800	300	
Total	1,500	50	6,500	6,600	100	
Gen. Expense						
Selling	500	4	4,500	4,700	200	
Admin.	1,000	1	2,000	1,800		200
Total	1,500	5	6,500	6,500		
Grand Total	$3,000		$13,000	$ 13,100	$100	

FIG. 14

factor of 25 per cent and adding to this result the fixed expense of $700, for a total of $1,950.

Similarly, the other factory expense accounts are computed as shown.

The general expense accounts are computed in the same way, except that net sales is the base used for converting the budget formula into the budget amount. In actual practice, all these accounts are broken down into the detail that corresponds to the actual accounting control.

After the budget amounts are figured, the actual expense is entered against the corresponding budget account, and the over- or under-budget is *variance*-figured. Unless there is a very good reason for doing otherwise, it is preferable to use over and under columns rather than a single column with red or black entries. They not only simplify the mechanical preparation of the budget reports but also, more important still, make the budget understandable to department heads in the factory, when the over-all budget is broken down departmentally. Red and black figures are confusing to a shop foreman and should be avoided if at all possible.

With reference again to Figure 14, it may be noted that on high volume the same formula will apply to the larger direct labor and net sales bases. The budgets clearly indicate that, when activity is doubled, expenses do not necessarily double too. For example, at $50,000 volume, total expense is budgeted at $8,000; but, at $100,000 volume, total expense is budgeted at $13,000. In other words, a 100 per cent increase in volume requires only a 62½ per cent increase in expense.

THE BREAK-EVEN POINT

As has been pointed out in Section 1, the field of operating profit lies in this expense differential for varying volumes above the break-even point. That is why budgetary control plays a vital part in a business and why it must be adequate in its scope and method of application. It profits business but little to figure gross margins and potential volumes, unless there is realistic knowledge as to where the break-even point lies. Too many concerns determine this point from a historical accounting experience and accept it as an unchangeable fact not greatly affected by pricing policy or cost reductions, or the fixed cost of being in business.

As a matter of fact, the break-even point is definitely dependent on these very factors. It can be easily and accurately determined after *all* the direct and indirect expense accounts have been analyzed for their fixed and variable contents.

This is done by, first, adding up all the fixed expense amounts and all the variable expense ratios; then, by subtracting the latter from the gross sales after they have been expressed as a percentage of the sales dollar, and, lastly, by dividing the fixed expense by the variable difference (marginal income) thus found.

For example, suppose the fixed expense totals $10,000 per month, and the variable expense totals 75 per cent of gross sales. The difference between gross sales and variable expense is therefore 25 per cent.

Dividing the fixed expense of $10,000 by this marginal income of 25 per cent gives $40,000 as the break-even point.

This is a convenient formula to remember. It can be worked out for individual lines of products as well as for the over-all operation, providing the ledgers are sufficiently detailed to carry income and expense accounts by products.

If such analysis by products can be made, charts similar to Figure 15 can readily be devised, enabling management to test the effect of given sales volume combinations on the resulting profit.

A change in fixed expense materially alters the break-even point if the variable expenses remain constant. It is very easy for a business to add a clerk here and a clerk there, to provide a larger advertising budget, to project a more extensive research and development program, without realizing that it is materially changing the location of the break-even point in its sales or production volume.

The break-even point has other management aspects that are important from a budgetary control standpoint. First of all, the break-even point should not be too close to normal operating capacities because of the small profit attainable.

Back of this statement are the equally important considerations of plant operation itself. A break-even point that lies close to normal capacity gives a business a very small factor of safety

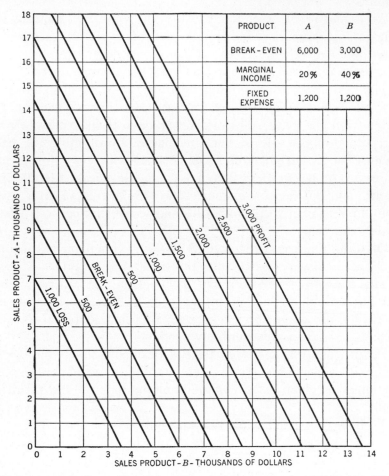

PRODUCT	A	B
BREAK - EVEN	6,000	3,000
MARGINAL INCOME	20%	40%
FIXED EXPENSE	1,200	1,200

FIG. 15.   Profit–Loss Chart for Two Products Having Different Marginal Incomes

on profits and gives management a constant marketing headache in its struggle to maintain the essential volume.

The break-even point should never exceed 75 per cent of the normal sales or production volume. The satisfactory and safe proportion is between 50 and 60 per cent for sound profit control.

Another important consideration of the break-even point is its relation to inventory costs. If the *normal* expense overhead can be set at this break-even point, low cost inventory is manufactured. The unabsorbed overhead variance that usually excites management into criticism of the operating control can be eliminated.

PROCEDURAL APPLICATION OF BUDGETARY CONTROL

The procedural techniques of budgetary control are important in the successful application of a budget. As mentioned previously, errors of judgment must be minimized as much as possible. It is modern practice to maintain currently the same type of charts described for every account carried in the factory and general ledgers.

These charts are laid out on standard 8½-by-11-inch graph paper, with horizontal and vertical scales selected to cover the possible range of values used and yet throw the line diagonally through the sheet. Back of each chart is a sheet that carries the account number and name, the budget formula, the definition of the account, the distribution of the charges, and, if desired, the values used in plotting the chart.

At the beginning of the year the budget line is laid on the chart, and each month's actual experience is plotted on the chart. As the year proceeds, the pattern of experience is developed. It shows how closely the control is operating and at the same time develops the trend for the determination of next year's budget. Such charts are similar to Figure 12 which was described previously.

In some plants entire control is exercised by such charts, which are blueprinted each month and given to the various department heads. This practice makes it unnecessary to figure and type the budget schedules and is most certainly the most simple and effective presentation that can be made.

However, if the organization is *not* chart-minded, the budget schedules must be prepared in conventional form. The charts then merely become the working tools of the budget manager.

Application

In rounding out the complete installation of a flexible budgetary control, certain procedural routines should be established. They will organize the entire control into an effective program for management's use. These routines are as follows:

1. The preparation of a *forecast* at the beginning of each year, by months and cumulative for the coming year. This forecast will be prepared for a low and for a normal volume of sales and will show the profit to be expected from those volumes when the budget standards are realized. See Figure 14 for form.

2. The preparation of a monthly forecast at the beginning of each month, in the form of a profit and loss statement for the coming month. Expected sales volume will be corrected for past experience, and budgeted expenses for that volume and profit will be indicated.

3. At the end of each month an actual profit and loss statement will be prepared, as well as a budgeted profit and loss statement based on the *actual volume realized*. These statements will measure the effectiveness of the operations for the month and, cumulatively, for the period to date.

4. The accumulation of controllable expenses daily or weekly, wherever possible. This will permit comparison of actual expenses with the budget *during* the month as well as at the end of the month, for earlier corrective action.

Current, that is, daily and weekly, accumulation of elements of sales, expenses, finances, and manufacturing will also simplify the work of accounting and tend to reduce monthly peaks in accounting procedure.

Sales, purchase material commitments, material received, production by departments, direct labor by departments, indirect labor by accounts, supplies received or disbursed from stores, traveling expenses, scrap, engineering time by projects, and all other pertinent data can be accumulated daily or weekly with little if any more effort than that required by monthly accumulations.

Having *current* data, it will be possible to apply the variable factors of the budget standards to sales and production at any time during the month, to determine the budgeted amount for the sales and production actually realized, and to forecast the profit that should result by the end of the period.

The foregoing comparison of actual and budgeted performance will then indicate the need for remedial action and show where such action must be taken. The allocation of such corrective action to the various organization levels responsible will give added emphasis to the control and make it an effective tool for profitable company operation.

BENEFITS

The benefits, both tangible and intangible, derived from a budgetary control application are:

1. Management will have a sound plan of operation for the year.

2. Management will quickly know when results are below expectations.

3. Management will be able to take remedial action promptly, and variations will be held to a minimum.

4. Management will be able to predetermine cash requirements, whether it will be necessary to borrow, and, if so, how much.

5. Expenses will be held to a minimum, and profits will be larger.

6. Management will be able to plan its disbursements more accurately and to predetermine the condition of the accounts payable and the accounts receivable.

7. Management will have a sound expense control *policy*.

CHAPTER 16

CASH FORECASTS

•

Definition

Supplementing the budgetary control is the *cash forecast*. This is derived from the standards and objectives determined for the budget. The cash forecast translates the company income into company assets and regulates the amount and time at which this disposal may be made.

The cash forecast may be defined as a projection of income and expenditure data. It reveals to management the origin and disposal of all cash of the business and the balance sheet effect of such transactions.

For these reasons the importance of developing a cash forecast for a company is secondary only to the establishment of sound budgetary control.

Purpose

The cash forecast informs management in detail as to the income and outgo of cash, month by month, during the fiscal year. It establishes a sound guide on which to maintain the proper cash position. It also indicates whether borrowings are necessary and, if so, how much, during what periods, and when they can be repaid.

APPLICATION

The cash forecast is built up before the beginning of the fiscal year and immediately establishes the degree of soundness of the proposed yearly operation plan. Completion of the forecast should show:

1. Whether the cash position throughout the year will be satisfactory.

2. What borrowings will be necessary but might be avoided if a revision were made in the manufacturing program.

3. What borrowings will be necessary but can be repaid during the year without any change in the operating plan.

4. What borrowings will be necessary for which there will not be cash available at any time during the year to repay the loan. In this event it may be necessary to revise the entire program of operation.

The forecast, when completed, serves as a standard for management to use in measuring the result of operations as far as the cash position is concerned. It is a measure of sales against the forecast, the collection rate, the inventory changes, and similar factors.

The forecast should be revised each month for the remainder of the year in accord with actual accomplishment and the initial forecast compared with actual accomplishment as a means of control.

CONSTRUCTION

A cash forecast is shown in Figure 16. The following elements are necessary to its construction:

1. *A sales forecast* in order to determine the income.

2. *A determination of the collection rate based on the sales terms;* the actual collection rate for the past year should also be checked to determine whether the collection policy is being followed and, if not, what must be done to correct the condition.

3. *Projection of the inventory picture,* which requires a management decision as to what the company's inventory policy

CASH FORECAST AFTER ECONOMIES

	July	Aug.	Sept.	Oct.	Nov.	Dec.	Jan.	Feb.	Mar.	Apr.	May	June	Total for 12 Mos.
GROSS SALES	$180,000	$180,000	$170,000	$170,000	$170,000	$150,000	$170,000	$180,000	$210,000	$230,000	$240,000	$250,000	$2,300,000
Cash Income from Sales	126,000	126,000	119,000	119,000	119,000	105,000	119,000	126,000	147,000	161,000	168,000	175,000	1,610,000
	June 44,000	45,000	45,000	42,500	42,500	42,500	35,500	42,500	45,000	52,500	47,500	60,000	544,500
	May 7,600	June 9,000	9,000	9,000	8,500	8,500	8,500	7,500	8,500	9,000	10,500	11,500	107,100
Other cash income	1,260	1,260	1,190	1,190	1,190	1,050	1,190	1,260	1,470	1,610	1,680	1,750	16,100
TOTAL CASH INCOME	178,860	181,260	174,190	171,690	171,190	157,050	164,190	177,260	201,970	224,110	227,680	248,250	2,277,700
DISBURSEMENTS													
Material	85,000	85,000	85,000	75,000	85,000	90,000	105,000	115,000	120,000	125,000	125,000	125,000	1,220,000
Direct Labor	16,200	15,300	15,300	15,300	13,500	15,300	16,200	18,900	20,700	21,600	22,500	22,500	213,300
Indirect Labor	8,710	8,390	8,390	8,390	7,810	8,390	8,710	9,520	10,090	10,380	10,660	10,660	110,100
Oper. & Maint. Supplies	3,570	3,570	3,570	3,160	3,570	3,750	4,340	4,740	4,930	5,120	5,130	5,130	50,590
Services and Other Mfg. Expense	6,350	6,020	6,020	6,020	5,350	6,010	6,350	7,350	8,010	8,350	8,680	8,680	83,190
Taxes, Mfg.				1,690						1,690			3,380
Taxes, Gen.				1,560						1,560			3,120
Product Engineering	3,040	2,920	2,920	2,920	2,890	2,920	3,040	3,370	3,590	3,710	3,820	3,820	38,960
Selling Expense	8,560	8,560	8,440	8,440	8,440	8,190	8,440	8,560	8,930	9,170	9,290	9,370	104,390
Service Expense	2,390	2,390	2,310	2,310	2,310	2,150	2,310	2,390	2,640	2,810	2,890	2,970	29,870
Admin. Expense	4,230	4,230	4,150	4,150	4,150	3,990	4,150	4,230	4,480	4,650	4,730	4,810	51,950
Life Insurance												10,380	10,380
NET CASH REQ. FOR OPERATION	138,050	136,380	136,100	128,940	133,020	140,700	158,540	174,060	183,370	194,050	192,700	203,320	1,919,230
Probable Excess & Gains	13,000	10,000	7,000	4,000	2,000	1,000			7,000	8,000	10,000	12,000	
TOTAL CASH REQ. FOR OPERATION	151,050	146,380	143,100	132,940	135,020	141,700	158,540	174,060	176,370	186,050	182,700	191,320	1,919,230
Research & Develop.	1,923	1,923	1,923	1,923	1,923	1,923	1,923	1,923	1,923	1,923	1,923	1,923	23,076
Betterments		5,000	5,000	10,000	10,000	10,000							40,000
Engineering Fee	1,500	1,500	1,500	1,500	1,500	1,500							9,000
Appropriated Cash Total	3,423	8,423	8,423	13,423	13,423	13,423	1,923	1,923	1,923	1,923	1,923	1,923	72,076
TOTAL CASH REQUIRED	154,473	154,803	151,523	146,360	148,443	155,123	160,463	175,983	178,293	187,973	184,623	193,243	1,991,306
MONTHLY CASH BALANCE	24,387	26,457	22,667	25,327	22,747	1,927	3,727	1,277	23,677	36,137	43,057	55,007	286,394
CUMULATIVE CASH BALANCE	24,387	50,844	73,511	98,838	121,585	123,512	127,239	128,516	152,193	188,330	231,387	286,394	286,394

Notes:

Noncash items—Depreciation
Losses on Returns
Returns & Allow.

Material—Figured 60 days ahead
Labor —Figured 30 days ahead
Supplies—Figured 30 days ahead

FIG. 16

must be, and the setting of the month-by-month inventory balance to maintain this policy.

FIXED AND VARIABLE EXPENSE FACTORS

	Fixed $ per Mo.	Variable % of Base
GROSS SALES		
Cash Income from Sales.............		70% of current mo.
		25% in 30 days
		5% in 60 days
Other Cash Income		
TOTAL CASH INCOME		
DISBURSEMENTS		
Material........................		50% Gross Sales
Direct Labor.....................		9% Gross Sales
Indirect Labor...................	$3,536 per month	31.7% Direct Labor
Oper. & Maint. Supplies..........	200 per month	21.9% Direct Labor
Services and Other Mfg. Expense..	340 per month	37.1% Direct Labor
Taxes, Mfg.....................	Calendar	
Taxes, Gen.....................	Calendar	
Product Engineering..............	1,012 per month	12.5% Direct Labor
Selling Expense..................	6,367 per month	1.22% Gross Sales
Service Expense..................	900 per month	.83% Gross Sales
Admin. Expense.................	2,740 per month	.83% Gross Sales
Life Insurance..................	Calendar	
Research & Develop..............	1,923 per month	

Fig. 17

4. *Production determination,* normally the forecasted sales, plus or minus the inventory change. Often it is set at a uniform figure to avoid the penalties inflicted on a business when there is too great a fluctuation in employment.

5. *Determination of the cash cost,* which requires a knowledge of the fixed and variable cash expense of the company and is found by adding the monthly cash fixed expense to the variable cash cost of production (see Figure 17).

6. *Determination of the cash gain or loss,* the difference between the collections and the cash cost.

7. *Determination of the cash on hand,* the cash gain or loss added to or subtracted from the cash on hand at the beginning of the month.

Consideration should be given to any increase or decrease in the receivables and payables, which will affect the amount of cash available. If these two accounts remain uniform, they need not be considered, but, if terms of sale, or purchase, or seasonal fluctuations are important, they must be worked into the forecast.

Detail Notes

Sales

The sales forecast should be most realistically and carefully determined. If it is not the result of an organized study of the market potentiality, based on past experience and correlated with the industry and general economic picture, any fiscal projection will be waste of effort. The wise management will *understate* rather than overstate its anticipated sales volume.

Collections

The cash position of a company is affected most easily by the collection policy of the company. In fact, the company cash is more sensitive to this influence than any other fiscal policy of operation. The collection policy must be an aggressive one; otherwise, earnings are frozen in receivables, and cash is immobilized by the customer himself.

It is not difficult to determine the collection rate, if the receivables are aged properly. An analysis of the ledgers will readily show how much of a given month's billing was paid for according to terms, 30 days late, 60 days late, and so on. If the sales terms are 30 days net, the outstanding receivables should not average over 45 days of sales. In forecasting the cash position, however, the account aging method is preferred.

If the collection policy of the company is an aggressive one pointed at keeping customer's accounts current, the forecast of collections based on sales terms of 30 days net should follow these ratios for each month's billing:

70% within 30 days
25% within 60 days
5% within 90 days

If installment selling is a part of the sales terms, longer collection periods will be required. For example, if the sales terms are 10 per cent down payment, 12 monthly installments, the turnover of receivables is very slow and will average six months. Current business practice, however, provides for the handling of these types of accounts through acceptance or discount corporations, thus relieving the manufacturing company of the financial burden of carrying them.

Inventories

Second only to the effect of receivables on the cash position is that of inventory. Cash tied up in large inventories yields no profit and may result in a loss if the inventory is not kept on a current basis. Chapter 30 in Section 4 should be read carefully in this connection.

Production

Although uniform production schedules are the most profitable in a manufacturing program, they are not always feasible in a job-order type of business. However, a business that has a *stable market,* even though it manufactures to a customer's individual order, will find that the production pattern is consistent through the year. Though it may involve wider fluctuations in the manufacturing schedules, a definite production plan can be established nevertheless. Custom grey-iron job foundries illustrate the character of this job-order type of manufacture.

STATEMENT OF DAILY BALANCES

Date...................

	Today		Month to Date	
Cash:	$		$	
Bank A				
Bank B				
Other				
Total				
Receivables:				
Current				
30 days				
60 days				
Over 60 days				
Less:				
Collections				
Balance				
Orders received:				
Field Acct.				
House Acct.				
Total				
Purchases:				
Commitments				
Less Invoices				
Balance				
Payables:				
Invoiced				
Paid				
Balance				

Fig. 18

Cash Cost

In placing the fixed cash expenditures on the forecast, the fact that the general books may be on an accrual basis is not to be considered.

The spot outlay must be determined for the month in which the bill is due and placed accordingly.

In particular, capital commitments for betterments should be watched out for and satisfactory terms arranged well in advance of such purchases. Otherwise the borrowing requirements, if there are any, may be pyramided to a point where the banks will be unwilling to make the accommodation.

Other factors to watch out for are mid-season or other price or cost changes that affect the variable cost ratios. For example, a price decrease of 10 per cent on products with a 50 per cent material cost ratio will require refiguring of the cash cost, with a 55½ per cent material cost ratio. Or, if economies are worked out reducing the material cost 10 per cent, the material cost ratio must then be refigured at 45 per cent.

STATEMENT OF DAILY BALANCES

Effective control over the cash forecast and, for that matter, over the fiscal operation of the business itself lies in the establishment of a satisfactory *daily* fiscal control.

This is accomplished through a statement of daily balances which should be required from the accounting department each day. Such statements take the form shown in Figure 18 and can be amplified to whatever extent may seem desirable. However, they should not be too complicated. Otherwise the time required for their compilation will nullify their control value.

Although some items on the statement require submission of data from other departments (such as *orders received* from the sales department and *purchase commitments* from the purchasing department), this information should be funneled into the accounting department. The statement should be published in its entirety by this department.

The statement of daily balances should be closed out each month and started anew with each accounting period.

CHAPTER 17

COST CONTROL

•

Definitions

In defining cost control, analogous phrases too often are considered as synonymous terms.

The phrases most commonly used as substitutes for cost control are cost finding, cost accounting, costing, and cost determination. Their explicit meanings follow:

Cost finding means just what it says—the accumulation and proper classification of the direct and indirect expense details chargeable to the unit of production or activity, to discover the cost.

Cost determination may be dismissed as merely a synonym for cost finding.

Cost accounting reaches into a somewhat broader field. It arranges and records, through established accounting principles, the elements of cost about which the books of account are concerned. These must, however, be recorded in the books of account in such a manner that an analysis of the various cost elements can be made quickly and easily.

Costing is such a vague expression that it is hard to pin its meaning down. It is generally used to define more closely some other equally indeterminate expression, such as costing procedure, costing method, or costing practice.

Cost control, however, has a specific meaning and an explicit purpose. Cost control is the method by which material, labor and overhead elements of cost are controlled or regulated, so that the actual elements of cost will be equal to or less than the amount estimated as being satisfactory to operation. Therefore, cost control is not a part of cost accounting. It consists of a material control, a labor control, and an expense control that currently regulate, to predetermined standards, the inflow of cash into the production of units of goods to be sold.

ORGANIZATION

A control is not an end in itself but a *means* to an end. Cost control is a tool by which management attains certain results in a productive enterprise. Therefore someone—an organization member—must exercise that control.

In modern industrial organizations cost control is allocated to a particular person concerned with the accounting functions of a company. His title varies; cost accountant or controller are the most common designations.

The job is more closely defined by the responsibilities and duties assigned to it by management's conception of the function.

Since this is a job of *control,* the organization for cost control must necessarily be a *management* function. In modern industrial organizations, this places it close to the administration of a company and makes it *executive* in its relation to many other functions. This relationship is graphically shown in Figures 7, 8, and 9 used in Chapter 12 of this section.

THE EXCEPTION PRINCIPLE

This leads into another important principle of control, the "exception" principle. Because cost control is essentially a *control of exceptions,* a precise definition of this basic principle is desirable.

The exception principle merely establishes and segregates the deviations from the normal and expected results, so that attention and remedial action can be focused on them. Correction of such deviations insures that the total result will meet the desired objective. To use a common saying, "a stitch in time saves nine."

This exception principle is fundamental to the whole philosophy of cost control. It is so necessary to the practical application of such controls that a reiteration and re-emphasis of its importance is necessary.

THE BASIS FOR COST CONTROL

Earlier it was stated that cost control is a tool for management's use. It is not a single simple tool but is composed of one major and several minor tools.

Standards are the major tool in cost control. A standard is defined as a recognized, acceptable, and carefully determined measure. The subject of standards is here being considered in its larger sense, that is, as it relates to *all* the components of a cost. Therefore, standards for labor, for material, and for factory indirect or overhead expense, must be considered as separate entities. Each has different but measurable characteristics, and all lend themselves to precise determination.

Unless this is accepted as a basic premise of control, no control can be effectuated. It is essential, therefore, to consider control as the result of the application of standards derived for each cost component.

THE TOOLS OF COST CONTROL

Cost standards fall into two general classes:

1. "Current" standards.
2. Basic or "measure" standards.

The first class merely represents a sloppy philosophy of management and is characterized by the word "guesstimate." Current standards have a place in cost control and, lacking a more precise measure, serve a better purpose than no standards at all.

But real control cannot be attained by halfway measures. For that reason the second class of standards, which are "measure" standards, represent the real tool of control.

"Measure" standards are built on the solid foundation of fact and analysis. They are determined from carefully and elementally measured basic factors of activity, such as time, size, and quantity.

They are the real measuring sticks of cost control and are divided and subdivided into the necessary classifications. A single cost will not be correct for all volumes of production or sale. Consequently, the standards are divided into standard material cost, standard labor cost and standard overhead cost.

These are characterized by certain specific differences in the "measure." Thus, standard material cost and standard labor cost are "simple" standards. That is, the "measure" is single and constant—dollars per quantity or hours per unit.

However, standard overhead cost is a "complex" standard composed of two elements, a fixed and a variable measure, resolved into a unit measure of overhead cost.

In other words, a standard material cost will consist of a specific quantity of material (scientifically determined from the drawings, specifications, and bills of material) priced at a normal unit price of the raw material. A standard labor cost will consist of a specific time determined by time study and priced at the sound or normal wage rate for the occupation. A standard overhead cost will consist of fixed expenses inherent in the total operation (reduced to a unit charge under conditions of normal operation) plus a variable unit expense. These are derived by analysis of the total expense charges in relation to the activity that produced them.

Fundamentally, cost control is based on unit "measure" standards and, in turn, is the basis for the next degree of control, namely, managerial control of the total cost of the company's total operation. This managerial control is called budgetary control and was discussed in detail in Section 2, Chapter 15.

DIVISIONS OF COST CONTROL

Cost control consists of three control elements: material cost control, labor cost control, and overhead cost control.

This breakdown is necessary, as cost control must be applied at the origin of costs if the desired results in total cost are to be obtained.

Each of these three subcontrols originates in a different division of the company's operation. Each requires a different routine for administration, and each has a different method of presentation to management.

The general principles of budgetary control apply to cost control; that is:

1. It must cover current periods of operation.
2. It must be based on current activity.
3. Results must be reported promptly and accurately.

Material Cost Control

Fundamentally, material cost control is based on a material control procedure incorporated into the production control routine. It is not based on the prices of raw material, although naturally these have an important bearing on the final material cost.

The production control department is primarily concerned with quantity, or *physical* units of material, rather than with the unit cost of the raw material. Basically, therefore, the control of material is quantitative rather than financial—qualitative rather than monetary.

To plan the work properly for the various factory departments, adequate records must show the quantity of:

1. Material on order.
2. Material in process.
3. Finished material.
4. Material spoiled.

These routines are described fully in Section 4, Chapter 29.

Such records, currently maintained, will produce a satisfactory control of material. The cost department function is then limited to recording the money value of these material transactions.

In order to have an effective material cost control, it is important that all transactions be recorded currently. Discrepancies or variations from predetermined standards will thus be observed immediately. Ordinarily cost accounting procedures do not record such transactions currently. Generally an entire month of transactions must be completed before any data or information can be laid before management for corrective action. Such delay emphasizes the need for controlling material cost through the production control routine rather than through the cost accounting routine.

Labor Cost Control

Direct labor costs are best controlled by a labor control which will indicate *daily* the effectiveness or rate of performance of the various workmen or working groups. Such daily performance reports are illustrated by Figure 19.

DAILY PERFORMANCE REPORT

Date....................   Department................

Clock No.	Employee Name	Act. Hrs.	Std. Hrs.	Efficiency
Total				

FIG. 19

In order to establish such a control, labor standards must be set by the time study department and a timekeeping procedure established to apply those standards to each workman's daily performance. This will establish his effectiveness or rate of performance.

If the cost accounting routines are depended on to supply such information, practically no control will exist because of the time lag between the actual performance and its recording. Weeks are required for application of the cost routines, and the transactions are reported in money. Such delay in presentation of data would, of course, make it impossible to apply corrective measures in time to secure beneficial results.

Therefore, with the proper labor control of performance properly integrated into the payroll functions, the cost accounting procedures can be limited to recording the total productive labor dollars in the general books of account, with no further classifications other than by departments if desirable.

Cost finding for products thus becomes a statistical effort rather than an accounting effort. Cost sheets by products can be assembled easily from the detailed routines and records established for material, labor, and overhead cost control.

Overhead Cost

The overhead element of cost always contains a certain proportion of fixed expense, that is, an expense that does not vary with changes in production.

The actual overhead cost for a single unit will be one value when production is low and will have another value when production is high. With the overhead cost changing with production, the total cost per unit will also change with changes in the volume of production.

For example, assume that the overhead cost consists of $10,000 fixed expense plus a variable expense of $1 per unit. The overhead cost per unit would then be as follows:

No. of Units	Fixed Exp.	Var. Exp.	Total Exp.	Unit Exp.
5,000	$10,000	$ 5,000	$15,000	$3.00
10,000	10,000	10,000	20,000	2.00
15,000	10,000	15,000	25,000	1.67
20,000	10,000	20,000	30,000	1.50

The control of such overhead expense items is best exercised through a budgetary control. Under a budgetary control, standards should be determined for each expense account in terms of fixed and variable factors as described in Chapter 15 of this section. Furthermore, these expenses can best be controlled when the *actual* expense is accumulated in total for the originating department, rather than by allocations of the expense to various departments or pieces of equipment.

For example, more attention will be paid to a power cost expressed as a single figure for all departments than to the same power cost prorated over various departments. As an illustra-

Acct. No.	Acct. Name	Standard		Activity Base	Std. Amt.	Act. Amt.	Variance	
		Fix.	Var.				Over Std.	Under Std.
Total								

OVERHEAD EXPENSE CONTROL

Date or Period....................

Fig. 20

tion, a total power bill of $5,000 per month will be more informative to and *more subject to control by* management than a power cost charge of $500 per month to each of ten cost sheets, each sheet representing a different department. Especially is this true when it is known that the distribution may not be accurate.

Another example to illustrate this problem is found in the handling of overtime costs, that is, the premium half-time paid for extra hours.

There is a question as to whether all the overtime amount in labor costs is a variance in overhead cost or is to be budgeted as an allowable expense, with only *excess* overtime shown as a variance.

It is obvious, because of its departmental significance and ease of accurate determination, that it should be shown as a controllable expense by department, whether or not a budget allowance is set for it.

DEPARTMENT EXPENSE CONTROL

Date or Period.....................   Department...................

Controllable Items

Acct. No.	Acct. Name	Standard	Actual	Variance	
				Over	Under

Noncontrollable Items

Taxes

Depreciation

Etc.

Fig. 21

The budgetary control should provide for accumulating actual expenses by expense accounts and by departments, so that they may be compared with the amounts set up by the budget formulas.

Figure 20 illustrates a typical form for overhead expense control of basic expense accounts.

Figure 21 shows a typical form for overhead expense control

within a department. It should be noted that the departmental control form divides the overhead cost into controllable items and noncontrollable items. The display of the noncontrollable items affords the department head an opportunity to assist the budget manager with constructive criticism; such noncontrollable departmental items may be distributed so that any *cost finding* procedure can realistically portray the actual cost of the product.

With a sound budgetary control of overhead expense, the cost accounting procedure need then pertain only to the final recording of the total amount of each expense.

STANDARD COST ACCOUNTING

As evidenced by the previous discussion, any effort to establish a single control for all elements of cost, as part of the cost accounting routine, will be of little value from a control standpoint.

The cost accounting procedure should be as simple as possible. The major purpose of the cost accounting system is to record the transactions of the business so that they can be thoroughly analyzed and clearly understood by management and easily applied in the financial statements of the company.

Frequently, however, costs for accounting purposes are developed in a complicated manner and by a confusing procedure. Just as frequently, very little use is made of such data.

The most practical method for simplifying cost accounting procedures is to establish standard costs. Material, labor, and overhead cost control afford the logical method for installing standard costs. The standard cost procedure will then consist of the following routines:

1. Establishing standards for material, labor, and overhead.
2. Using such standards for inventory pricing, cost of sales determination, and all other accounting purposes.
3. Determining the variation between the actual and the standard for the various detail and total costs.
4. Charging that variation against the profit and loss of each month.

In order to operate under a standard cost procedure, the following routines are necessary:

1. Provide bills of material (see Figure 44) and operation sheets (see Figure 45) which show in detail every single item to be manufactured or purchased and every operation to be performed by direct labor.

2. Establish standard *unit* material costs and the standard (or average) earning rate per hour for the various operations.

3. Multiply the quantities specified by the bills of material and operation sheets by the standard unit material prices and standard hourly rates, to determine the standard cost for material and labor for each unit or product.

4. Check the prices on all incoming invoices for material against the standard unit price, and accumulate the variances on the proper ledger account. At the end of the month this variance is totaled and charged off as a material price variation in the cost of sales.

5. Indicate, on the current production reports, any excess material usage or consumption. Price it at the standard unit material cost, and accumulate these variances on the proper ledger account. At the end of the month treat this usage variance exactly like the price variance, and charge it off in the cost of sales.

6. Determine from the labor control the excess labor cost, and handle this variance in the same manner as the material cost. If the same refinement is desired, excess labor costs can be analyzed by accounts. They may also be separated by usage variance based on performance and by price variance due to nonstandard hourly rates.

7. Determine the standard overhead rate from the budget or, if not available, from past normal performance. The standard overhead amount is found by multiplying the standard direct labor by the standard overhead rate. The variance between the standard overhead amount thus determined and the actual overhead costs accumulated in the ledgers is expressed as a variance, charged to that ledger account, and closed out into the profit and loss statement monthly. This practice fixes the overhead in the inventory at a constant and standard rate.

Standard costs will permit the inventory always to be priced uniformly and will also provide a uniform costing of shipments by multiplying the number of units shipped by standard material, labor, and overhead costs.

Whenever an inventory is priced, or the cost of sales determined, these three elements of cost should be listed individually. Current checks can then be made readily, as by comparing the actual payroll for the month with the labor charge in the cost of sales, or by comparing the amount of material purchased or received or both with the amount of material actually shipped.

The overhead cost in the inventory should be kept as low as possible. When liquidating obsolete inventory, the selling price of such material may not exceed the labor and material cost and may be even less. Therefore, it is extremely important to watch the amount of overhead charged into the inventory. Too large an amount may require a disastrous write-off at some future time.

The one factor which can easily complicate a cost routine is the allocation of overhead. With standard costing in effect, and with material, labor, and overhead control completely operative, it is not necessary to allocate actual overhead costs for either cost accounting or cost finding purposes, with any degree of refinement.

A complicated cost system hinders rather than helps management. An understanding that the control of costs is quite separate from pricing (which can be done by a separate analysis whenever it is required) will provide, through standard cost procedure, a simple cost accounting system which will serve all basic purposes.

Cost Finding

Every business should determine the cost and price of each product. A cost is necessary for pricing or estimating purposes, for control purposes, and for cost accounting purposes. The cost should always be expressed to show material, labor, and overhead separately, regardless of the use to which the cost is to be put.

An estimated cost or a standard cost can be usually determined from properly established bills of material, operation sheets, and overhead analysis. Actual costs are difficult to determine and, in many cases, cannot be determined accurately; the fixed elements in the overhead cause different costs to be obtained for different volumes of production.

Every effort should therefore be made to establish standard costs as accurately as possible and to use such standard costs for all purposes. Variations from standard costs or the difference between an actual cost and a standard cost should be obtained from each of the three controls previously described.

It is not considered essential in all cases to allocate too accurately the difference between standard cost and actual cost. For example, a certain department may have an excess labor cost of $1,000 for a month. Allocation of this $1,000 among the various products made in that department during that month will require a great deal of clerical effort and will be of no value to management for control purposes. Furthermore, it is doubtful whether the selling price of any product can be increased whenever an excess cost is incurred.

An excess cost may be incurred, not because a particular product is being manufactured at that particular time, but because of some factor which has no relation to any specific product. Therefore, penalizing a certain product with additional expense, simply because it happened to be in manufacture at the time when the excess occurred, does not furnish a true indication of the actual cost of that product. Other products made in other periods should bear part of such excess costs.

Knowledge of the actual cost of each individual product is usually desired so that management can determine whether or not the selling price is adequate or the product is profitable. The selling price of a product has been established from an estimate. Once it has been established, it cannot easily be changed. Therefore every effort must be made to establish the estimated costs, or standard costs, as accurately as possible.

When establishing selling prices, the material and direct labor elements of cost can be precisely itemized on bills of material. Operation sheets will also show, in detail, every single item of direct material that enters into the finished product and every direct labor operation that has to be performed.

Overhead, however, cannot usually be determined so accurately. A common method of applying manufacturing overhead is, first, to determine what percentage of direct labor has been overhead, either during the past year or during the past few months. Then another overhead percentage is added to the total of labor, material, and manufacturing overhead, to provide for sales and administrative expense. Finally, a profit percentage is added to the total of all these elements to determine the selling price. The cost, however, is correct only when actual production or sales volume is equal to that on which the overhead percentages were originally based.

Instead of attempting to apply a single overhead percentage, the preferred method is to separate the fixed and variable elements of all overhead expenses. Apply only the variable elements to the direct labor and material, so that a total variable cost can be determined.

A selling price, based on variable costs thus established, will be much more accurate and much more informative to management than the conventionally determined cost. For example, management finds that variable manufacturing overhead is, say, 100 per cent of the direct labor dollar, and variable sales and administrative expenses are 5 per cent of the sales dollar. The direct labor and direct material costs are known, and a selling price, properly reflecting the desired margin of profit, is easily found by adding the desired marginal income to the total variable cost thus found.

To determine the fixed and variable elements of expense, an analysis should be made as described in Chapter 15. This analysis can be independent of the cost accounting procedure, as it merely requires the total amounts of expense as recorded by the cost accounting procedure.

Cost Reports

The activation of cost control, after the standards have been set and the accounting procedures established, requires that a regular system of cost reports be established. These will currently focus management's attention on the variations in cost from the established standards, so that remedial action can be taken promptly at the appropriate organization level of responsibility. And "currently" should mean "daily" for the prime cost elements of direct labor, direct material, and direct variable expense.

Such reports should provide, at each level of cost responsibility, complete information on the cost elements originating there. Only those cost elements over which this level has actual and direct control should be reported.

As the control responsibility flows upward through the higher echelons of management, the cost reports should be combined into more comprehensive and less detailed summaries. Where they reach the highest organization level of cost responsibility, they become in effect the profit and loss statement, as illustrated in Figure 22.

This flow of tributary reports into summary reports may be likened to the pattern of a river system. Such reports must point out at every level the difference between the actual cost and the standard, by means of variance figures. Otherwise there can be no cost control.

The detailed manner in which such reports are made up, the way in which the variances are accumulated, and the procedures by which final figures are gathered into the profit and loss statement are all matters of systematic installation. They are to be regulated by the character of the business thus placed under control.

There are many techniques of presentation, but they divide into two general classes—statistical and graphical. The conventional method is the statistical one and consists of comparing actual against standard costs in whatever detail and order of accounts seem desirable.

The newer method and one that has received much impetus in the past few years is graphical. It consists of charts which visually picture the same information.

The use of charts provides a readier and a much simpler presentation than the statistical method. It requires, however, a "chart mindedness" on the part of management and organization. Too frequently this is lacking.

OPERATING STATEMENT				
	This Month		Year to Date	
Gross Sales				
Less Disc.—Returns—Allow., etc.				
NET SALES				
Standard Material				
Standard Labor				
Standard Burden				
Standard Cost of Sales				
Variances: Material Price				
Material Usage				
Labor Price				
Labor Usage				
Burden				
Total Variances				
Total Cost of Sales				
GROSS PROFIT				
Selling Expense				
Administrative Expense				
General Expense				
Total Expense				
OPERATING PROFIT				
Other Income & Expense				
NET PROFIT BEFORE FED. INC. TAX				
Reserve for Fed. Inc. Tax				
NET PROFIT				

Fig. 22

The cost control principles outlined in the *Cost Accountant's Handbook* summarize this whole subject most adequately:

"1. Accounts should be fitted into the organization chart so that costs can be segregated by individual responsibilities.

"2. Cost accounts should be subdivided by individual responsibilities under uniform classifications to show nature of expenditures.

"3. Goals should be set in standards, budgets, and allowances, and constantly kept up-to-date.

"4. Where justifiable cost varies with the rate of activity, variable or flexible budgets should be developed.

"5. Standards and budgets should be prepared for each cost item with the co-operation of the person responsible and should be agreed to by him.

"6. Variations of actual costs from standard or budget should be segregated and shown in detail. Responsibility for each variance should be determined definitely.

"7. Frequent reports of his costs should be supplied to each person who is responsible for control of any cost element. These reports should emphasize variances of actual costs from standards or budgeted figures.

"8. In these reports, apportioned or prorated costs over which an executive has no control should not be combined with costs over which he does have control."

CHAPTER 18

EXECUTIVE
REPORTS

•

DEFINITION

Executive reports are those records by which management obtains the information required to measure performance, to make decisions, and to execute the affairs of the company.

Executive reports will vary in number and kind, dependent on the nature and size of the business, but all such reports should have certain characteristics in common. They should be:

1. Pertinent. They must pertain to and only to the functions with which the executive is concerned.

2. Informative. They must present the subject in an understandable manner and give proper emphasis to the matters requiring action.

3. Brief. They must be short and concise and require a minimum of management time for review.

4. Accurate. They must be 100 per cent accurate.

5. Comparative. They should compare the information being presented with a standard, automatically showing variations which require correction.

6. Current. They must be up-to-date.

7. Prompt. They must be presented promptly on definite dates.

Purpose and Necessity

It is the purpose of these reports to provide information. The necessity for reliable information, presented currently, is unquestioned. Practical control of activities and the initiation of corrective measures are impossible unless such information is compiled and made available in accordance with a definite plan.

Character of Content

The character of the reports should be the result of careful examination and decision as to what is actually required. Such decision will depend on the character and size of the business. Only essential information should be compiled and presented; there is a cost associated with the compilation of information. Therefore in this, as in all activities, proper economy should be the watchword.

Character of Presentation

Reports for executives divide into two broad classifications: that is, *standard reports,* containing basic information, which are adapted to continuous presentation; and *special reports* which provide information pertinent to some current activity or which amplify information contained in the standard reports.

Unless some safeguard is established as a definite policy, the whole system of reports can and sometimes does develop ponderous proportions. It grows beyond the ability of executives to digest and use in accordance with their intent. Special reports, initiated for a temporary purpose, may continue to be presented after the need for them has expired. This represents wasted energy for those engaged in their compilation and for the executives who receive and examine them.

Positive control should be established to confine these reports within limits that will provide only essential information. Such control naturally falls within the province of the controller, or whoever exercises control functions affecting procedures. In the exercise of such control, all reports should be subjected to frequent and careful examination to determine what information or reports should be deleted. Other information may be found to be essential for improved control of the business.

Character of Frequency

Every business has an individuality which requires reports peculiar only to that business. However, there are certain reports which are common to and considered essential by every business. These cover:

1. Sales, shipments, and unfilled orders, in units and dollars, compared with a standard or a budget. This report should show the information both daily and as accumulated from the first of the month.

2. Financial data, on cash, collections, disbursements, receivables, payables, and purchase commitments. This report should show daily and month-to-date figures.

3. Number of hourly and salary employees, classified by departments and major occupations where possible. Indirect employees should be separated from direct. This should be a daily report showing the number of employees working on that day.

4. Payroll distribution, classified as to direct and indirect by departments, showing excess direct labor compared to standard and actual indirect labor compared to budgets. These should be reported daily, weekly, and monthly.

5. Capital expenditures classified by major types of projects, showing annual budget, commitments, and actual disbursements made. This report should be made monthly, but the data should be cumulative from the beginning of the fiscal year.

6. A budget forecast in the form of a profit and loss statement of operations, sales, and profit or loss for the coming month. This should be issued monthly, supported by a manufacturing forecast and detailed schedules of expenses for the manufacturing program.

7. A monthly profit and loss statement showing the actual performance and the budgeted performance built around actual sales. Supporting schedules of each major class of expense should accompany the condensed statement. This should be issued monthly and show monthly figures compared with the

actual budget for the month, as well as cumulative figures from the beginning of the fiscal year. It should be available by approximately the tenth of each month.

8. A cash forecast for the fiscal year showing estimated sales, collections, and disbursements by major classes of expense, including capital expenditures and cash available or required month by month. This forecast should be prepared yearly but adjusted each month for the following months, when any large variation makes this necessary.

9. A weekly production report showing the number of units scheduled and actually produced, classified by types. There can be many variations of this, and the amount of detail will depend entirely on the particular business. Some companies find it essential to issue this report daily.

10. An engineering project report showing the projects completed and their cost, the contemplated projects with their estimated cost, and the status of the projects being worked on with their cost to date, as compared to the estimated cost. This should be issued monthly.

11. An inventory report, showing the amount and quantity of inventory, aged by groups according to their degree of obsolescence.

12. In addition to these basic reports, certain special reports may be required and devised. Such special reports may be a combination of the several types already listed, designed to show the effectiveness or performance of the plant as a whole or by departments or both. Figures 23 and 24 illustrate the more common types of such reports.

SUMMARY

With these as a basis, the development of a system of reports should present no great difficulty. The program to be followed should include:

1. Determination of what constitutes information necessary to control of the business activities.
2. Decision as to the form to be selected for the presentation of such information.

Dept.	Output in Units		Performance %	Force Count (No. of Employees)	Effectivity (Employees per Unit)
	Produced	Scheduled			
A					
B					
C					
D					
Plant Total					

PERFORMANCE REPORT

Date or Period.................

Fig. 23

| Dept. | Hours | | Performance % | Remarks |
	Standard	Actual		

PERFORMANCE REPORT

Date or Period................

FIG. 24

3. Establishment of a schedule indicating the time for presentation of the reports, and their frequency.
4. Assignment of responsibility for preparation of the reports.
5. Establishment of a control to keep the reports within the bounds of essential current requirements.

An organized, simple, and accurate system of executive reports eliminates need for following the details of operations, simplifies executive tasks, and allows attention to be given to major problems in the further development of the business.

CHAPTER 19

COMPENSATION
POLICIES

•

IMPORTANCE

In any business there is no one factor more important to its employees than their personal compensation. Practically every personnel problem that confronts a company springs from this source. Consequently, proper compensation of all employees plays an important part in establishing and maintaining co-operation and good industrial relations throughout the organization.

The problem of proper compensation policies should be a matter of deep concern to the management of every company. Too often such policies are completely lacking, and an attitude of "let matters take their own course" establishes the working relationship between the management and its employees.

Such an attitude has no place in a modern enterprise. It can only result in the eventual strangulation of the business. The constructive attitude is represented by compensation policies that express an awareness of the social and economic obligations of a company. These are rewarded by an organization spirit that can only result in profitable operation.

The development of such policies can be readily implemented by a sound compensation program affecting all organization levels consistently and equitably. It is the purpose of this chapter to deal only with the employees of the salaried group. Salesmen and factory employees are separately covered in Chapter 23, Section 3, and Chapter 31, Section 4, respectively.

METHODS

Compensation programs for salaried personnel fall into three categories:

1. Base pay.
2. Incentives.
3. Profit sharing.

Bonuses are excluded from compensation as they are usually arbitrary in basis, and are not related to the basic performance requirements of a compensation plan. If they are, they automatically classify themselves into some form of incentive or profit sharing.

DEFINITION

Compensation is defined as the remuneration of an employee for the thought and effort he exerts and the results he obtains in behalf of the company. It is an earned reward, and its payment is a moral and legal obligation of the company.

COMPENSATION PLANS

Salaries (Base Pay)

If some employees receive greater compensation than others whose work requires more effort or skill, it is well-nigh impossible to maintain the proper co-operative relationship between these employees or to secure the loyalty essential to the company's continued welfare and success.

There are two aspects of salary compensation. The external one relates the company's salary levels to those of other industries in the community. The internal one provides an equitable relationship within and between the various organization levels.

The first aspect may be dismissed briefly, providing compensation rates are comparable to those paid by similar companies in the same locality. Higher rates of compensation will draw the more capable and more personable types of personnel. Rates below the community average generally require some added incentive, such as permanency of employment, or imply some tolerance of effort such as "easy work" to keep an able group of employees in the organization.

To establish a satisfactory and equitable internal salary plan, the following procedure is recommended:

1. Analyze the various positions. Determine the amount of skill and other abilities required to perform each function, the responsibility involved, the amount of authority that must be exercised, the amount of direction received, the period of time necessary to train someone to perform that function, and any other pertinent factors.

This analysis can be made in a systematic manner by using one of the accepted salary evaluation techniques (see Section 5, Chapter 35). If an empirical method rather than a systematic evaluation is used, errors of judgment and a lack of consistency will invalidate the ratings applied to each position.

2. Determine the current compensation being paid to holders of similar positions in the surrounding community, and compare them with salaries actually paid within the company.

3. Classify the various positions into occupational groups so that all the positions in each group require similar skills, abilities, and other qualifications. For example, one group may consist of typists, another of clerks, another of certain junior department heads, and so on. There may be as many as 25 occupational groups, though the number is usually much less.

4. Establish a high and low scale for each occupational group, within the limits of any statutory regulation. The low rate would constitute the hiring rate, or starting rate, and the high rate would represent the maximum earnings which could be realized by anyone in that particular occupational group. In setting these rates, give consideration to the community levels of compensation.

5. Acquaint all employees with the method of and reasons for the classification of positions into occupational groups. They may then determine their earning possibilities in their present

types of work and the earnings they may expect if they are transferred or upgraded to another occupational group.

6. Provide for a systematic review or rating of all employees at periodic intervals, to determine their eligibility for salary increases or upgrading. Such merit rating plans should be carefully devised and should follow the established practice in such matters.

The outlined procedure for establishing a proper salary compensation plan should not and need not always apply to senior executives. It need not apply to those doing unusual work of a creative or highly technical nature, nor to those doing work which can only be accomplished because of some unusual personal characteristics. Some individuals may have particular ability along certain inventive or executive lines. This ability, if it permits the company to be a leader in new products, new designs, or new processing techniques, or enables it to rehabilitate itself and operate profitably instead of at a loss, cannot be priced by ordinary standards of compensation. Such positions should not be included in the salary classification plan.

It is practically impossible to establish definite rules of compensation for such employees. Fair salaries in these cases must be determined by mutual agreement between the employer and employee, but limited by the requirements of the budgetary control. This will establish the boundaries for various classes of expense, and the compensations that can be paid to special employees or senior executives. For extra performance such individuals should be included in a profit sharing plan, as described later in this chapter.

Incentives

An incentive is always desirable and should be established whenever possible.

An incentive plan is defined as the method by which an employee receives additional compensation for greater output, or for better performance of his assigned duties.

Although the administrative group ordinarily consists principally of office employees and junior executives, it may also include certain factory employees such as foremen, plant engineers, and factory office employees. There are several different forms of incentives which may be offered to this group:

Indirect Incentives

1. Establishment of classifications for all positions, as described under the heading Salaries.

2. Adoption of the policy of adhering to this classification and making all promotions from within the organization. This establishes a very decided promotion incentive for each employee.

3. Statement that, when an employee starts in a new group, his compensation will be at the minimum rate for that group; but, that by performing his job satisfactorily, he can increase his compensation while still remaining within that classification. It should be made clear that his earnings can be still further increased by his becoming familiar with the duties and the work involved in other higher paid groups so that he will be given such a position, if eligible, when the opening occurs.

4. Assurance that it is basic company policy to employ all new personnel in the lowest classification proper to their experience, and to make all promotions from within the organization.

5. Recognition that this plan does not provide for the promotion of *every* individual one step upward every time a vacancy occurs. Certain individuals can never rise above certain minimum levels of ability or capacity. This makes it inevitable that some employees will eventually supersede their former supervisors. Such practice is perfectly in accord with good management policy and actually becomes an added indirect incentive for every employee to develop himself for promotion.

Direct Incentives

1. In large office organizations, a certain amount of work is of a highly repetitive nature, as addressing envelopes, posting transactions, typing orders, sweeping floors. For such types of work it has been practical at times to apply *piecework prices* to various jobs and thereby to reward the worker for a larger amount of work produced.

2. This type of incentive is limited in its application to fairly large groups of employees doing identical, repetitive, routine work. It should not be applied generally to all office positions, because it will be too difficult to establish the proper standards. Too much clerical work will be required to measure the performance, calculate the additional earnings, and keep up the necessary records.

Savings Incentives

1. An incentive may be applied to various groups or departments by establishing a budget of expense for each group or department. The personnel within these units is then paid additional compensation in direct proportion to the savings in actual expense as compared to budgeted expense.

2. Generally the incentive established by this procedure is not sufficiently great to warrant its universal application. If the budgets are correctly and accurately established, it will be difficult to gain on them unless an allowance is arbitrarily made in the budget for such incentive. There is always the danger that economies will be made at the expense of satisfactory work.

3. There is also the added hazard that, if the budgets are established on the basis of past performance only and not on a basis of careful analysis and measure, certain departments will be able to better the budget by a considerable amount. In this case the departments which have been operating most inefficiently will receive the largest amount of added compensation, and a premium will be paid for poor performance in the past.

Profit Sharing Incentive

1. An incentive may be established by means of a profit sharing plan. A certain proportion of the profits is distributed among the employees as additional compensation, in accordance with a plan that measures their proportionate contributions to the profit actually obtained.

2. Such an incentive plan has so many desirable features from the standpoint of operating efficiency that it is presented in detail in the following pages.

PROFIT SHARING

A profit sharing plan is considered to be generally the most suitable form of incentive for the management and administrative groups.

It is impossible to formulate a single profit sharing plan that will be applicable to all types of businesses. Instead, each one must be established for the particular conditions existing, in order to be equitable to both the company and the employee. Certain general principles can be outlined, however. These include:

1. Establishing all salaries in accordance with the classification method previously mentioned, but with the compensation rates set at a low level so that they can be paid during bad business periods as well as good.

2. Determining the amount of profit the company should earn before additional compensation is paid to employees. The amount to be set aside for the company before distributing a proportion of the profit to employees should not be too excessive.

Instead, the current rate of interest that invested capital can realize should be determined. This percentage applied to the amount of profit that should be set aside before paying added compensation to employees. That is, the amount of profit to be paid to stockholders should be a nominal amount only and should be considered as wages to capital.

3. Making a projection of the profit possibilities of the company under various conditions and various volumes. This determines the maximum profit that may be realized, as well as the normal profit to be expected.

Once the amount of profit that may be realized has been determined there should be deducted that amount of profit which is to be used as wages to capital before added compensation is paid to employees.

4. The remaining profit will then be available for profit sharing, for company reserves, and for additional disbursements to capital accounts. For a company that is not contemplating extensive capital expenditures for expansion or other development

purposes, it has been found practical to divide the remaining profit in about the following proportions:

One third in the form of profit sharing to employees.

One third to be retained by the company for future developments.

One third to be paid to stockholders as additional compensation on their investment.

5. Analyzing the classification of positions to determine how many employees there are in each classification. Each classification of employees should then have a factor or a percentage established for that group.

This factor will indicate what percentage of each employee's salary he will receive as additional compensation for a certain amount of profit. For example, a certain classification may reveal that there are six employees normally in that group, and that the compensation rate is from $200 to $250 per month, per individual.

The profit sharing factor for this group may be established at 1 per cent for each $10,000 of profit earned over and above that portion of the amount to be set aside before any profit sharing. This means that each employee in this group will receive 1 per cent of his salary for every $10,000 of profit earned over and above the amount to be set aside as wages to capital.

6. Calculating the total amount of the profit to be disbursed when the established factors are applied. If it is found that too large a proportion of the total profit is used for profit sharing, all of the factors must be adjusted. These factors must continue to be adjusted until the total amount disbursed is in proper proportion to the amount paid out in profit sharing.

7. Providing for the inclusion of factory employees in the plan. Although disbursements may not be made to factory employees, they should be included in the calculations so that a proper and not an excessive amount will be paid to the administrative group. Furthermore, should it be desirable to include them at some later date, no revision of the plan will be necessary.

8. Consideration must also be given to the fact that some classifications of work require a greater incentive than others.

Some incentive is obtained merely by the existence of a sound classification of jobs and compensation. Additional incentive may be established by using larger factors of profit sharing disbursement for the more important job classifications.

For example: A group of junior executives may receive 5 per cent of their salary for each $10,000 of profit above the predetermined amount, whereas a classification of clerks may receive only ½ per cent of their salary for each $10,000 of profit above the predetermined amount.

Profit sharing plans have not been widely adopted in industry and business, but surveys have shown that an increasing number of companies are adding this policy to their management programs, in spite of the modest number of failures that have occurred.

Surveys have also shown that, where a profit sharing plan has been soundly conceived, it has become completely accepted by the organization as an established policy of the company operation and plays an important part in the industrial relations phase of the business.

The advantages of a profit sharing plan may be summarized as follows:

1. It encourages every employee to make the company's earnings as large as possible.

2. It avoids the disastrous effects of possible future salary reductions, because compensation is directly related to profits.

3. It makes expenses variable and proportionate to income.

4. It gives greater job security.

5. It establishes minimum pay levels which can be maintained in bad times as well as good.

BONUSES

Unfortunately, the word bonus has been confused with incentive payments in the modern industrial vocabulary, partly through lack of an accepted definition, and partly because management has frequently used it to designate some form of profit distribution.

A bonus is correctly defined as an arbitrary gift made at the discretion of the giver, without regard to an established measure of award. It is based on the personal relationship existing between the giver and receiver.

Bonuses have a proper place in the remuneration of employees, provided they are based on proper factors of award and represent payments for such forms of service as cannot be rewarded otherwise. For example, a bonus based on years of service with a company rewards the employee for a spirit of faithfulness and loyalty that cannot be measured properly in any other way.

Bonuses paid on a discretionary and personal basis are merely "largesse" and should have no place in American industry. If management wishes to give extra compensation to its organization members for performance beyond the normal requirement and in proportion to occupational rank, it should find no difficulty in devising a profit sharing plan to include these considerations.

Wage Administration

The problem of wage administration, after a satisfactory plan of compensation has been set up, is one that requires careful consideration to be successfully answered.

Wage administration comprises the method of applying all policies affecting the earnings of an employee. It should concern itself, therefore, with:

1. The manner of determining hourly or salary rates for various occupational classifications.
2. The method of establishing and granting increases in these pay categories.
3. The rate of overtime to be paid for time in excess of the statutory work week, Sundays, and holidays.
4. The amount of differential to be paid to second and third shifts.
5. The amount of vacation time to be granted for given terms of employment.
6. The amount of sick leave, if any, to be granted.
7. The amount of absenteeism or tardiness that will be tolerated.

8. All other questions that affect the employee's individual earnings.

In addition to these questions, the employer must keep in mind the regulatory influences that emanate from either Government agencies or labor unions. If they affect his plant, he must absorb them into his compensation policies.

To secure consistency of policy and action in all of these matters, it is most desirable that the details be administered by a well-organized industrial relations department. Such a department is in a position, because of its other personnel functions, to make the administration of all compensation policies an integral part of the entire industrial relations program.

3

Sales Management

CHAPTER 20

MARKET STUDIES

•

PURPOSE

The basis for all preparatory work in the merchandising activities of a company is a *market study*.

A market study may be defined as an investigation among the users or sellers or both of the product, and of the statistical data available, to determine the acceptability of the product, the potential volume available to the company, and the method of merchandising it to best advantage.

Without proper preparation for the market, either in potential exploitation or in routine application, the following weaknesses may be expected:

1. *A volume of sales less than anticipated.*
2. *High selling cost.*
3. *A product that does not meet the customer's wants.*

No sound manufacturing activity starts without a design for the product. Carefully engineered through research and preplanned in detail for the market desired, good design will properly relate the component parts and accomplish the results required.

The same care must be taken in preparing the merchandising

activities. Because such work is less tangible than the development of a product or the manufacturing facility itself, generally it has not been developed to the same degree.

In the field of merchandising, however, the same opportunity exists for finding and attaining valid objectives. The same scientific methods of investigation, analysis, and development are used, implemented by accepted techniques.

It may be concluded, therefore, that, when the merchandising problem is concerned with a new product, the market study should precede the final designing of the product, even though it may have gone through its preliminary development.

Of equal importance is the definition of the type of market to be reached. An early decision as to the economic class for which the product is or will be designed is fundamental to the success of the market study.

If merchandising is considered as a business science and not as an art, less misdirection of the selling effort of the company will result.

Scope

If a market study is to have the proper scope, it must obtain *all* the facts concerning the product, the customer, the customer's wants, the market potentiality, and such other data as may be required by management to make its decisions safely and intelligently.

From these facts a merchandising plan can be developed that will permit the company to sell its products to the greatest number of users in the most economical and effective manner, at prices the consumer is willing to pay, with profits satisfactory to the company.

The following outline summarizes the facts which must be secured by market study, if these objectives are to be realized:

1. The correct selling price.
2. The kind and number of units of the product that are now sold over a given period.
3. The undesirable and desirable points of the product.
4. Desirable improvements in the product or packaging.

5. The potential volumes.
6. The degree and character of competition
    (*a*) Prices.
    (*b*) Number.
    (*c*) Strength.
    (*d*) Methods.
7. The type and location of the consumer.
8. The amount of service required or desirable.
9. The consumers' buying habits
    (*a*) How *much* of the product is purchased at one time?
    (*b*) How *often* does the regular user purchase the product?
    (*c*) *Where* does the consumer buy the product?
    (*d*) *How* is the product purchased?
10. The customers' likes and dislikes
    (*a*) *Why* do present consumers buy the product?
    (*b*) *Why* do nonusers refuse to buy the product?
    (*c*) *Why* did former users discontinue buying?
11. The right sales promotion plan
    (*a*) To indicate the advertising media and methods which will reach the greatest number of present and potential users of the product.
    (*b*) To co-ordinate the advertising with the selling effort.
12. The method of selecting salesmen.
13. The salesmen's routes and territories.
14. The salesmen's compensation plan.
15. The selling aids
    (*a*) Are catalogs required?
    (*b*) Are samples required?
    (*c*) Are follow-up calls necessary?
    (*d*) Is sales engineering required?
16. The best channels of distribution.

METHODS

To secure these facts requires a two-fold approach to the market study:

1. The accumulation and analysis of statistical data covering every phase of the past selling activities of the company and the industry.

2. An investigation of the market by making actual contacts in the field, with present customers and prospective customers in the various areas served or to be exploited.

Statistical Preparation

The accumulation and analysis of statistical data may be made largely from company records, if they are available. Results must be comprehensive, factual, and so organized that their

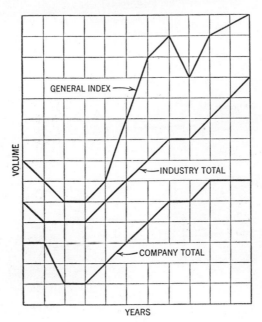

FIG. 25. Comparison of Company and Industry Sales with General Economic Picture

presentation will permit clear and valid conclusions. The following data analyses should be made first:

1. The tabulation of sales by total and by products for the past 5, 10, or 15 years, or longer if necessary. This will help determine any increasing or decreasing trends. These trends can be readily discovered by charting the sales and by correlating the curve with charts available from various commercial statistical agencies.

These cover the industry and the general economic picture of the country at large. Figure 25 shows a typical charting of such information, correlated with the industry trend and the general economic trend.

2. The accumulation of sales by products for the industry as a whole for a similar period of years. This determines whether or not the company is retaining its factor position in the industry. In the case of a new product, it indicates whether there is a place for the company in the market. Such data may be obtained from either government agencies or trade associations, or by a direct canvass of the entire industry.

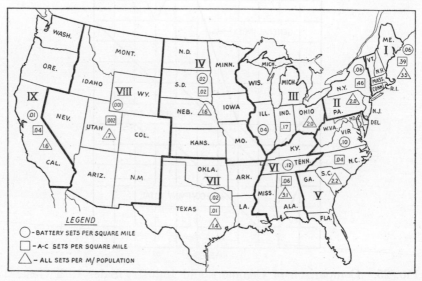

Fig. 26. Geographical Analysis of Sales

3. A geographical analysis of sales to show the market density of the sales by population or trading areas or both. This is an important consideration and may show, in areas of equal population and income density, that the dollars of sales per thousand population varies too greatly from the normal expectancy of the company's sales.

Such data should be charted on outline maps of the territory covered by the company. These maps, of states or sections or the United States as a whole, are available in metropolitan book stores in various sizes. Figure 26 illustrates such an analysis charted on a map.

4. A tabulation of sales by customers for a period of years, classified by size of account. Such data will provide information

on the turnover in customers. They will show whether a few customers provide a large proportion of the sales or whether the volume is uniformly distributed among all customers.

5. A determination of the sales made by the individual salesmen for a period of years. This should be compared with the salesmen's salaries, commissions, and expenses, to determine whether satisfactory earnings have been made by the salesmen and whether their expense has been in proper relation to sales. By reducing such figures to percentage ratios, comparisons can be readily made between the over-all figures and the individual salesmen.

6. A determination of the total number of potential customers by geographical areas, if it is possible to secure such data. Recourse may be had to the Census Bureau and to other Government and statistical agencies for such information. Where available, it should be charted on maps as described in paragraph 3.

7. An analysis of the salesmen's calls and territory to determine whom he calls on, how much time he devotes to these calls, and whether satisfactory territorial coverage is being obtained.

8. A careful analysis of each general selling expense account to determine its necessity and amount. This will also build up the proper relation between the total selling expense and the sales volume.

As a part of the internal statistical study, an investigation should also be made of the procedural methods pertinent to the selling activity. The two principal objectives are:

1. A review of the entire office selling procedure, including the handling of orders, the degree to which delivery promises are kept, the manner of billing, the credit policies, and the liquidity of the accounts receivable.

2. A careful analysis of the method by which salesmen are selected and trained, including the manner and frequency with which they are assisted in the field by their superior officers.

Field Investigation

The second phase of the market study calls for a comprehensive series of field contacts to secure valid data on customers and products. This program must be most carefully organized in order that a representative cross section of the market may be contacted.

	RANGE OF ERROR IN SAMPLING						
Range of Error, Per Cent	Opinion Divides Percentagewise as Follows:						
	20/80	25/75	30/70	35/65	40/60	45/55	50/50
2.0	3,600	4,219	4,725	5,119	5,400	5,569	5,625
3.0	1,600	1,875	2,100	2,275	2,400	2,475	2,500
4.0	900	1,055	1,181	1,280	1,350	1,392	1,406
5.0	576	675	756	819	864	891	900
6.0	400	469	525	569	600	619	625
7.0	294	344	386	418	441	455	459
8.0	225	264	295	320	338	348	352
9.0	178	208	233	253	267	275	278
10.0 *	144	169	189	205	216	223	225
15.0 *	64	75	84	91	96	99	100
20.0	36	42	47	51	54	56	56
25.0	23	27	30	33	35	36	36

* Range usually required.

FIG. 27

Much money can be wasted in unnecessary contacts if these calls are not carefully planned ahead, both as to number and location, and as to the allowable error in the information required. The most satisfactory method is the method known as "sampling," used by Gallup, Roper, and others in conducting national opinion surveys.

The first determination to be made is the degree of accuracy required. The higher the degree of accuracy required, the greater

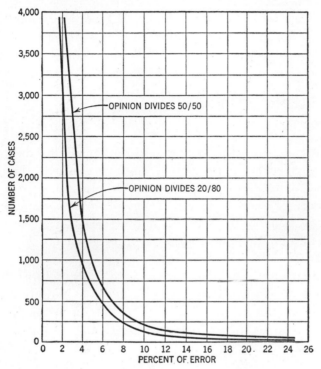

Fig. 28.   Opinion Survey Ratios

the number of calls that must be made. Figures 27 and 28, which are based on the formula used in conducting national opinion surveys, illustrate these ratios.

For the purpose of a field market study a probable error of 10 per cent is usually allowable. This will require a maximum of 225 calls, if it is assumed that opinion is divided 50–50. If it is discovered, after field contacts are started, that opinion is running 80–20, for example, the number of calls can be reduced accordingly. The field contact program should provide for this possibility.

Having determined the total number of calls required, the next determination to be made is their allocation to territories, outlets, and customers. Contacts should be made in large and small territories with good and poor sales volumes, large and small customers, various channels of distribution, and limited and complete product accounts.

If the number of contacts selected in each group has the same relation to the total contacts made, as has each group to its total field, a true sampling of the total field will be secured. It will be comprehensive as to data and authentic as to the conclusions drawn.

Questionnaires

Before going into the field, a questionnaire must be prepared listing the specific points of information required. Frequently, it will be found necessary to prepare several different questionnaires, one for each of certain types of customers, another for each of certain products if the line is varied and lacks homogeneity, and another for each of the different channels of distribution or types of selling.

Particular emphasis must be given to those points, developed from the statistical analysis, which appear to require correction or further amplification. That is, if it has been found that the salesmen turnover is very high, the questions must be so arranged that the cause will be determined. Or, if the statistical data reveal that the company is losing a certain portion of its customers, particular emphasis must be given to questions that will bring forth the reasons for such losses.

Sometimes it is found desirable to make up the questionnaire tentatively, and to conduct a brief field trip of ten or more calls to determine whether the phrasing is adequate and whether the questions proposed are sufficiently comprehensive in scope. The final questionnaire can then be corrected and printed for field use.

The questions should be so prepared that "yes" or "no" answers can be entered wherever possible. If this is done, the tabulation of data at the conclusion of the field study can be readily made. Figure 29 illustrates a typical form of questionnaire.

QUESTIONNAIRE NO.......

Date........

1. Name.................
2. Location.................
3. Products Made.................
4. Name and Title Persons Interviewed.................
5. Class: Industrial......Auto......Marine......Received Catalogs.....
6. Present Specifications:
   (a) Type and Make...........   (g) HP...........
   (b) Cycle...................   (h) Displace cu in...........
   (c) Bore...................   (i) Weight...........
   (d) Stroke...................   (j) Mounting...........
   (e) No. Cyls...................   (k) Accessories...........
   (f) Size dim...................   (l) ....
7. Cost.................
8. Engines/year.................
9. Applications (equipment engine is used on)
   Nature of Equipment.................
   (a) Size...................   (f) HP Required...........
   (b) Weight...................   (g) Adequate Power?...........
   (c) Rating...................   (h) Weight Correct?...........
   (d) Position...................   (i) Can larger space be provided
   (e) Load...................   for?...........
10. Desired Requirements, or Trend:
    Nature of Equipment.................
    (a) Type...................   (g) Idling Speed RPM...........
    (b) Weight...................   (h) Max. Speed RPM...........
    (c) Price/HP...................   (i) Supercharging...........
    (d) Size dim...................   (j) BMEP...........
    (e) Displace. cu in...........   (k) Accessories...........
    (f) Normal Speed RPM.......   (l) Maintenance...........
                                                     Accessibility...........
11. Is fuel economy required?.................
12. Which is more important, performance or fuel economy?...........
13. Is smoke and smell important?.................
14. Is noise very objectionable?.................
15. Prefer engine as original or replacement equipment? (For users only)....
16. Is method of selling replacement parts satisfactory?...........
17. Which is more important in first cost, price or quality?...........
18. Prefer a *supercharged* engine, or a new engine not supercharged, with same power characteristics?.................
19. Which would you be willing to pay more for?...........
20. Operating Peculiarities:
    Which is most important?
    (a) Weight...................   (d) First cost...........
    (b) Speed...................   (e) Upkeep...........
    (c) Economy...................
21. Is smoothness of engine performance very essential?...........
22. General Remarks:

....

....

....

FIG. 29

The field investigators must be coached carefully as to the manner of approach to be used and the handling of the questions. If an outside organization is engaged to make the study, the degree of anonymity of the sponsor must be decided on. The advantage of using a professional organization usually outweighs the cost, because of its specialized experience in this field, and because it can obtain frank and unbiased opinions from its contacts.

If the study is conducted by members of the company organization, usually more field contacts must be made. These will serve to average out the bias or lack of frankness in responding to inquiry from a vendor on whose good opinion their business must depend.

In either case the questionnaire must be used with great tact. Usually it is better to memorize the contents rather than to display it to the contact. Immediately on conclusion of the interview the investigator should fill in the answers in personal privacy. He will then note any comments in the space provided, which will later help to interpret the answers or characterize the authenticity of the data secured.

Personal contact should be made only by a skilled investigator. Only he will know how to make a proper contact that will result in maximum dependable information. An unskilled investigator may receive replies to his questions which were sincerely expressed by the person being interviewed, but which were incomplete, or true for only a limited set of conditions. The skilled investigator will recognize such situations and, by supplementary interrogation, draw out a complete answer.

Wherever possible, the investigator should make a number of calls with various salesmen in order to become acquainted with their approach. He can thus determine the relationship between the salesmen and the customer, evaluate the assistance that could be given the salesmen, and generally appraise the effectiveness of their representation of the company and its products.

In rare cases it is possible to use a mail questionnaire. Usually the difficulties encountered when questionnaires are mailed are the small number of returns and the lack of complete and representative responses.

PRODUCTS

Much contributory information on the company's products can be and should be secured from the field survey. A good investigator will elicit much valuable information in his contacts, particularly if the questionnaire includes queries on this subject.

Technological developments in natural and synthetic material fields, in the mechanical and electrical industries, are obsoleting many present products. Companies whose products are affected by these developments (which includes practically all) may find themselves in dwindling markets and must either change their present products or find new ones.

The market study must therefore determine the requirements as to design, performance, price and competition; the total size of the market, and the proportion of total business which the company can obtain for its products.

If it is found that a nominal expenditure for redesigning, engineering research and development will produce a product which will meet the market's requirements, such a review should be embodied in the management program for the company.

If it is found that the present market is disappearing as a result of technological advances and that new products are necessary, or if it is found desirable to add new products to expand the business, the merchandising decision must be influenced by the following factors:

1. Whether the new product must be manufactured by the same facilities being used for the present product.

2. Whether the new product will require, for its manufacture, the same type of labor now employed in the plant.

3. Whether the new product can be sold through the same channels of distribution as the old, using the same sales organization.

4. Whether the company should consider a product that is a departure from what is commonly sold to accomplish the same purpose. In a real sense this requires pioneering with its attendant risks.

5. Whether the company should or could buy another company that has already established a market for the products desired to complete its own line.

6. Whether the money needed for merchandising a new product is available.

7. Whether the company wants to add more volume to what it now has.

PRODUCT PERFORMANCE STUDY

Frequently the market study will reveal unsatisfactory performance of the product in the field. Product performance must be first determined by laboratory analysis, tests, and proving ground trials, before it is actually ready to be manufactured and sold in quantity. However, its suitability must be finally determined by field use.

For this reason (although normally it is a function of the engineering department and in large measure must still remain so) the study of product performance in the field can be conveniently handled as a later part of the merchandising program, either through a regularly organized market study, or as a specialized investigation with the engineering department.

Too often it has been found that, although one product may be superior in performance in the engineering laboratory, the customer will select a competitor's product. This occurs not on the basis of performance but because of some minor "gadget" that caught his fancy. Endless tests in the laboratory will not reveal such consumer reactions, and for this reason the final proving ground must be the customer himself.

Included in this phase of the study is that of service requirements. The investigation should determine how frequent and how much servicing is required. This is true with respect to replacement of parts, as well as purely service maintenance. In addition, every effort should be made to discover how competitors handle this problem and with what success.

The investigator should keep this fact constantly before him, and endeavor to learn what the actual product performance may be. His findings, after analysis for customer reaction, should be passed on to the engineering department, to which the data will be of inestimable value.

PRODUCT DEVELOPMENT

Although product development is a matter concerning all the major divisions of the business, so much of it springs from the merchandising objectives of a company that it is included in this chapter.

Definition

Product development is defined as the process or program through which changes or improvements are made in existing products to:

1. *Satisfy the wants of the market.*
2. *Provide for reduced manufacturing costs.*
3. *Improve performance and service requirements.*

It is an activity in which all divisions of the business are concerned and in which management, merchandising, manufacturing, and engineering must participate.

Product development must be carried on continuously. In the competitive industrial world "he who stops, dies," and the pathway of industrial success is strewn with the remains of companies who rested on their laurels and let their products atrophy.

Too strong an emphasis cannot be placed on this subject. The general management of the company should include product development as an important objective in its statement of basic policies.

Participation by Management

The specific and detailed function of management in the development of its products is to direct the work of the engineering department, so that a proper and balanced consideration is given to the requirements of:

1. *The market's wants.*
2. *Manufacturing limitations.*
3. *Good engineering practice.*

If such over-all direction is not exercised, too frequently it will be found that the responsibility for product development is left solely in the hands of the engineering department. As a result:

1. The product may be adequate in quality and performance and yet lack market acceptance because of deficient styling and appearance, or

2. The product may prove too costly to manufacture, thus making it impossible to meet competition profitably.

In order to activate this project with the maximum results, management must arrange for and regularly receive:

1. Comprehensive programs stating the purpose and scope of procedures undertaken to attain any stated product development objectives.

2. Periodic reports, properly organized and related, which will give a clear picture of the progress to date, on every phase of every product development project.

Participation by Merchandising

The problem of incorporating the requirements of the market into the development of the product is management's continuous and most difficult problem.

Usually this problem is first called to management's attention by the sales department. Reports are continuously being received from salesmen calling attention to these requirements and to what competitors are doing about them. Before such information is passed on to management, however, the sales department should carefully weigh and check it for reliability. It should then be classified and properly organized for presentation to the management.

In making up such reports, care must be taken not to give undue emphasis to any one source of information, such as one salesman who is more aggressive and has more selling ability than his fellow workers.

Neither should special emphasis be given to a local market activity which may be temporary in nature. For instance, small engines of low horsepower for pumping in oil fields under quota restriction do not represent a stable market, since the regular line of engines built for this purpose also serve many other industrial uses.

If the sales department can weigh its judgments carefully in such matters, it will greatly aid management in setting a proper course for the product development program.

Wherever possible, information regarding the requirement of the market should also be checked by some agency with a fresh and unbiased viewpoint toward the problem, the opinions and findings of which will reflect this attitude.

Such work should be done directly for management, so that the report will be impartial and serve as a cross-check on other information received on the same subject. It may be performed by an individual or a group, selected from the organization or engaged especially for the purpose from outside. In either case, even though the investigation may receive detailed direction from the sales department, final responsibility should be to top management.

If conditions permit, the chief executive of the company should personally make enough contacts in the market to satisfy himself as to the validity of the problem and to obtain at first hand an indication of the requirements to be met.

Participation by Manufacturing

Many worth-while product development programs die aborning because the facilities of the manufacturing division were not taken into account when the product was designed.

The chain of events to be guarded against is common: A design may be excellent from an engineering standpoint but involve high actual manufacturing cost on available equipment. Capital expenditures are therefore required for new equipment in order that the product can be made at a cost which will permit it to be sold at a profit. Such expenditures may constitute a serious drain on the finances of the company or may involve it in a borrowing program dangerous to its credit. The entire program is then rejected, in spite of the fact that the new product may be essential to the continuing operation of the company.

Participation by Engineering

The engineering department has major obligations to management in its endeavor constantly to improve the product on the following counts:

1. Better appearance.
2. Greater performance.
3. Newer materials.
4. Wider field applications.
5. Lower manufacturing cost.
6. Minimum and easy servicing.
7. Lower operating and maintenance cost.

An important source of information in these respects is the salesman of vendors supplying the company with materials or equipment. Proper contact and interrogation of these individuals will frequently reveal much valuable data for product improvement in all of these directions.

Even though all new developments are not incorporated immediately into the design, such improvements and changes should be readily available. They can thus be made when the time and circumstances are opportune, competition and inventory being taken into consideration.

If the company is so prepared, it will be in a better position to fight competition for the market and to weather the economic storms which constantly beset every business enterprise.

FINALIZING THE MERCHANDISING PROGRAM

On the completion of the market study, including any special studies on new products or product development, a complete tabulation of all findings should be made, carefully classified by subject, and logically arranged.

From these data a merchandising program may be prepared which will outline in detail:

1. *The changes to be made in present selling methods.*
2. *The new methods or procedures to be adopted.*
3. *The volume to be realized, which can be integrated into the manufacturing facilities.*

4. The finances available and required.

5. The manner in which volume is to be obtained, with reference to territories, salesmen, and products.

An important decision must be made when newer and better products are developed and experience and the market study indicate that they are more acceptable to the user than the older models. The decision as to whether to allow the older models to remain in competition with the newer ones can only follow one course—the older models should be withdrawn from the market as quickly as possible.

RESEARCH AND DEVELOPMENT

In conducting product research and development projects, the most satisfactory results are attained only if such project programs are properly organized. In nearly all research programs, there is a great deal of repetitive action and detail. They lend themselves very readily to the same principles of control that are applicable to the production activities of a company.

If they are considered in this light, the organization of the research program can follow a regular pattern of control, for example:

(a) Planning
(b) Budgeting
(c) Scheduling
(d) Reporting

Planning

The planning for product research and development takes into consideration several factors:

1. The organization of the department (usually the engineering department) charged with this function. Development work should be a separate function from all other engineering activities, so that the work assignments are given the consistent and continuous effort required for the consummation of product development projects.

2. The facilities available in the form of reference material, testing laboratories, shops for the construction of prototype models, and field testing equipment.

3. The planning procedure itself. This takes into account the importance of the project, its urgency with respect to time, and the method to be used to schedule the development work and follow its progress.

Budgeting

No research or development work should be instituted unless it envisions a definite objective result. Money is easily frittered away on unplanned research effort. To control the applications of such funds, budgets are necessary. They usually start with an appropriation for each project approved by management, the amount of which is determined by the estimated benefit to be secured from its successful conclusion. The project appropriation must then be divided into its basic components of labor, material, and overhead, if applicable. Detail reports of time applied by engineers, craftsmen, and others must be arranged for, as well as materials purchased outside or requisitioned from plant stores. A form should be devised showing the project name, the serial number assigned, the purpose of the project, the schedule for significant actions during the project's existence, the amount of the appropriation granted, and space for detail accumulation of the costs applied against the basic cost components budgeted. With these controls the entire research and development program can be kept in harmony with the financial and operating policies of the company.

Scheduling

After the project is planned and its cost budgeted, it can be scheduled into the work program of the staff and the facilities to be used. The schedule must take into account the urgency of the project, the availability of man power and equipment, and the work load capacity of both. The problem therefore becomes identical with that of the control of a product through the plant, and the same principles will apply (see Chapter 29, Section 4).

Reporting

Final control by research and development projects is effectuated by reports to management from the executive responsible for this work and by reports to the responsible executive by the project leaders appointed to carry out each project. Although the budget report will convey to management considerable information on progress, it should be supplemented by a report from the responsible executive appraising the progress made in actually solving the problem.

Frequently a company may consider itself too small to maintain the permanent staff and facilities necessary for effective research and development. In such cases, there are available the very complete facilities of educational institutions and commercial research laboratories, many of which have a national reputation for the character and scope of work they undertake.

However, even this method should not be attempted unless it is co-ordinated under the direction of a full-time employee of the company who will organize and direct these activities. No company is too small to have at least one person definitely assigned to the function of product research and development. If the enterprise is very small, this may be a part-time function. In the final analysis, the proper staffing of the function will depend on its importance in the enterprise.

CHAPTER 21

SELLING METHODS
AND QUOTAS

•

OBJECTIVES

In the preceding chapter on market study the basic first step for organizing a merchandising plan was outlined and described in detail.

The second step in its preparation is to establish selling methods and quotas. These will put into effect the conclusions and decisions resulting from the market study and provide the objectives necessary for accomplishment of the fundamental purpose, to operate profitably.

SALES VOLUME

Prior to determining the sales method to be employed, a more important decision must first be made. What sales volume is to be chosen for the merchandising plan?

The market study should have revealed the total potential market throughout the country for each of the products and areas to be exploited. The decision which management then faces is: What proportion of this total market can the company reasonably expect to secure? If the statistical study has indicated that the company has a participation, or share, of 5 per cent in the actual sales of the industry, a reasonable increase of 10 per cent to 25 per cent may be selected. Or the participation

162

position of 5 per cent may be retained for the discovered potential, which may be much larger than the present volume enjoyed by the company. In either case the decision must be realistic.

The next step is to give consideration to the finances and manufacturing facilities available. If the company volume objective is too large a proportion of the total market, and a sales organization and selling methods are established to obtain this objective, it is quite likely that the company will find itself without sufficient funds to finance such volume or with insufficient manufacturing facilities.

On the other hand, the decision may be to place the expected sales volume at a figure less than that which can be produced by the available manufacturing facilities. In either case an unbalanced condition will occur which immediately creates a serious handicap to the merchandising plan.

If a sales volume is selected in excess of the manufacturing capacity or the available finances, delayed deliveries and broken delivery promises may result and may completely disrupt the company organization and operation. If a sales volume is selected that is less than the manufacturing capacity, production costs will be high. It will be difficult or impossible to make a satisfactory profit on the sales volume being realized.

A third difficulty may also enter the picture. In spite of the selection of a sales volume that is in balance with manufacturing facilities and finances, the desired sales volume may not be economically obtainable.

Other companies must live, too. They need their portion of the potential volume to exist. They may also have special advantages which give them a favored position. Some may have special patented features for their products. Some may have social or financial connections which pre-empt the business of a potential customer.

Or transportation costs may be too great to permit the company to tap certain potential market areas against local competition. Or years of successful service by a competitor may be a barrier to the customer that no consideration can overcome. All these factors are important and should be given careful weight.

If the merchandising plan contemplates an increase in sales volume without benefit of new products, then these added sales must be obtained from a competitor, or at the expense of some of the existing products of the company, unless the market can be widened.

In any case of increased volume, some or all of the foregoing difficulties must be overcome. They may therefore require abnormal selling expense, new or unusual selling effort, more extensive advertising and sales promotion, lower selling prices, or a radically improved product.

Consequently, in selecting the sales volume when preparing the merchandising plan, finances, manufacturing facilities, and selling effort must be carefully balanced and properly co-ordinated. Alternate provisions must be made to overcome any obstacles which may develop later.

Sales Quotas

Sales quotas are the sales volumes desired in various territories, by products and in total. Too often they are *guesses* as to the volume that management hopes it can obtain from each territory. More frequently they are mere arbitrary targets set up as psychological incentives for the salesmen. Usually they are based on past experience and do not sufficiently consider the real potentiality of each territory.

Seldom are sales quotas based on a scientific determination of the market. If quotas are to be set competently and equitably, therefore, it is important to establish a definite and realistic method for evaluating the potential of each territory.

In setting quotas, consideration should be given to the following factors:

1. Market potential (derived from the market study).
2. Capacity of the sales organization (based on its past activity and an appraisal of its potential effectiveness).
3. Cyclical trends (general business conditions which affect the company; see Chapter 20, Section 3).
4. Seasonal trends (the *normal* variation of volume during the year; see Chapter 3, Section 1).

5. Type and degree of competition.
6. The company's reputation.
7. Consumer acceptance of the various products (see Chapter 20, Section 3).
8. The sales promotion program.

All these factors should be used to evaluate the volume that might be realized from each of the various territories. In many cases they can be reduced to unit market measures, as described in the preceding chapter, which will greatly expedite the sales quota determination, and enhance its statistical reliability.

In a sense, a sales quota is a measure or standard and should be used as such. It will provide the means for measuring sales volume performance when the merchandising plan is put into effect. If that volume is not actually obtained, an analysis should be made to determine the reason for any variation from the standard. Some of the pitfalls to be watched for in uncovering low sales volume performance are:

1. Local competition firmly entrenched in the territory.

2. Certain areas where a different styling or design of the product is required.

3. Territories so far removed from the plant that adequate service and sales coverage cannot be given (unless branch offices and warehouses are established).

Sales quotas are an important factor in any merchandising plan. They are the basic standard for its application. They supply the sales administration with its primary and major objective and the manufacturing organization with a basic schedule for its operation. For this reason alone, sales quotas must be given the same careful preparation that the financial program itself receives and should receive equal importance in the general management program.

CHANNELS OF DISTRIBUTION

Having determined the total volume that can be properly financed, manufactured, and sold, the next logical step is to decide on the type of outlet that will be most desirable in accomplishing the merchandising plan.

Primary market products, to be retailed directly to the consumer, may be sold through department stores, drugstores, chain stores, specialty stores, and similar retail establishments. Or the entire output may be sold through a mail order house, or through house-to-house salesmen, or through syndicate buyers. The retailing method to be selected will be largely influenced by the type of product and its end use.

Products sold to the secondary market of manufacturers, contractors, and other users are to be incorporated or assembled into still other products. They offer little choice in the type of sales outlet. The problem is not one of selecting the type of outlet, but rather of selecting the most suitable method of contacting the known customers, and is characteristic of this type of market.

If it is assumed that market study has indicated the type of outlet from which the consumer is accustomed to buy, management should give careful consideration to the characteristics of each before coming to final decision.

Department Stores

Large department stores usually deal in large volumes and to that end will frequently be willing to apply appreciable and specific promotional effort. The better department stores have made careful studies of their customers wants and select their merchandise with discrimination and care. Stores catering to low-income customers require products having mass appeal, with low price and high utility emphasized.

Stores catering to the high-income group require products with superior and exclusive styling, in addition to an implied high quality. Frequently these outlets insist on the exclusive use of a line or part of a line, which prevents other outlets in the same locality from carrying it.

Private brands or the use of the outlet's name on the product are frequently required and may limit, to some extent, the number of sales outlets in a given territory. This is not such a serious requirement as that of exclusive styling, however, and, unless the product is a distinctive article, it can easily be met. If such private brands are also "national brands," however, the identical product under other brand names may not find sufficient sales volume in other outlets.

Hardware Stores

Hardware stores carry a large variety of products, termed "hard goods." These include not only true hardware items and tools, but also sport goods, stoves, electrical equipment, kitchen ware, and garden equipment and supplies.

Such stores are usually small, cater only to the particular community or neighborhood in which they are located, do little advertising and promotional work, and generally do not sell in large volumes.

Their purchasing is usually done through large distributors and supply houses, and the real promotion of the products must be done by the manufacturer.

Mail Order Houses

The mail order houses are few and offer a highly concentrated outlet for huge national volumes. They purchase in tremendously large quantities, with great emphasis on price and an equal requirement of high quality. Frequently, they will take entire outputs and often supervise the design and functioning of the product.

A company selling its products to a mail order house may have difficulty in selling its products to other retail outlets. This is especially true of neighborhood-type stores in competition with the retail stores of the mail order house.

If a company has its own selling and distributing organization, this handicap is not serious. It may be turned into an operating advantage in fact, if the mail order volume is limited to 50 per cent or less of the company's products.

Careful cost analysis and pricing and simplicity of line are needed to take full advantage of such a connection. The merchandising plan should not overlook the volume and profit possibilities of an outlet of this type.

Specialty Stores

So-called specialty stores dealing in a restricted line of products have many limitations as satisfactory sales outlets. Generally, their volume is small, since they operate on a neighborhood basis and must compete with stores where the customer can shop for other needed items.

Being less successful than other types of retail outlets, they have a high rate of business mortality and pose a serious and frequent problem in re-establishing outlets.

House-to-House Sales

As mentioned earlier, house-to-house sales have been successfully developed in relatively few cases. This selling method requires an exceptionally strong and well-organized personnel to overcome the high turnover in salesmen and to train and direct a group of salesmen that are generally of less than average ability.

An alternate method of house-to-house sales is that of using agents who actually buy the product and sell it as individual retailers. This method has certain administrative and financial advantages.

House-to-house selling requires the office processing of many small orders, with a proportionately large office cost for personnel to operate the detailed procedure of receiving and shipping orders.

National advertising must be planned for this selling method, and the brand name must be well established in the public mind. The sales promotional costs can easily become prohibitive.

Drugstores

Drugstores have been extending the number and variety of their products to the point where they are practically variety stores. This is particularly true of the chain drugstores (and some large individual stores) in which everything from meals to household supplies can be purchased.

The small neighborhood stores usually limit their lines somewhat but are more and more being forced into general merchandise lines in order to stay in business.

Drugstores generally cater to the community or neighborhood in which they are located and do little sales promotional work except by display or in neighborhood papers. The larger stores or chains advertise more extensively but generally feature only price.

Limited lines of mechanical goods are carried, with few models or sizes, usually in the lower price ranges. These stores are not prepared to render service. The customer buying mechanical, electrical, or household equipment from them will find it difficult to obtain maintenance service.

Chain Stores

The chain stores of the 5¢–10¢–$1 class are large volume outlets. Promotional activity consists of merchandise display, local advertising, and sales appeal made on a price basis.

However, an increasing variety of products is being merchandised through such outlets, and many nationally advertised products are now carried on their counters. Smaller unit packages than those sold in the larger department stores must be provided, although in recent years both types of outlets have modified their requirements, with the "five and ten" adding larger packages, and the department stores adding smaller packages.

In buying for their stores, chain buyers give careful consideration to the needs of the neighborhoods in which their stores are located and select merchandise accordingly. For companies making the gadgetry and supplies handled by these outlets, the chain stores offer a quick and concentrated market, but a tremendously competitive one. It is an ideal market for the small manufacturer, but requires alert and ingenious management to adjust to sudden changes in consumers' tastes.

SALES ORGANIZATION

The two major steps of the merchandising plan have now been completed, that is, the decisions on the total volume to be realized, and the channel of distribution to be established.

The type and size of sales organization to reach this market must next be determined. The volume to be achieved and the number of outlets to be reached will limit the sales organization possibilities. The selection of the type of outlet will have a very direct bearing on selling costs.

There are six common forms of selling instruments:

1. Direct salesmen.
2. Agents.
3. Distributors and dealers.
4. Jobbers.
5. Branches.
6. Direct mail.

The advantages and disadvantages of each form are discussed in the following pages.

Direct Salesmen

The most effective coverage of the market is secured by the use of salesmen working directly in the territory on prospective and current customers of his company.

However, there are many conditions which qualify the choice of this type of selling effort.

1. It is most satisfactory when the market is concentrated and when accounts are large and relatively few and do not have to be contacted too frequently. The sales volume must be sufficient, within a reasonably sized territory, to justify such selling effort.

2. During periods of low volume, excessive selling expenses may be incurred because of the necessary permanency of this type of organization.

3. High selling costs may also be incurred through high turnover of salesmen, unless adequate provision is made for suitable compensation, selection, and training.

4. Whenever the sale to each of a large number of outlets is small, the use of direct salesmen becomes impractical. For example, there are approximately 160,000 department stores in this country. It is easily seen how prohibitive the selling costs would be if these outlets were contacted individually.

5. However, by direct field selling to its accounts, the company is in a most satisfactory position to be informed promptly and accurately of trends, changes, and competitive activity in the market.

Also classified under this heading are the so-called "house accounts." Such sales are generally made through contacts by the principals of the company and usually involve important customers and large orders. Managerial sales of this type are frequently of a critical nature because of price or quantity or both and are permanently reserved from the salesmen for these reasons.

Agents

Agents are sales representatives who usually work on a straight commission basis, or on consignment account, or more rarely on an outright purchase of the product. They are not direct employees of the company except in the legal sense and may sell the products of more than one company.

Usually the company is required to carry the customer's account, and the only financial participation by the agent is in his receipt of the commission.

When the agent is employed on a consignment basis, his financial and moral responsibility should be carefully checked. He collects from the customer on his own account and remits to the company only the cost price of the merchandise. Some companies selling on a house-to-house basis find this method desirable, as the "agent" in this case is really a small retailer in business for himself, and the company has no employer responsibility for him.

The use of agents involves consideration of the following factors:

1. Maximum control over his efforts is seldom if ever possible.

2. The line of products may not be exploited to its utmost. Usually the agent will push those items in the line which can be sold most easily and which carry the largest amount of profit.

3. Periodic contact by a representative of the company is required to educate the agent, to help him sell, and to apply promotional effort.

4. The company obtains only limited information as to trends, changes, and competitive activity in the market.

Distributors and Dealers

Distributors and dealers, in general, handle only a limited number of products, usually only one make in a competitive group. They buy the product from the company, warehouse it, frequently on a consignment basis, and handle all financial transactions between themselves and their customers.

They may themselves have a direct field sales organization and engage in considerable promotional activities.

Unless distributors are well financed and have an aggressive sales management, they frequently constitute a merchandising hazard. The company may eventually find itself directing the detailed activities of the distributor and finally taking over his operation as a branch of the company itself.

The use of this type of selling effort is further influenced by the following conditions:

1. A distributor may be better known in a specific locality than the manufacturer.

2. Although the company may not be obliged to carry the retail accounts of the distributor, it may be compelled to render extensive financial assistance to him through large consignment stocks, special discounts, and trade-in allowances.

3. The control over a distributor's activities is limited unless the sales effort of the company is well and extensively organized.

4. Periodic contact by representatives of the company is required to educate and assist the distributor.

5. The field selling cost is established through the standard discount, which may vary considerably.

The selection of the distributor or dealer method of selling is based primarily on the need for local concentrated coverage, and, secondly, on demands for continuing service to the customer after the sale is made.

For this reason, *franchise dealers* are generally established to guarantee these results. In return for the franchise, which grants him exclusive selling rights in a defined territory, the dealer contracts to take a certain quantity of the product. He must maintain required standards of price, selling effort, and service to the customer, and engage in an adequate program of sales promotion and advertising. Typical examples of this method of selling are automobile agencies, household appliance dealers, and certain classes of plumbing goods dealers.

Branches

A branch is a company-owned distributor or dealer, functioning in a similar manner but under the direct control of the company. A branch handles the company's products only, unless a special situation permits it to carry complementary lines.

The adopting of this type of selling effort is governed by:

1. The need for locally directed sales and service effort.
2. Inability to secure properly qualified distributors, or
3. The necessity for meeting a geographical problem in the merchandising plan.

Branch operation is substantially a form of direct selling, and the sales organization requirements are the same. When sales decline to a low volume, the usual hazard of unprofitable operation is attached to branch selling, owing to the inherent security of its personnel as permanent salaried employees of the company.

Jobbers

Jobbers serve the same purpose as distributors in merchandising. They handle a variety of lines, whereas the distributor handles only one or a few. In some cases, a jobber is recognized as both a distributor and jobber.

Usually the jobber is purely a merchandiser, sometimes merely brokering the account. Seldom, if ever, is he in position to render service to the customer after the sale is made.

Direct Mail

Of all the methods of selling, none is more typically American than direct mail selling. It may be used as the only merchandising effort or merely to supplement some other form of selling. In this case it becomes a part of the advertising function.

Direct mail selling requires a distinct type of sales organization and a well-organized procedure for planning, dispatching, and following up every phase of the direct mail campaign.

The heart and soul of direct mail selling lies in the prospect mailing list. The maintenance of such lists is the vital function in direct mail selling, and, unless the necessary time and effort are spent to keep them up-to-date and complete, the money spent in making the mailings is completely wasted.

The percentage of sales effectiveness (sales orders per 100 mailings) normally runs very low in this type of selling, although special offers of value at opportune times may bring in a very large volume of orders.

The product to be merchandised by this method should be one for which there is a mass consumer market. Generally price appeal is paramount. The product must also be one which can be distributed readily without undue transportation costs, usually via parcel post. It should not require servicing.

The large mail order houses do not exactly typify direct mail selling, although practically all their merchandising is based on this principle. They are actually retailers of practically every commodity required in the economy of our people. Direct mail selling is considered in the foregoing paragraphs solely from the standpoint of a manufacturer producing a somewhat limited line of products.

The selection of this type of selling effort should therefore be based on the type of product to be sold and the type and size of market to be reached.

Sales Administration

The form of sales administration required for the direction of the sales organization will be governed largely by the selling method selected.

The sales administration, no matter what method is used, must be prepared to cope with personnel problems. It must understand how to measure performance, how to secure effective activity, and how to maintain a co-operative and co-ordinated effort in the field.

It must also be constantly alert to maintain good customer relations, through the selling organization's efforts, and constantly guard against any deviation from the merchandising policies established by the general management.

In addition, an effective sales administration must keep itself informed on economic trends and on the operation of the company itself with respect to its financial and operating problems. At all times the direction and application of all selling effort must be in harmony with the company's progress and tied into the general management program.

CHAPTER 22

SELLING COSTS

•

DEFINITION

Selling costs include all of the expenses that pertain directly to advertising and selling the product. These include:

1. Salesmen's salaries.
2. Salesmen's commissions.
3. Traveling expenses of anyone engaged in the selling activities.
4. Sales administrative and clerical salaries.
5. Sales office expense.
6. Advertising expense.
7. Sales promotion expense.

Discounts and allowances may sometimes be included in the selling cost also, if the general books are set up on a gross or list price sales basis. This is particularly true if distributorships are used as a sales outlet. Any decision to include them in the selling cost should be influenced by the tax and financial considerations involved, as well as by the corporate structure of the company itself.

SELLING COST RANGE

Selling costs vary widely with different types of industry, with different companies within the same industry, and even with different products within the same company. They range from a low of 1 per cent to a high of 50 per cent of the sales dollar for industrial products. Other lines, such as proprietary drug and toilet sundries, are known to have selling costs as high as 75 per cent.

Selling costs, therefore, are governed by the type of outlet used and the kind of market reached. There is no hard and fast rule to apply. The general principle of market size (that is, the size of the unit sale and the number of customers) will, however, largely influence the selling cost.

For example, a company making a product to be used by very few other manufacturers or retailers, in large quantities, can generally afford only a low selling cost. Such sales are influenced to a large extent by the reliability of the company manufacturing the product, and by the unit selling price. Advertising and extensive sales promotion will be of little value, and the company can best apply its effort to the design of the product to meet the customers' needs, and in assisting the customer in overcoming any problems that might be encountered.

Mail order houses, for example, take the position that no selling cost exists in placing a product with them, as the sale is consummated by the general management on a basis of quality, price, and delivery. This is also the attitude of certain large automobile companies regarding the purchase of tires. If any selling cost is allowed in the selling price, it is usually a very nominal amount. Under such conditions, the top management itself must play a leading part in maintaining the customer contact and in consummating the sale.

On the other hand, a company selling its products to a large numbers of users, scattered widely over the country, who make small unit purchases only at infrequent intervals, may find its selling costs approaching the upper limits. The reason is that the sales representatives are required to make many contacts, even though they know that the prospect is not immediately in the market for a new product or additional quantity. Such contacts must be made, as a sales promotional effort, to keep the company's name and products before the potential customer.

Or the user may have to be shown, by demonstration and actual trial, that the product being offered will reduce his costs, or improve his service, or benefit him in some other manner. Such sales effort requires the expenditure of much time and attention for each customer. If, in addition, the product is expensive, requiring the financing of the sale on a time basis or large trade-in allowances or both, this becomes an important factor in producing a high selling cost.

Illustrative of the variations in selling costs for a number of representative companies, the following tabulation shows the actual direct selling cost ratios to their primary outlets:

Product	Outlet	Sales Cost % of Sales Dollar
Warm air heating equipment	Dealer	9.0
Diesel engines	Dealer	6.5
Automobile engines	Manufacturer	2.0
Plastics	Jobber	10.5
Molded rubber goods	Jobber	5.5
Furniture products	Dealer	7.5
Radios	Mail order house	1.5

SALES PROMOTION COSTS

A large element of selling cost is sales promotional expense. This is the cost of advertising, demonstrating, and otherwise preparing the market and customer for the sale. Here again the range between the low and high limits is considerable.

Such promotional expense usually lies in advertising the product through media (which are publications of all kinds), the distribution of free samples, exhibitions, or direct mail.

For industrial products the ratio of the advertising cost to the sales dollar is restricted to rather narrow limits, usually from 3 to 7 per cent. For mass consumer products, such as cigarettes, chewing gum, and carbonated drinks, it may range much higher.

The cost of advertising by direct mail is influenced by the number of names reached and the character of the mailing piece, which determine its unit cost. At one extreme is the simple form letter, with or without a stuffer enclosure, which will cost from 5¢ to 15¢ for each address, including printing, postage, and mailing. At the other extreme is the catalog, which may cost up to several dollars for each mailing.

The sales returns from direct mailing should be carefully checked as to results. If the unit cost of the mailing is high and the mailing list is large, a definite sales volume should be expected. Otherwise the selling cost will go beyond control.

Direct mail costs, if used to supplement the advertising, should be included as a subaccount under advertising and controlled by the same appropriation procedure used in establishing the advertising budget.

Media advertising is best handled through an advertising agency, regardless of the size of a company. Agencies are especially equipped to analyze the "pulling value" of any media and to prepare and place the advertising copy. Their fee is usually included in the space rate of the publication, so that little advantage accrues to a company that endeavors to prepare and place its own advertising copy directly.

SELLING COST CONTROL

Standards are commonly accepted by industry as the proper method of maintaining control over its several activities. For example, standards for direct labor operations are carefully determined and are used to eliminate unnecessary work or wasteful operations.

It is of equal importance and, in many instances, of extreme importance to analyze and control in detail and in the same manner the various elements of selling costs. One of the inconsistencies in industrial management is the close control given direct production costs and the loose control of indirect costs in the office and selling activity. Selling costs may range between 15 and 30 per cent of the sales dollar, and direct labor costs only 10 to 20 per cent. Yet the average company will devote much effort to careful analysis and control of direct labor operations, while giving but cursory attention to selling costs.

Too often management takes the attitude that selling costs are beyond its control, that they are determined by conditions outside its regulation and must be suffered as a concession to the selling effort.

This is a false philosophy. Standards for each element of the selling cost may be established as accurately and as completely as standards for direct labor. The method of making such analyses will vary, of course, depending on the character of the selling expense being analyzed.

For example, salesmen's salaries or commissions or both, generally a large item in selling cost, may be analyzed by:

1. Comparing each salesman's actual salary with his actual sales and determining whether or not this ratio is excessive, thereby establishing the proper fixed and variable costs that are proper to this item.

2. Determining whether his territory is being completely covered at proper intervals, by dividing his total actual calls into his prospect list and determining the "turnover" rate. Thus, if he has 1,200 prospects to call on in a year, and makes only 10 calls a day, he can only call twice a year on each one. If the business requires 4 calls a year, and 10 calls is the most he can make in a day, then his prospect list or territory should be reduced to 750 names or less.

3. Determining whether the products he is selling have the correct relative proportions, that is, that he is not concentrating on the ones most profitable to him.

4. Determining whether proper pricing levels are being maintained.

Another example might be sales office expense, which can be analyzed by:

1. Reviewing each routine for its necessity and effectiveness.

2. Examining all reports for their utility and frequency.

3. Checking the dispatch of incoming orders and correspondence.

4. Establishing, by the method described in Chapter 15, Section 2, the proper fixed and variable expense allowance for each office expense account, after the routines have been analyzed as in 1, 2, and 3.

After proper standards for each element of selling cost have been established in accordance with sound principles of budgetary control, provision must be made for accumulating the actual expenses for comparison with standard. This can be accomplished by the budget department, using the regular routines of budgetary control.

It will then become the responsibility of sales management to take such action as will correct any unfavorable variance revealed in the control reports.

CHAPTER 23

SALESMEN'S COMPENSATION

•

TYPES

Many forms of incentives have been devised to spur salesmen to greater activity and better results for themselves and their companies. Some of the more common types of compensation and incentive are listed here and described in detail in the subsequent subject headings:

1. Point system.
2. Special incentives and prizes.
3. Straight commission.
4. Straight salary and expenses.
5. Salary and commission.

POINT SYSTEM

The point system of incentives establishes a certain number of points for various selling activities and results and then places a dollar value on each point. The salesman will then earn or be credited with a number of points which, when multiplied by the dollar value per point, will fix his compensation.

All selling activities can be included in this plan, by allowing points for:

1. Each new account opened.
2. Quotas reached.

3. Quotas exceeded by various amounts.
4. Total volume of sales.
5. Varying proportions of profit in the sales.
6. Number of calls made.
7. Repeat orders.
8. Travel expenses held within the budget.

Invariably this plan becomes somewhat complicated. It requires additional clerical effort in the office and involves many detailed records and calculations. Although presumably it causes the salesman to watch each of his activities carefully, it is doubtful whether this actually occurs in all instances. Furthermore, it affords frequent sources of argument between the salesman and the office that calculates his earnings.

Actually this plan is rarely used. It has been described only because it frequently seems to be a logical method of placing the selling activities on a "piecework" basis. It is generally impractical and should not be considered, except as a basis for additional compensation to salesmen in the form of prizes and special awards.

SPECIAL INCENTIVES AND PRIZES

Regardless of the regular type of compensation, additional compensation or incentives can be offered to salesmen for unusual services.

If quotas have been established accurately and properly, added compensation can be offered for exceeding the quota. This may be a lump sum, or a higher commission rate.

Or an incentive may be offered to each salesman in the form of a certain amount of money for each new account opened.

Variants of these two major objectives in the merchandising plan may be selected by the sales management for cash awards. All should have a time limit in order that their special characteristic may be recognized. They can be renewed whenever sales lag or an additional spur is needed.

Sales contests with prizes produce excellent results at low cost, since they play on the psychological factors of competitive effort. They are particularly applicable to a well-organized sales division where the men have been equally trained and developed in sales work and have uniform opportunity in their sales territories. No contests should be initiated unless these conditions prevail. Otherwise the contest becomes one-sided, and the "star" salesman wins all the prizes.

Any contest should be arranged to accomplish certain and definite results, such as:

1. Securing added volume during a low volume period.
2. Opening up new territory.
3. Introducing new products.

Wherever prizes or premiums are offered, care must be taken to see that the award brings a proportionate increase in volume or the accomplishment of certain desired results. The point system, described earlier, finds a logical application in this plan. It is generally used in some form by all companies organizing and operating sales contests.

Straight Salary and Expenses

Under this plan the salesman receives a fixed and stated salary, regardless of the volume of business he obtains. This plan can be made to provide some incentive by establishing sales quotas which the salesman must consistently attain if he is to continue receiving his regular compensation.

The straight salary form of compensation is most suitable where it is difficult to define territories accurately or where salesmen may be required to work in certain territories simply because of their familiarity with local conditions.

It is also particularly applicable where sales involving large sums are made at infrequent intervals, as with large pieces of equipment.

Where a large sales organization is maintained in extensive territories with only moderate supervision, a straight salary type of incentive plan is not considered practical.

In compact territories with close supervision the straight salary plan affords a means of reducing the selling cost and of exercising complete control over the *time* and activity of the salesman.

STRAIGHT COMMISSION

The straight commission form of incentive provides for compensating a salesman directly, in proportion to the volume of business he obtains. In other words, for every dollar of sales, he receives a certain amount as his commission.

The principal advantage to the company under this plan is that it establishes a definite direct selling cost. The principal disadvantages are that it does not automatically give a low cost and that it is difficult to obtain the maximum degree of control over the salesman. The salesman can object to doing missionary work, good will work, or even service work for the company because he can argue that he is receiving no compensation for such work.

When this form of incentive is used, it will frequently be found that advances must be made to the salesman during periods of low sales. These often become difficult to liquidate because, at some future time, accumulated commissions may not prove sufficient for this purpose. Regardless of this contingency, commission salesmen are usually provided with drawing accounts, or advances, to cover traveling expenses and a minimum living wage.

The straight commission plan is most suitable to the agent method of selling. A company may be endeavoring to sell its product in certain outlying territories which it does not feel justified in covering with direct selling effort. Instead, it will employ an agent, who might sell not only its line of products but also products manufactured by other companies. As already stated, the agent is operating his own business in that case and is not subject to very much direction or authority from the manufacturer.

Straight commission compensation requires slightly more clerical work than straight salary, in that careful record must be made of each salesman's orders so that his commissions may be accurately computed.

The employment agreement must also provide that commissions will be paid on actual collections and not on orders booked, for the obvious reason that commissions are collectable on actual sales income only.

Salary and Commission

Under this plan the salesman receives a fixed but usually small salary, which should be sufficient for living expenses. He also receives a commission in the form of a percentage of all sales credited to him.

This plan is considered suitable for practically all kinds of sales organizations. Although it creates a fixed as well as a variable element in the selling expense, it provides the sales administration with complete control over the salesmen's activities.

Salesmen can then be asked to do a certain amount of missionary work, or service work if they are qualified to perform it, without making them feel they are doing work for which they are receiving no compensation. Furthermore, it provides the salesman with a greater degree of security by insuring him at least a certain amount of regular compensation.

Under this plan it is essential that adequate control of the salesman's performance be established, in order that the salesman will produce a volume from his territory at least approximating that expected by the company.

Usually this is accomplished by setting a quota which must be attained before commissions are paid. For example, a salesman may be paid $300 per month salary against a monthly sales quota of $2,500. For all sales above $2,500 he will be paid a commission of, say, 10 per cent. The total compensation and selling cost will then appear as follows:

Sales	Salary	Commission	Total Comp.	Total Selling Cost
$ 1,000	$300		$ 300	30.0%
2,000	300		300	15.0
3,000	300	50	350	11.7
4,000	300	150	450	11.2
5,000	300	250	550	11.0
6,000	300	350	650	10.8
7,000	300	450	750	10.7
8,000	300	550	850	10.6
9,000	300	650	950	10.5
10,000	300	750	1,050	10.5

Summary

No hard and fast rule can be applied to the selection of the salesmen's compensation plan. However, with well-organized sales direction and a firmly established selling cost control, the salary plus commission method of compensation is considered the most desirable plan. It provides the proper incentive to the salesman and the necessary protection and advantage to the company.

CHAPTER 24

SALESMEN SELECTION, TRAINING, AND DIRECTION

•

SELECTION REQUIREMENTS

A knowledge of the character of each sales territory is essential to the proper selection of a salesman.

The conditions of sales coverage in a small town may be entirely different from those peculiar to a large city. A salesman with a successful record in a small community may be a failure in a large city.

Size of territory has an important influence on the type of salesman employed. A scattered far-flung territory may require an energetic youthful personality. By contrast, a compact metropolitan area may demand a mature and persistent personality.

Similarly, the location of the territory can determine the type of salesmen to be employed. Territories south of the Mason–Dixon Line may require a different sales personality than those in the Midwest or the East. Rural territories, too, produce selling conditions quite dissimilar to those found in a large metropolitan center and impose special requirements.

Another important factor in the selection of salesmen is the amount of personal experience required. If he is to introduce the product in a new territory, experience is necessary to gain entree and develop quick interest. If his calls are to be made on established customers, his experience can be more limited. If the salesman must render service, his experience qualifications will be other than if the service function is to be supplied by another individual. If the salesman is expected to call on various officers, ranging from engineers to executives, he must be well-grounded in the technical details of his product.

The personal finances of the prospective salesman must also be considered. What standard of living is expected of him? Does he have private resources of income, or savings, that will carry him over periods of low income?

Such factors lead to the question of what compensation should be paid, a most vital condition of sales employment. A salesman expected to service a product, or to talk technicalities with an engineering department as well as to sell a chief executive, or to address a group of high officials of a company, must be in a position to earn a rather high income.

On the other hand, a salesman who is merely an order taker, who travels about with a catalog from which the customer makes his own selections, requires a lesser degree of compensation. The customer can be greatly influenced by the reputation of the company, and the salesman's prime function then becomes one of maintaining friendly relations.

Last, but not least, the personality background, interests, and temperament required of the salesmen for a particular territory must be given the most careful consideration. Such characteristics must complement those of the prospects to be called upon. Effective presentation of the product can only be made by the salesman who gains the compatible interest of the prospect.

SELECTION METHODS

Many methods exist for selecting salesmen, ranging from spot intuitive engagements by the interviewer to scientific testing procedures. Both methods attempt to determine attitudes, aptitudes, and personal attributes. In other words, they attempt to discover whether he likes to talk to people, is easily discouraged or offended, or is at ease, alert, and vocal at the proper time.

No matter what method is used, the primary requirement is a thorough check of the applicant's moral and credit character and experience. This should be satisfactorily concluded before any commitment toward employment is made.

Such investigation can be made through any accredited agency doing such work, particularly if the salesman is to be bonded. In this case the bonding company will automatically make such an investigation. Because all salesmen have some amount of company funds in their possession, the bonding requirement affords a dignified and open method of securing the character information desired and should be a regular part of the engagement contract.

TESTING

While the applicant's references and character are being checked, a study of his selling ability should be made. As mentioned earlier, this may be done by a trained interviewer through interrogation, or it may be accomplished by the standard psychological testing procedures developed in recent years.

For the average company, a happy medium between the two should be struck. A sympathetic and friendly interview with the applicant will get the "feel" of his personality and disclose the details of his experience and habits. A few simple tests will discover whether he has the basic characteristics for the work.

Such tests take various forms, as described in Chapter 34, Section 5, and they should not be brushed aside as impractical and theoretical. Their extensive use throughout business and industry has completely validated their practicability and pertinency. They should therefore be considered as desirable and workable tools in the employment procedure.

TRAINING

Depending on the kind of work the salesman is to do, different methods of training must be used. Such methods cannot be haphazard. They must be the basis of a well-organized training program, planned to give the salesman a complete background of the company's history, policies, products, and selling techniques.

A salesman expected to discuss the function of the product

from an engineering standpoint must be given a thorough training in the manufacturing operation and a sound knowledge of the basic principles inherent in the product.

On the other hand, a salesman who is primarily an order taker need be trained only in the policies of the company, the general deportment required of him, and the correct method of developing and maintaining friendly relations with and creating the goodwill of the customer.

In an effort to obtain volume quickly, a salesman is too often sent out into a territory with an order book and price list, an expense account, and an admonition to get sales. When sales do not materialize he is condemned as a poor salesman. If the sales administration is indifferent or has sufficient patience, the salesman may eventually train himself and become productive. Needless to say, the cost of this method of "training" is excessive.

A well-organized plan of selecting and training salesmen will materially assist in reducing selling costs in the long run, even though the apparent first cost seems high.

The final result will be an effective and economical sales force, uniform in its method, and working in a co-ordinated and co-operative manner.

Organization

No training program should be started unless it can be activated by:

(a) A competent and well-organized training staff.
(b) A comprehensive and balanced training curriculum.
(c) A working manual for the salesman after his graduation.

The training staff may be permanently assigned if the company is large and employs many salesmen, or it may be appointive for stated teaching periods or as the need appears. In neither case should it be large. It should have a permanent secretariat so that the records and the continuity of the training program can be maintained.

Method

The training period must be definitely organized as to time and place. It must provide sufficient time in the office, factory, and field to give the salesman proper background and knowledge for a running start on his job. Actually, some training can best be done out in the field, under the direct supervision of a representative from the factory. Other training must be had in the factory itself, so that the salesman can acquire the necessary knowledge of the processes, the product, the organization, and the various procedural routines. Usually both of these training phases are needed to produce a well-rounded salesman.

A comprehensive program covering the foregoing subjects should be developed by the training staff before any training whatever is started. The training should follow a systematic plan. The curriculum should include the following subjects and activities:

1. A complete history of the company from its inception, and its policies.
2. A complete explanation of the positions, titles and functions within the organization, with particular emphasis on the sales organization function and its relation to other divisions of the business.
3. A thorough study of the product with respect to:
    (*a*) Functional operation.
    (*b*) Field applications.
    (*c*) Engineering principles.
    (*d*) Method of manufacture.
    (*e*) Service requirements.
    (*f*) Selling points.
4. A detailed study of the company's sales policies and operation with respect to:
    (*a*) Prices, terms, and credit.
    (*b*) Sales procedures and records.
    (*c*) Customer relations.
    (*d*) Sales promotional activities.
    (*e*) Territories and coverage.
5. A detailed explanation of the company's position in the industry with respect to:
    (*a*) Its participation or share position.
    (*b*) The character and amount of competition.
    (*c*) Its technological progress.

6. The furnishing of a complete salesman's kit, which should include:
   (a) The sales manual.
   (b) Catalogs and price lists.
   (c) Promotional material.
   (d) Records and forms for interior use.
7. A training period in the factory to learn the control procedures, the manufacturing methods, and the problems of production.
8. A training period in the sales office to learn the procedural routines and the method of sales control.
9. A training period in the field, with an experienced representative, to learn:
   (a) The selling techniques required to convert a prospect into a customer.
   (b) The problems and methods of servicing the product when necessary.

No one training method can be adopted universally. Each company must develop its own methods to meet its particular objectives and requirements. Sales policies, methods, procedures, and routines which are a part of the company's operation, should be systematically recorded in a sales manual. Every procedure and the reason for it should be thoroughly understood and accepted by the sales organization, so that consistency and continuity will mark the entire selling effort.

The truism that fundamental principles are common to all activities of all business applies to the problem of training. The detailed methods may vary for each company, but the basic requirements, indicated by the subject headings of this chapter, are universally pertinent. There is little advantage in trying to uncover a different approach.

ADMINISTRATION

When the salesman has finished his training and has been placed in his territory, the real work of making him effective starts. Sales administration must furnish intelligent and aggressive direction of his effort, organized around a definite plan of control and pointed towards a stated degree of performance.

Such direction requires an organized program of contacts with the salesman in the field so that there is continuous control of his activity. The aim of this direction is to keep the salesman informed of changes in methods and procedures, profitable practices in other territories, new or urgent prospect calls, lack of proper results, and so on.

Follow-up

Important also in the direction of salesmen are the administrative sales office routines. Call reports, which the salesman may think unnecessary and burdensome, are essential to the sales administration. They not only inform it clearly as to the conditions in the territory and the attitude of prospects and customers, but also record the history of the solicitation and afford the means for helping the salesman.

It may be found that a salesman is not planning his work carefully but is constantly jumping from one town to another. He may be making only one or two calls in each town, simply because he believes that those particular customers should be contacted or followed up on that particular day. Or it may be found that salesmen are calling upon certain customers too frequently, merely because they are friendly with the customer and know that they will receive a cordial reception.

An analysis of call reports to determine the manner in which a salesman is making his calls is frequently illuminating, and constitutes the essential follow-up on his work. A typical form of call report is shown in Figure 30. The form used should fulfill the particular requirements of the company.

Direction

A stereotyped approach is frequently unsatisfactory. A certain approach may match the personality of one salesman, yet not suit another man's personality at all. Each salesman develops certain methods of his own, and it is the duty of the sales administration to see that these are encouraged to the utmost.

Salesmen left almost entirely to their own resources, without close direction, will create high selling costs. Salesmen have difficult tasks and can easily become discouraged. It is the responsibility of the sales administrative personnel to see that this condition does not become aggravated, that the salesman is always sold on his company, and that he displays the required enthusiasm for the product and the company at all times.

SALESMAN'S CALL REPORT

Employees	Type of Business	Contact		Phone Call	Length of Call	Waiting Time	Recall	Date
		New	Old					

Officers
(Underline Man Contacted)

Salesman

Used Engineers? — Who — When — Results

Literature left

Presentation

Company — Address — City — State

FIG. 30

4

Manufacturing

CHAPTER 25

ORGANIZATION

DEFINITION

The general requirements for effective organization have been described in Chapter 12 of Section 2, "Organization." Usually most of a company's money is spent in the factory. Because the greatest variety of activity lies in manufacture, the manufacturing organization of a company takes on greater significance than the other divisions of the business.

In recent years another factor has emphasized the need for a complete and carefully planned manufacturing organization. It is the specialization of functions resulting from the complexity of modern industrial operation.

For example, it is no longer good practice for a foreman to keep time records, or to regulate the release of work orders into his department, or to hire the men needed, or to establish the performance standards and the resulting labor costs.

Experience has also shown that, when there is lack of control in the factory operation, there is also an increased cost of performing these indirect functions, a very low effectiveness in their accomplishment, and a much higher manufacturing cost. In order to eliminate inefficient practice of this nature, manufacturing functions have been developed into line and staff positions.

Today these are practically standard requirements in all manufacturing plants.

MANUFACTURING FUNCTIONS

As previously defined in Chapter 12 of Section 2, "Organization," a staff function is essentially advisory and directive. It may or may not be repetitive in its application of effort. A line function is essentially authoritative and repetitive in its activity and is definitely limited to the manufacturing process itself.

Organization Problems

Manufacturing organization can be defined as a grouping of functions. It gives consideration to line and staff activities assembled into groups of related functions. These are co-ordinated as departmental divisions for economical effective performance.

The detail design of the organization will vary widely, depending on the character and size of the business. An organization for a job shop might be inadequate for a process operation, such as a flour mill, or a chemical plant. A still different arrangement would be necessary to meet mass production requirement.

Here, again, a different requirement is encountered. An organization arrangement satisfactory for a company engaged in the production of machine tools would be unsatisfactory for a company producing rubber products in a large variety of shapes and sizes. Companies engaged in the production of automotive equipment have yet other organization problems.

Variety and volume of products have a distinct bearing on the character of the organization arrangement required, which still further complicates the problem of organization. The volume of certain products may necessitate the creation of separate divisions, or the erection and equipping of separate plants, for their manufacture.

A statement often heard is: "This business is different." In a sense, this is a true statement. Each business, even within an industry, has its own peculiarities. These may be due to any of several factors including, among others, location, management and its policies, availability of labor, management and labor relations, limitations of plant, equipment layout, and certain peculiarities relating to the manufacture of the product.

Despite this fact, the fundamental principles of good functional organization remain unchanged. They apply regardless of detail arrangements which must be taken into consideration.

Organization Plan

Each business presents a distinct organization requirement. The greatest complication of the problem is found in the manufacturing division. Consequently, the established form of organization for that division should be founded on careful study. Full consideration of all factors will assemble groups of related functions, co-ordinated as departmental divisions, for economical effective performance under adequate direction.

Dependent on the character and size of the business, its products, and its manufacturing methods, certain specialized functions will be encountered. These present a problem as to designation and placement in the organization. Because of their number and variety, no positive rule can apply to them. Each of these problems must be solved by the exercise of judgment, the objective being economical effective performance.

Manufacturing functions commonly found in most companies are:

1. *Line Functions:*
   (a) *Supervisory;* consisting of the works manager, superintendent, foreman, and any other person directing employees actually engaged in the manufacturing operations.
   (b) *Manufacturing or processing;* consisting of those employees actually engaged in the processes of manufacture.
   (c) *Maintenance;* consisting of those employees responsible for the operating condition of buildings, machinery, and equipment.
   (d) *Service;* consisting of watchmen, janitors, and other employees responsible for safe and sanitary working conditions.
2. *Staff Functions:*
   (a) *Production control;* which determines what should be made, in what quantities, and when and where the work shall be done.
   (b) *Product engineering;* which designs the product for ease of manufacture and low cost and prepares drawings, parts lists, bills of materials, and specifications for the manufacturing departments.

(c) *Purchasing;* which procures all direct and indirect materials used in the factory.

(d) *Inspection;* which determines whether the quality of the product conforms to the standards set by general management.

(e) *Methods and standards;* which determines the best method of fabricating the product and sets the performance standards for its manufacture.

(f) *Personnel;* which secures the necessary manufacturing personnel, is responsible for their selection and training, maintains all the necessary records on the employees of the factory, and handles welfare and industrial relations activities.

It is sometimes rather difficult to decide whether a function is a line or a staff function. The size of the company and the nature of its manufacturing process frequently do not permit a clear distinction between many of the activities. When this is the case, it is better practice to accent the line aspect rather than the staff aspect of such a composite activity, and to place it in the organization plan accordingly.

Allocation

A still more frequent problem encountered in setting up a manufacturing organization is that of deciding where certain staff functions belong. In many companies they are not considered a part of the manufacturing operation at all. For example:

1. *Product engineering* is sometimes so important that it is placed directly under the general management rather than under the factory management.

2. *Inspection* may require such a high degree of precision and customer satisfaction that it must be completely divorced from the manufacturing authority.

3. *Production control* may assume such importance, because of the commitments planned, that it, too, may require close direction from the general management itself.

4. *Methods and standards* may lack the importance necessary to give it a separate character, and it may be included in some other staff function.

5. *Personnel,* if it handles all office, sales, and factory personnel and is responsible for the training and welfare of all employees,

may require direct supervision from a general officer of the company, rather than from the manufacturing executive.

6. *Purchasing* may frequently be responsible for procurement of costly materials in large quantities. In that case it should report to a senior officer of the company. If it merely buys to small quantity specifications, it may report directly to the factory executive.

In these instances the location of any debatable function must be decided by carefully weighing the full effects of such placement. Judgment rather than rule must guide management in debatable cases. It will frequently be found that time and training will cause a staff function to shift gradually from one division to another.

Organization is not static. It must not be crystallized around a given set of conditions, because conditions change. Any organization plan must be based on the premise of flexibility, so that it can be adjusted to meet changes that develop from time to time in every factory operation.

Of all the staff functions proper to the manufacturing operation, the most important is production control. Because it is concerned with time and quantity, it must be most carefully co-ordinated with the manufacturing functions and with other general functions as well, including sales and accounting and general management itself. Frequently, therefore, general management must dominate the production plan, which in turn may require that production control be directly under its supervision.

The character of the organization of production control itself is an important factor in determining its placement. To be completely effective, production control should include all related functions, one of the most important of these being material control. Obviously, if correct materials are not available at the proper working places at the right time, the most carefully laid plans and schedules are doomed to failure.

Material control involves not only the administration of control records, which is a staff function, but also the line functions of receiving, storage, issuance, internal transportation, shipping, and warehousing.

Some managements insist on treating material control as an organizational entity, separate and distinct from production control. They are influenced in this determination by the size and value of the inventories and by the distribution of these inventories to various locations.

There is occasional justification for this, although it violates the organization principle of co-ordination of related functions under one directing head. This imposes a limitation on the effectiveness of production control. Under these circumstances production control offers no organization placement problem. It becomes a scheduling and control medium only and naturally falls under the direction of the factory management. If production control was complete and included the control of material, it could properly be placed under the direction of the general management.

Second in importance is frequently the methods and standards department. Under competitive conditions of operation, it may be necessary to regulate and to direct most carefully the physical operation of the plant. In this case methods and measures of performance become the most important tools for operating control.

Under certain circumstances, with a small operation, this department can satisfactorily be placed under the direction of the chief engineer. Increased size combined with keen competition may necessitate treating it as a separate department remaining, however, under the direction of factory management.

This does not mean that product engineering is of minor importance. Because it has long been recognized as an essential element of the manufacturing process, it has always had a place in the functional organization. As such, its long history of existence in manufacturing does not require the special emphasis given to other staff functions.

Frequently the personnel function is placed under the direction of factory management. There is a decisive trend toward closer co-operation of management and labor, with consideration for the increasing complexities encountered therein and consequent changes in policy and procedure. The necessity for placing this important function under the direction of general management is, therefore, being recognized by appropriate action.

Organization Chart

It is the purpose of these comments to stress the importance and necessity of careful study of each function. This will determine combinations of related functions and their proper allocation in the organization plan.

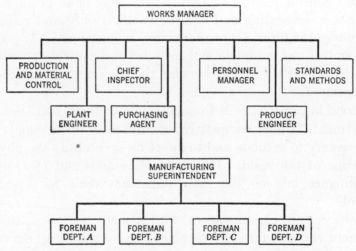

FIG. 31.   Manufacturing Line and Staff Organization

Effective application of organization effort can be secured only if there is a definite understanding of the relationship of various functions on the part of the personnel. This requires an organization chart showing the lines of authority and the lines of advisory or staff relationship.

Figure 31 is an organization chart which illustrates the relationship between line and staff functions and shows their positions graphically in an organization plan. Reference to both Figures 9 and 10, in Chapter 12 of Section 2, "Organization," will further aid in the design of the organization chart.

The organization chart will show graphically the functional divisions, their grouping under co-ordinating directive heads, their position in relation to each other, and the connecting lines of authority. It will present a picture of the adopted organization plan, which, being limited in scope, must be supplemented by an organization manual in order to complete the instruction.

ORGANIZATION MANUAL

The organization manual provides adequate description of the responsibilities and duties associated with each directive position shown on the organization chart. In combination with the organization chart, it should provide a clear definition of management organization policy, easily understood by all concerned as to its effect on their positions.

In the formulation of the whole plan of organization for the manufacturing division, the organization principles described in Chapter 12 of Section 2, "Organization," should be observed and applied for best results.

As described in that chapter, a manual of standard practice instruction and a booklet of rules and regulations are further requirements for a complete organization plan. Because of the complexities of operation and the greater number of persons involved, the need for these supplementary instructions is greater in the manufacturing division than in any other.

All these instructions should be distributed, with discretion, to those affected by them. None of these instructions are static; all are subject to change to meet changing conditions. It is necessary, therefore, to establish the responsibility for their distribution, change, and maintenance in an up-to-date condition with a highly placed official of the company.

SUMMARY

The development and installation of an adequate organization plan will result in many distinct benefits to the company. Some of these are:

1. Better-informed personnel.
2. Lower manufacturing costs.
3. Lower organization costs.

4. Better co-ordination and co-operation between departments.
5. Greater flexibility of operation.
6. A basis for measuring effectiveness of the personnel.
7. A better means of training employees and of maintaining a high standard of personnel.

CHAPTER 26

PROCESSING AND MANUFACTURING METHODS

•

DEFINITIONS

Processing and manufacturing methods is the name of that department of plant operation which tells the "how" of doing the work most effectively. Its job involves the art and science of finding and applying the one best way to do a specific task. *Processing* indicates the best sequence of operations for producing the product. *Methods study* brings out the improved means.

PURPOSE

The purpose of giving attention to processing and methods is to:

1. Produce the product in accordance with design.
2. Achieve low manufacturing costs.
3. Secure quality.
4. Co-ordinate and obtain maximum utilization of equipment.

Properly organized and controlled continual study of the "how" of doing work can be of great value to a company. It can spell the difference between success and failure. Our "American way of life," our ever-improving living conditions, have been founded on better ways of doing work.

Organizing the Methods Department

The size of the plant and the kind of product have a bearing on the size of the organization needed to study and control processing and methods. But under any conditions of manufactur-

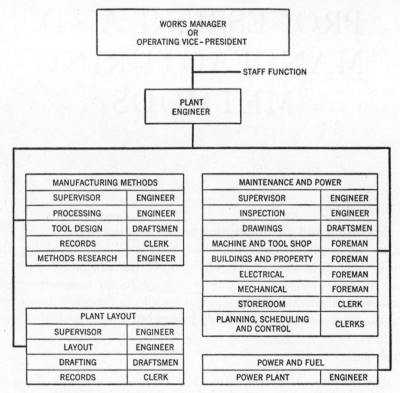

Fig. 32.   Manufacturing Methods' Place in the Organization

ing operation, some one individual should be given this responsibility.

Normally a methods department is a staff function as described in Chapter 25. Some plants list methods as a division of plant engineering (see Figure 32) and some have it as a division of production engineering, but in either case the department plans and specifies the manner in which the work should be done. In continuous process industries, methods can well be handled by engineering research.

To say that processing and methods must be allocated to a particular division of a business is, however, not the real issue. The important decision to make is that processing and methods shall be considered as an important function and that a definite program of study and action shall be maintained in these fields.

Personnel Qualifications

It is important that the department be headed by an engineer with vision, character, and broad experience. He must be a man who can secure the co-operation of the organization, solicit suggestions and ideas to supplement his own, and gain acceptance for them when they are presented.

It is a human trait to resist change, and hence the workmen, foremen, and supervisors will often resist new ideas. However, if they are shown the possibilities of an idea and are convinced of its benefits, the progress of the methods department will be speeded.

It cannot be expected that all new ideas will work; but, if many failures occur in changes made in the shop, confidence is destroyed, and future benefits are lost both to the company and to the men. If new ideas have been worked out sufficiently well on the drawing board, reduced to practice, and proved before they are introduced to the shop, then confidence is established and future acceptance easily gained.

Facilities for Methods Department

The organization of a processing and methods department should include a drafting room and a place to try out new ideas and innovations. Under present-day conditions of rapid changes in machinery, tools, and materials, and the influence of social and economic conditions on industry, the head of a methods department must keep informed and up-to-date. He must be in a position to learn the new techniques and to apply them promptly.

Thus an important function is the gathering and recording of pertinent information so that it will be readily available when needed. A library and file, under the direction of a competent person, are decided assets. In a well-organized company, many members will pass on information that might be helpful to the head of the methods department.

The methods department, being a staff function, should have no authority over other divisions of plant. It members should be permitted access to all departments for study and consultation, but any changes should be effected through the line organization.

PROCEDURE FOR A METHODS DEPARTMENT

When a new enterprise is being contemplated, or a new product has been decided on and is ready for manufacture, the first step for the methods department is to break the product down into its many operations. It then prescribes the way to do each operation; selects the machine, equipment, or work stations to be used; and estimates the length of time required to perform the operation.

Estimating Standards

Often these processing estimates are used by the accounting department as a basis for building up estimated costs, which in turn are used to compute selling prices. When the business is of the jobbing type, processing estimates are essential in arriving at a selling price. Processing requires the breakdown and analysis of each operation and the estimating of the time elements. This makes it possible to arrive at an accurate over-all estimate of the cost of the finished product.

Management will know the range of selling prices offered by competition. If the developed estimated cost will not allow a profitable selling price within that range, then it becomes the methods engineer's problem to find ways and means to lower the cost before production is started. Thus it is possible to avoid hazard or loss by proper processing before setting a selling price.

Use of Actual Standards

When a plant is established and correct element time standards are available, as described in Chapter 31 of this section, it will be possible for the processing engineer to use an actual time to guide him in his estimates. Estimating can also be made more accurate if the engineer will visualize the exact motions which will be employed to accomplish the operation, that is, go through them in pantomime, and time his motions. As time goes on and experience is gained, it is possible to group and compare estimated operations with actual performance. The estimates for new products then become very accurate.

Breakdown of Product

After the manufacturing drawings, complete specifications, samples and all information about a product are received by the process or methods engineer, he will analyze the product and break it down into its component parts, subassemblies, and assemblies.

Bills of material or parts list (see Figure 44), showing the list of parts; number of parts required; kind, size, and amount of material; patterns and finishes; are necessary to the processing engineer and should show the code numbers of parts. If such a bill of material is not furnished, then it is important for the processing engineer to make his own. It is, however, properly the duty of product engineering to make a complete bill of material. This department knows what is required, and the bill can be made as the design is being completed.

Each part is then studied, and the best possible way to make it is determined. This develops an operation and processing sheet, a sample of which is illustrated (Figure 45).

Data Sources

It is very evident that the engineer must know the departments, machinery, equipment, and facilities available if he is to make a good operation sheet. He must know the proper feeds and speeds, machine and equipment sizes, and the latest tools, cutting compounds, devices, and methods.

The information needed can and should be made a matter of simple record and is most useful in chart form. For example, various handbooks and trade publications give the economic cutting speeds, and machine manufacturers give the feeds of and speeds with which their tools are equipped. If this is brought together in one chart that can be applied to a variety of dimensions, it makes processing easier and more uniform.

The compiling of useful data and its cataloging for ready reference is very important to the processing engineer and should be considered as one of his prime duties.

OPERATION AND PROCESSING SHEET

The operation and processing sheet is used by other departments, that is, production control, cost, manufacturing inspection, time study, and standards, and sufficient copies should be made to furnish one to each of those concerned. The duplicating can be done by one of several different commercial methods, or even by blueprinting. Under any condition of duplication, it is the methods engineering department's responsibility to keep the files up-to-date and to see that obsolete sheets are collected and destroyed.

Each manufacturing department should be furnished with a file of operation and process sheets, and the foremen and supervisors should be instructed to follow the sequence as indicated on the sheets. Unless the practice of following prescribed plans is firmly established, the various manufacturing departments will follow whatever practice they think best and will change those practices at their discretion. This interferes with the smooth running of the plant and leads to confusion, particularly for the timekeeping and production control departments.

Management should insist that operation and process sheets be followed. If disagreement with the sequence arises, then the methods engineer should prove the soundness of his plans or concede his error and make corrections in the operation and process sheet.

After the correct number of copies of process sheets has been decided on, neither more nor fewer copies should be made. In case extra copies are needed for some specific purpose, each should be stamped "Extra Sheet—Not to Be Used." This prevents obsolete or incorrect sheets from finding their way into the plant. When changes are made, the changed sheet should be substituted in each of the files and the old one taken out and destroyed.

It is important that process sheets be maintained correctly if they are to be effective in control of plant operations. In spite of the utmost care, some sheets will be lost, destroyed, or altered, and a constant check must be made to keep them in order.

When parts being manufactured are few in number, it is well to have the sheets duplicated on heavy paper or cardboard and filed in a standard file, preferably of the visible type. When there is a large volume of different parts, then it is better to duplicate the sheets on lightweight paper and file them in book form.

Form of Sheet

The process sheet will, of course, vary with the type of industry and plant, and careful study should be given to the requirements for the plant under consideration. The following form of sheet is suggested as being applicable to many plants. There is usually a separate sheet for each part, for each subassembly, and for each assembly.

1. The part number.
2. The part name.
3. The drawing number.
4. The assemblies where the part is used.
5. The customer's name (when necessary).
6. Who wrote the sheet.
7. Who approved the sheet.
8. The date.
9. The total number of sheets for that part.
10. Number required.
11. Used on other models.
12. Material kind.
13. Material form.
14. Material rough size.

The sequence of data to be given on the body of the process sheet should include:

1. The operation number.
2. The operation name.
3. The department.
4. The work station number.
5. The work station name.
6. The tools required and their identification.
7. The gages required and their identification.
8. The setup time allowed.
9. The standard time for machine.
10. The standard time for labor (usually in man-hours per 100 pieces).
11. Equipment.

Other Uses of Sheet

When the process sheet is also used to serve the accounting department for estimate costs and for standard costs, then two more columns are needed. These are the hourly rate or labor grade and the extended cost for the operation, which is the standard time multiplied by the hourly rate. These cost figures are, of course, only for the direct labor, as this is as far as it is advisable to carry costs on the process sheet.

As previously mentioned, a complete set of process sheets is to be made out before the product is placed in the plant for manufacture. They constitute the preliminary planning and will be the basis for determining the kind and amount of machinery and equipment needed, the kind and amount of tools and gages, and the type and number of personnel required for direct labor.

If a new plant is being contemplated, they will be the basis for the required layout, from which the type and size of plant is determined. Hence the process sheets take a very important role. The best engineering talent will be needed to prepare complete and accurate sheets, as they constitute the basic manufacturing plan for the plant. They should be studied and checked and reworked to arrive at the very best plan of operations possible.

The more and better *parts* experience possessed by the engineers, the more realistic will be the setup of the plant, and fewer will be the costly errors that develop when this experience is lacking.

METHODS ENGINEERING

In a going plant the first process sheets for a new product are still very important, but past local experience is available, and the operations are generally done on equipment that is already in use. It is desirable to use the facilities and machinery that are available. Still, the methods engineer should not overlook the fact that savings can many times be made by doing the job in a manner entirely different from the old way. However, he must weigh the advantages and disadvantages of the change, and take many things into consideration, such as:

1. Investment in new facilities.
2. Amount to be produced.
3. Extra tooling needed.
4. Floor space available.
5. Labor available.
6. Quality desired.
7. Other work for both old and new equipment.
8. Delivery promises.

Checking Actual Operations

After work is actually started and is following the process sheets, the methods engineer should carefully check each and every step. The time study department should have made their studies, establishing setup and machine and labor standards by which the original estimates for these items can be corrected.

For example, the originally selected work station or machine may not have been the right one. If so, corrections should be made. In other words, the process sheets must represent actual practice. But, as a word of warning, the methods engineer should not concede to the actual practice unless it is proved better.

In preparing the process sheets, the methods engineer should specify the machines and facilities that will best perform the work at each work station, as well as the tools and gages needed. If standard machine tools are needed, he should show the special chucking and tooling needed to adapt the machine to the task.

Handling facilities, such as trucks, cranes, conveyors, slides, and vises should also be specified and shown on the process sheets.

Tools and Fixtures

It is the duty of the methods engineer to sketch up the jigs, fixtures, gages, special tools, chucks, or other special arrangements which he expects will be needed in the operations. These sketches and descriptions can then be turned over to a draftsman for designing and, eventually, to the toolroom, outside jobber, or manufacturer for construction.

Sometimes the designing of tools, special machines, and other arrangements are assigned to the methods department, and a drafting and designing department becomes a division of methods. At other times this work is assigned to product engineering so that all the draftsmen and designers are in one department. In either case it is the duty of the methods engineer to furnish the ideas and specifications for the required special features which will be used to expedite the individual operation. He must determine the need for replacing temporary tooling with permanent tools as quickly as possible when volume is attained, to avoid losses in production and high costs.

In lining up the operations on the process sheet, the methods engineer must not overlook any of the work stations even though they be minor, such as a table for inspection. He must include the operations in their sequence and indicate when the parts go to a stockroom or to a stock bank. In other words, the plan for making the pieces, from raw stock to finished product, must be complete.

Improving Operations

Although much emphasis has been given to the importance of the process sheet, it is not all that a methods department must attend to. When the plan of operations has been established, it becomes the duty of the methods department continually to improve the ways and means of doing work. There must be a constant search for new and better ways to eliminate effort and to improve the quality and quantity of output at lower cost.

The ideas and suggestions of the men at the bench or machine must not be overlooked. They are in a most favorable position to know the work and to originate possible short-cuts. With the proper approach, this source of knowledge can be tapped to great advantage.

If a well-designed and installed suggestion system is working in the plant, many improvements in methods will be brought out. Foremen and supervisors can and should produce many ideas which will improve operations. However, the maximum benefits of the potential thinking of the organization cannot be secured, unless a concerted effort is made and a planned procedure gathers the ideas and puts them into practice.

The methods engineer must gain the confidence of the men. He must let it be known that he is receptive to new ideas and suggestions, that he sincerely appreciates receiving them. He must give credit to the originator of the idea even though he himself works it out to a final conclusion.

By publicizing the desire for suggestions, and by giving credit for those received on plant bulletin boards, in house organs, on loudspeakers and in local newspapers, a vast fund of excellent and usable ideas can be built up. These ideas should be cataloged, studied, and developed to final conclusion with dispatch. Those that are good should be put into practice without delay.

An idea that does not seem practical should be discussed with the originator who may be able to supply the missing thought that will make it usable. If not, he should be given the reasons why his idea cannot be adopted. Every one thinks his own ideas are sound, and resentment follows if they are discarded without sufficient explanation.

As pointed out before, it may be advisable to set up a division of the methods department where new ideas can be tried out before they are put into production. The advantages of such a division are that it:

1. Prevents the introduction of false ideas.
2. Permits the expansion of new ideas.
3. Eliminates lost production time.
4. Fits in with a progressive program for reducing costs.

Improving Indirect Operations

From the foregoing it might be assumed that methods concerns itself only with direct production operations. This is not the case, as many appreciable savings can also be realized from a study of indirect operations. Sweeping, for example, is a very common indirect operation in most plants. How many times does the sweeper clean debris from the floor and stir up a cloud of dust that settles over everything? Perhaps a vacuum cleaner or a sweeping compound would be the answer, or perhaps proper containers for waste from the operations would reduce the amount of sweeping and provide a salvage return.

The operations of material handling offer an opportunity for improvement and savings. Each operation of material handling should have close scrutiny and analysis. In almost every plant much useless moving of stock, parts, tools, supplies, and other material takes place. Ask these questions: (a) Why is the move necessary? (b) Is useful work done in the move? (c) If the move is necessary, can it be done economically by mechanical means? (d) Can the part be moved by gravity? (e) Is the container the most efficient for handling? (f) Can the material be moved without loading or unloading? (g) Is the route of the move the most direct? (h) Are the trucks, skids, hoists, cranes, and so on, subject to improvement? (i) Can the moves be made with less effort?

The methods engineer can also find a fertile field for savings in most of the maintenance department operations. A study of them should be made to find improvements and to recommend beneficial changes. For example, such simple operations as window washing have been made easier and safer by using long-handled brushes and squeegees.

Limitations in Authority

Inasmuch as methods engineering is a staff function, it has no authority over productive or nonproductive plant departments. All the ideas for improvements and changes can only be put into effect as suggestions and recommendations. Hence, plant management must see that action is taken on the improvements, to realize the maximum benefits. If the methods engineer is an orderly and systematic thinker, he will crystallize his ideas in reports to his superiors so that they may be passed on to the proper place for action.

To see that action is forthcoming, the methods engineer should follow up each and every recommendation and report the results. It would be well for him and his department if he kept a record of results to be reviewed with management at periodic intervals. No doubt there will be many disagreements with the suggested changes, but, if the methods engineer knows and has proved them to be sound and good, he should be persistent in getting them adopted.

If plant meetings of heads of departments or shop committees are held for the purpose of discussing operating plans, the methods engineer should be present at these meetings. There he can get the real objections to his ideas and constructively sell his arguments to the group.

SUMMARY OF BENEFITS

The resulting benefits from a constructive and active methods program might be summarized as follows:

1. Savings through continual reduction of production costs.

2. Complete knowledge and information available for production planning.

3. Prescribed speeds, feeds, and instruction to maintain a constant rate of production in accordance with best practice.

4. Established performance based on best practice, eliminating guesswork, delays, and arguments on the part of supervision and workers.

5. Better estimates for costs, equipment, floor space, and labor on new products, due to preplanned operations.

6. Better over-all attitude due to a progressive search for and application of new ways and means.

7. Better utilization of plant facilities.

8. Better service to customers.

9. A more orderly plant operation.

10. More time for foremen and supervision to direct the activities of their personnel.

CHAPTER 27

PLANT LAYOUT

•

PURPOSE

Broadly speaking, the purpose of plant layout is to provide a systematic economical arrangement of facilities for the intended function of the plant. More specifically, this broad definition covers the following essential requirements:

1. The arrangement of departments or divisions of a plant so as to reduce to a minimum all interplant services, such as:
   (a) Material handling.
   (b) Traffic.
   (c) Communication.
   (d) Power distribution, etc.
2. The arrangement of buildings so as to accommodate most economically the departmental or divisional requirements for space and services.
3. The arrangement of equipment and facilities for any given operating schedule within each department or division, so as to reduce to a minimum:
   (a) Floor space,
   (b) Direct labor,
   (c) Expense labor,
   (d) Expense materials;
   and to increase to a maximum:
   (e) Output per man-hour,
   (f) Output per dollar of overhead expense.

Systematic arrangement of plant facilities will provide plant economies. On the other hand, improper arrangement makes for excessive handling, which may result in spoilage of material,

219

additional cost of handling facilities, and general confusion in the flow of material.

Plant layout is not always given the study and attention that it rightly deserves. Usually, although the original arrangement may have been good, changes have gradually upset the plan. The business then suffers the extra costs that result from poor layout.

Frequently, when new equipment is added or methods or products are changed, the new operations are started up in any available space, regardless of how they fit in with the rest of the plant. Sometimes, management starts an operation with the knowledge that it is improperly located. The thought is that it will be changed at some future time, but the change never takes place, and excessive costs go on and on.

To keep the purpose of plant layout constantly in mind, management should give and require of the staff continuous attention to the subject. In the mass production industries, with many repetitions of the same operations and the same movements, extremely low costs have resulted from a constant study of plant layout.

No one thing contributes more to low-cost operation than a good plant layout. When movements of materials or products are made, useful work must be done at the least expenditure of the four "M's" of industry—men, money, material, and management.

LIMITING CONDITIONS

Except on rare occasions, it is impossible to produce the ideal plant layout—one which embodies all possible advantages. Almost always there is some limiting consideration. If by chance such limiting conditions do not exist, there will still be contradictory factors inherent in the processes involved. In such circumstances, decision must be made in favor of the more important consideration.

Site Influence

Frequently, the plant site is a controlling factor in building arrangements. This is particularly true in layout for plants which are already going concerns, with building arrangements already established. It is best, however, not to give too much weight to such conditions until the layout problem is fully analyzed.

There is always the possibility that what appear to be limiting conditions, at first glance, may turn out to be not so limiting in the light of resulting benefits. A thorough analysis of the layout problem often reveals ways and means of avoiding the restrictions.

It is important that every layout problem be approached with an open mind. Current arrangements must be disregarded, temporarily, in favor of a completely new layout to correct all unfavorable conditions. The theoretical layout can later be modified on the basis of estimated cost and savings comparisons to suit the existing site and building facilities.

Departmental or divisional layouts are subject to the same problems as site and building arrangements. Frequently, there are items of equipment or facilities within a department or division which, because of the expense involved, apparently cannot be economically relocated to accommodate a better layout. As pointed out previously, however, such limitations should not be accepted until the theoretically correct layout has been planned, and comparisons of costs and savings have been made.

Volume Influence

The conditions and limitations heretofore pointed out all pertain to "static" problems. Another most important problem, which may prove to be a limiting factor, is the current operating schedule. At any given period changes in layout may seem impractical because the equipment cannot be shut down or withdrawn from operation long enough for the desired changes to be made.

As a matter of fact, this is the usual condition when layout problems are under consideration. Periods of high production bring out the inefficiencies of layout, and those responsible begin to think of improvements. Too often the result is a makeshift compromise to suit current conditions. When productivity drops to a point where a comprehensive plant rearrangement program might be successfully carried out, interest in such a program dies out. Nothing is done until the pinch of increased productivity again points up the inefficiencies in plant layout.

Summary

The conclusion is obvious: A comprehensive layout of the plant should be prepared for, theoretically, the most economical operation. This layout should be corrected periodically as operating policies change. It should be held "in suspense" and yet always available. When expansion of the plant is contemplated, it will assure the management that changes are being made in accordance with a planned program. It should also be used in periods of low productivity to make rearrangements which seem advisable but which were impracticable in periods of high productivity.

ORGANIZING FOR PLANT LAYOUT

In most large plants the importance of plant layout is fully recognized, and a departmental unit is established for the purpose of keeping the layout up-to-date. This departmental unit properly reports to the head of the plant engineering, who is responsible for economic manufacture. The function of plant layout is closely related to the other functions of plant engineering, or, as it is often designated, the methods engineering department.

Among the functions of the plant or methods engineering group, as discussed in more detail in subsequent chapters, are the following:

1. To make routing sheets or operation sheets for each product.
2. To determine the methods of manufacture.
3. To specify the processing equipment to be used.
4. To determine the handling methods and equipment.

Just as the production control department is responsible for specifying when and in what quantities the product is to be manufactured, so the plant engineering department must be responsible for specifying how the product shall be manufactured and at what cost.

It follows that the responsibility for plant layout logically belongs to the plant engineering department.

The number of people in the plant layout unit, of course, depends on several factors. When a plant is being laid out, with the processing of the product completed and the selection of equipment decided on, the layout project requires a large group of engineers.

After the layout is completed and the plant is in operation, the department may be reduced to one man or to part-time work.

The type of engineer best suited to act as the head of a plant layout department has vision and can see and work to a final picture. He should be well grounded in the manufacturing processes required. Generally, a man with an engineering education in the field under consideration is best suited to do plant layout. There is no substitute for experience when it comes to producing the best layout in the shortest possible time.

On a large layout project, it is well to have one experienced engineer directing several engineering draftsmen and clerks. As the layout nears completion, the staff can and should be reduced, but the subject should have constant attention.

In small plants, the responsibility for layout can be combined with that of other engineering duties. However, it is important that the responsibility be recognized and given constant attention. In small plants where engineering skills are not available on the staff, management can call in outside assistance. It is well to do this at stated periods or when major changes are made. The savings can be large, not only in money but also in better service.

METHOD OF MAKING LAYOUTS—NEW PLANT

It can readily be deduced, from the foregoing discussion of layouts, that the problems in making a layout for a new plant are entirely different from those in making a layout for a plant that is already in operation.

The purpose in both cases is the same, except that in the case of a new plant there is usually a time limitation. Normally, this does not exist in the case of a going concern where the layout is intended for improvement of existing conditions. There may, of course, be cases where the problems are twofold, embodying both the considerations of a new plant and a plant which is already a going concern. A typical instance is the construction of a new building, on an existing plant site, which may or may not be an extension of existing processes.

Inasmuch as the problems are different, the methods of making layouts for a new plant and an old plant must also be different. Consequently, the following discussion will be separated on that basis. Since layout considerations for a new plant best illustrate the purpose and method of making layouts, this problem is discussed first.

It is assumed that there is no urgent time limitation to prevent a complete and thorough analysis of the problems. Making a layout for a new plant begins with the establishment of the purpose of the plant. This must be well understood in respect to both processes and schedules and will be a management decision.

Preliminary Layout

Having established the purpose of the plant, the next step is to make a preliminary *processing and material handling* layout to determine the equipment to be used, the material handling methods and the floor space required. Complete detailed processing should be postponed until these more important determinations have been made.

The reasons for this are important. Floor plans for the building can be made and turned over to architects for building design. Orders can be placed for equipment. Installation specifications can be prepared. Contracts can be placed for construction and installation work. All this can be done while detail processing and departmental layouts are being prepared. If this procedure is followed, the different steps can be so worked out that all operations dovetail and a minimum of time is expended in putting the plant into operation.

Processing in some industries is a specialized technique, and a separate department is maintained for that purpose. In other industries processing and plant layout are the responsibility of the same department. Whether processing and layout come under the same responsibility or under separate responsibilities, the steps in making a layout are the same.

It is important, however, that the layout work be done by men who have a thorough knowledge of the processes involved. They need not know the technical details of operation processes, but they must know the characteristics of the equipment involved and material handling methods to be used. Finally they must have had enough experience in the use of such equipment to understand the layout requirements.

Floor Space Requirements

Preliminary processing having been completed and the quantity and type of equipment having been established, as a consequence of that processing, it then becomes the job of the layout division to determine floor space requirements. This can best be done by template layouts. The experienced layout engineer has certain rule-of-thumb formulas which are accurate enough for this purpose. To do the job correctly, however, templates should be made and arranged for the more important pieces of equipment.

Care must be used to avoid overlooking the so-called hand operations which go along with equipment operations. Inspection operations and equipment, for example, require space and must be provided for.

Indirect Floor Space Requirements

The processing previously referred to is normally interpreted as the "direct-cost" processing; yet the operations in that category seldom account for more than 50 per cent of the total floor space requirements in a plant. It is because of this unrecognized fact that many faulty and unsatisfactory layouts are made.

These ultimately result in inefficient and costly operations.

Too little consideration is given to the service departments, such as receiving, shipping, productive material stores, non-productive stores, toolrooms, and maintenance; and to the personnel facilities, such as washrooms, lockers, lunchrooms, and first aid. The result is that these departments finally are crowded into areas that are not suitable in either size or location.

This is further evidence of the too prevalent misconception of direct labor. In most industrial plants factory overhead cost is greater than direct labor cost. Much of this overhead cost is directly affected by plant layout.

It is of prime importance, therefore, that layout be given the most careful study, particularly in respect to plant services. This is the real job of the layout engineer. The processing division confines itself entirely to the direct labor operations. The operating divisions think only in terms of their own individual problems. It thus becomes the responsibility of the layout engineer to analyze the over-all conditions and to provide space and facilities for the plant services required for low-cost operations.

Consequently, while the so-called "processing" is under way, the layout division must be developing the proper equipment, processes, and facilities for the indirect departments. There are a few operating policies which must be established by plant management, after which past experience and knowledge of similar operating problems must be the guide.

The policies which must be decided are in regard to extensions of the processing methods to include service and supply. They include decisions on whether the plant will operate on a finished stock bank or whether products will be processed to customers' orders. Will operations be seasonal, causing peaks and valleys, or evenly distributed over the year? Will purchase commitments be for scheduled deliveries in accordance with operating schedules or by drop shipment? If the latter, in what quantities? Which parts and subassemblies are to be manufactured within the plant, and which are to be purchased?

Armed with the answers to these questions, the layout engineer must make his calculations of floor space requirements from knowledge of similar operating conditions in other plants.

Building and Site Requirements

Having developed the floor space requirements for the direct labor departments and the indirect departments, the layout engi-

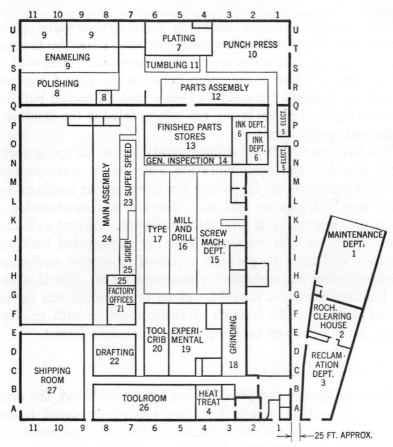

Fig. 33.   Schematic Layout of Departments

neer is ready to put the pieces together and arrive at his building and site requirements (see Figure 33). Suppose, as is frequently the case, that the site has already been determined by outside influences. He is then faced with the necessity of making his building arrangement conform to the site, which immediately affects his layout.

If the site has not been determined, he is then at liberty to develop the ideal layout. He will piece together individual segments of a plant, represented by departments, so as to form an integrated layout. This should have such obvious symmetry and continuity of processing as to make a recognizable planned design.

When this job has been completed, building floor plans can be turned over to the architects with the necessary specifications on building design and construction characteristics. It is well to point out that close co-operation between the layout engineer and the architect is necessary to assure that all special building features required by the layout are incorporated in the architect's plans and specifications.

The location of railroad sidings, receiving and shipping docks, main trucking and communication aisles, with corresponding building entrances, are frequently not given proper consideration when new buildings are laid out. The size and construction of doors, also important, is frequently neglected. Absurd as it may seem, there are still instances in newly constructed buildings where a wall must be partially removed to receive equipment specified before the architect's plans were made. Specifications on building entrances should be given to the architects by the layout division. The location of these, together with trucking aisles, must be shown on the plant arrangement layout.

Departmental Layouts

Building layouts and plans having been established, the over-all layout should be broken down into sections for detail departmental layouts (see Figures 34, 35), including equipment and installation specifications. In order to synchronize timing elements to insure earliest completion of the whole project, it is important that layouts for equipment which require elaborate installation specifications be completed first. This gives proper time for engineering work and specifications which must be included in the general contract for the building, or written as separate installation contracts.

There is also the problem of miscellaneous equipment which cannot be properly specified by the processing division, since characteristics and quantities depend on layout.   In this class of equipment are included such items as: benches, shelving, trucks, conveyors, cranes, hoists, heating, and lighting and power requirements.   Preliminary layouts must be made in sufficient detail to determine the quantity and type of such equipment.   The

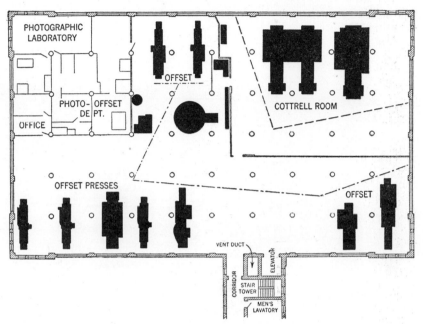

Fig. 34.   Machine Tool Template Layout

necessary specifications must be prepared for placing purchase orders and securing deliveries as required.

Those essential "first" items having been disposed of, detailed final departmental layouts can be prepared.   The problem and procedure in making a layout for each department, or division, is exactly the same as described earlier for making the over-all plant layout.   The problem now consists, however, of individual pieces of equipment instead of departments.   Scaled templates to the exact dimensions of each piece of equipment must be prepared.   The scale of such detailed layouts should not be less than ⅛ inch to 1 foot.   Some engineers prefer cross-section paper; others plain.   This is not important.   What is important is that all details of the building be accurately located and dimensioned on the floor plan layout and that all templates be to exact scale.

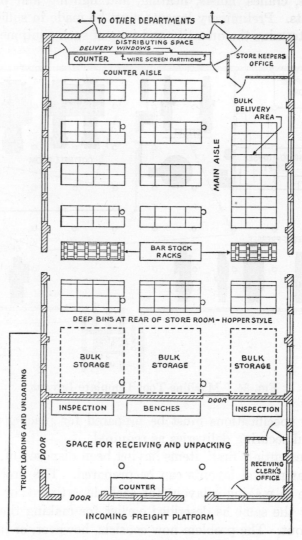

FIG. 35. Equipment Template Layout

They must conform to the outlines of the equipment when placed in position for operation.

For the direct labor departments, the processing division

should have prepared final routing sheets showing the sequence of operations and the processing equipment planned for each operation. These routing sheets will automatically determine certain features of the layout, such as whether the department will be "straight-line" processing and layout, or "job-shop" processing and layout, or "semistraight-line" processing and layout.

These decisions should have been agreed to in principle during preliminary processing and over-all plant layout. However, borderline cases will usually develop where the processing and plant layout divisions may be at variance. Conditions unforeseen during preliminary processing and over-all plant layout may develop. Final processing and layout will require adjustments between processing plans and layout plans. These must be reconciled by administrative procedure within the organization.

Once agreement has been reached on processing and routing, the routing sheets now become the basis for layouts in the corresponding departments, thereby placing very definite restrictions on the detail layouts. Nevertheless, the layout engineer still has ample opportunity for the use of judgment and technical ability. The working arrangement of process equipment and the use and arrangement of miscellaneous auxiliary equipment, mentioned earlier as a direct responsibility of the layout division, must take into account the machine loads and the operation flow as illustrated in Figure 6.

In those departments where the processing division normally makes no attempt to specify equipment, the layout engineer also becomes process engineer. He must analyze operations, determine the equipment required, develop operation sequence and technique, and then make the layout.

Although such departments are generally the so-called indirect departments, they may include productive departments such as assembly or finishing. Such operations do not require processing equipment and are confined to hand or hand-tool operations. Such departments frequently comprise a majority of the man power and are, therefore, important in the control of labor. Taken as a whole, the opportunity for cost reduction through improved layout in such departments far exceeds that in the process divisions.

Inasmuch as these departments cover a wide variety of operations, most of which have not been standardized, layout technique becomes a matter of generalization. A few basic principles have already been pointed out on preceding pages. Operating experience and judgment, supported by a knowledge of layout principles, must point the way to analyses and conclusions.

This is particularly true in laying out a new plant where the benefit of current operating conditions cannot be used as a guide. The layout engineer must develop the details of his layout from knowledge and previous experience, supported by advice from the operating organization.

Layout Approval

When detail department and division layouts have been completed in template form, the corresponding foremen and superintendents must be called in for consultation and approval of the layouts. Reactions of this responsible operating group must be carefully noted. If they do not approve the proposed layouts, then they must be sold into approval, or the necessary compromises must be made to secure approval.

These are the responsible individuals who must live with the layouts and secure operating results. If they are not properly sold from the beginning, they will be inclined to blame all their subsequent troubles on improper layouts. Only in rare cases, where experimentation is advisable, should a foreman or superintendent be forced to accept a layout which he does not approve from the beginning.

Layout Publication

When template layouts have been approved, they must be reproduced on vellum or other suitable blueprint tracings. Equipment templates must be faithfully reproduced to scale and location with respect to building details, such as columns. Each layout tracing must be supported by a bill of materials, listing all equipment involved by number or suitable symbol, which will indicate its location on the layout drawing. References must be made to purchase orders, or detail drawings, for all equipment which will require installation service connections, foundations, ventilation, or the like.

Prints of layouts are then turned over to the plant engineering division for preparation of installation details and specifications.

METHOD OF MAKING LAYOUTS—OLD PLANT

The procedure in developing layouts for a plant that is already in operation requires one first step and several intermediate steps, additional to those taken in laying out a new plant.

Analysis of Data

The first step is to secure a complete set of detailed departmental layouts and a schematic plan of the plant arrangement. If these are not available, and in most plants they are not, then such layouts must be made.

In either case, the objective of the layout engineer is to analyze existing conditions in detail and to secure the information which will be necessary in making subsequent revised layouts. For example, he must have accurate quantities, descriptions, and dimensions of equipment and buildings, in order to make the templates required for revised layouts.

His first concern, however, is to analyze conditions in each department and determine what is necessary to bring about a satisfactory layout of that department in relation to the plant arrangement as a whole. To do this, he will check layout details on the floor and make analyses of operations in sufficient detail to draw accurate conclusions.

Too hasty decisions, made from "paper" analyses, often result in revised layouts which do not accomplish the desired results. In laying out a new plant, it is necessary to rely on "paper" analyses; but, when working with a department in operation, it is inexcusable not to take into consideration whatever conditions currently exist.

Use should be made of whatever process and routing sheets exist. Time studies should be used, if available, to build up machine and operation loads. Ultimate schedules, on which capacities are to be based, are assumed to have been established when the need for layout analyses is determined.

All departments of the plant should be analyzed as described. Then the procedure follows the same general steps as described for laying out a new plant, with the following exceptions:

Equipment and floor space requirements should be listed by the exception method, that is, by items and quantities required over and above existing quantities, and by items and quantities that are surplus.

Schematic Layout of Plant

When the revised floor space requirements for each department or division have been established, the ideal schematic plant arrangement should be developed. This is limited only to the existing plant site and such buildings as obviously cannot be removed or changed. If it develops that additional plant floor space is required, then the location of such additional space becomes a major consideration.

Thought must be given to possible future expansion, as well as the current expansion. That is why it is important to make a theoretical plant arrangement for best results. The theoretical arrangement is then modified only to the point where the cost of changes cannot be justified by corresponding savings.

One important problem in the case of an old plant, which is not involved in the layout of a new plant, is a "maneuvering space." It is easy enough to change the location of departments of a plant on paper. There may be no serious obstacles in the form of physical restrictions in buildings or equipment. The change may still be impractical, however, owing to the lack of space in which to make the first or "unlocking" move.

In a plant which is running and must keep on running, the "unlocking" move is difficult and sometimes requires considerable ingenuity. It may be possible to make the first move over a weekend, or on the second and third shift, or during an inventory period when the plant is shut down.

If this is out of the question, it may be possible to make the first move to a temporary location, such as aisles or stockroom.

By using a tent or temporary sheet-metal shelter, whole departments have been moved to the yard to solve the "unlocking" move.

Completing Detail Layout

When due consideration has been given to the plant arrangement, when proposed changes have been justified by estimated cost and savings comparisons, and when management has approved the proposed arrangement, then the method of completing detailed layouts proceeds as described for making detailed layouts of a new plant.

Only one additional problem is involved: a schedule of departmental moves must be worked out with the operating division. When this has been done, then detail layouts must follow the same schedule.

The moving schedule is one of the important parts of planning. Not only must the physical handling of equipment be thought out and moving facilities procured, but a time schedule for each step of the rearrangement must be planned. What men are available? Do they have the necessary skills to perform their work with dispatch? Under the very best conditions, the rearrangement of a plant produces some confusion. Without good preplanning much time is lost, work must be done over, and hazards are increased. It is, therefore, important that the preplanning be done thoroughly and completely with particular attention to the following:

1. Sequence of moves.
2. Time of moves.
3. Handling equipment.
4. Foundations.
5. Routes of travel.
6. Tools required.
7. Supplies needed.
8. Sufficient personnel and skills.
9. Interference with going operations.
10. Availability of services.

The sequence of moves and the time of moves can best be pre-planned together on one large schedule sheet. First the equipment to be moved is listed in the order in which it can best be shifted; then the time required for each step of the move is estimated. This time estimate is converted into a time schedule showing the date and hour on which work is to be started and finished.

A Gantt or bar chart with time shown across the top of the chart and the steps of the move down the left-hand side is a satisfactory way of scheduling the plan. This has the additional advantage of showing the progress of the move on the same chart. Use different colors for the bars showing the planned schedule and the actual accomplishment. When the progress bar shows that the planned schedule is not being met, steps must be taken to bring it back to schedule. The planning chart can also be used to show management and others interested when the moves will take place and what interference, if any, will be caused.

In determining the moving equipment required, the type and kind of machinery must be considered. Much small equipment can be placed on skids and easily moved from place to place. Other equipment requires special rigging. This special moving equipment should be thought out in advance and made available. A handy piece of rigging is a movable "horse" with a chain fall which can be moved over a machine. The machine is picked up, and "horse" and machine are pushed to the new location.

Some equipment requires special foundations, and, where this is the case, they should be built in advance. Many equipment manufacturers supply foundation drawings and specifications, and these will prove helpful in making the correct foundation.

In moving equipment from one place to another, the route of travel should be considered in advance. Conditions may hinder or even prevent taking the shortest course. Perhaps the overhead clearance is not sufficient, or a floor may not be strong enough, requiring changes in the building. If this is the case, the changes should be made ahead of time.

In taking down and setting up machinery, special tools and supplies are needed. These also should be provided in advance.

As each step in the move is thought out, lists of tools and sup-plies should be made. Nearly every going plant has these tools on hand, but they should not be taken for granted until a checkup has been made.

Good planning should also include the assignment of the proper personnel to each step of the move. If the plant organi-zation does not include millwrights, helpers, plumbers, me-chanics, and so on, they can be secured from companies who do this kind of work.

When it is necessary to make major rearrangements of a plant which must continue in production, the problem is more diffi-cult. Plan to have sufficient material in advance, or provide other means of continuing the operation while the move is being made. A meeting of minds and a discussion with those con-cerned always brings to light some means of solving this prob-lem. The important thing is to plan in advance so that confu-sion and expense will be reduced to the minimum.

If services such as electric power lines, water, sewer, air, and gas lines are planned for and made available well in advance of the move, much time can be saved, and machines can be put into operation sooner. Along with the layout of equipment should go a layout of all service lines. It is well to make these layouts in considerable detail, showing sizes, switches, valves, and so on. Not only will these drawings prove useful while the original in-stallation and changes are being made, but also they will have future value for maintenance and further moves.

Some Techniques That Help in Making a Layout

The scale of the layout is quite important. As stated before, the largest possible scale for convenient handling is best, as tem-plates are easier to handle. There is a choice as to whether it will be on fractions or decimals of 1 inch. It will be found con-venient to make the layout on cross-section paper. The outline of the building showing columns, partitions, crane ways, and the like, can be drawn on the cross-section paper with a heavy pencil or in ink without the use of T squares by following the lines of the paper. Templates can be placed by counting the divisions to get the distance.

Cross-section paper can be purchased in scales of $\frac{1}{8}''$, $\frac{1}{10}''$ and $\frac{1}{20}''$ divisions. The $\frac{1}{10}''$ and $\frac{1}{20}''$ are made in rolls, and the other comes in sheets. For that reason, it is well to choose the $\frac{1}{10}''$ or $\frac{1}{20}''$ with preference given to the $\frac{1}{10}''$. However, the $\frac{1}{8}''$ can be used by placing sheets together, using Scotch tape or other means, and fastening them to plywood or other types of wallboard. This is a convenient way to handle the layouts, as the plywood or wallboard can be used in meetings or carried to the job easily.

The machines and equipment can be represented by paper templates or by models, but they should be in the same scale as the cross-section paper, that is, if $\frac{1}{8}''$ paper is used, the templates or models should be $\frac{1}{8}''$, $\frac{1}{4}''$, $\frac{3}{8}''$, and so on, to the foot, and, if $\frac{1}{10}''$ is used, the scale should be 0.1", 0.2", 0.3", and so on, to the foot.

Models of machines made in wood, plastic, or metal are excellent to show the placing of equipment. The third dimension brings out any interference with headroom, the layman can get a good idea as to how the plant will look, and the layout can be used for display purposes.

However, scale models are expensive, and paper templates serve the practical purpose (see Figures 34 and 35). When making the templates, colored paper may be used to show classes of machines and is helpful in selling the layout to those concerned. By referring to catalogs, the sizes of most standard equipment can be found.

It is sometimes necessary actually to measure the machines. The measurements should then be reduced to the scale selected and line drawings made of each piece of equipment. If all of one kind of machine is made on one sheet of paper, the identifying names and numbers can be easily typed on the templates. When templates and models are being made, the overhang and travel of machine parts and material must be taken into consideration so that ample space will be allowed. There will then be no interference when the time comes to install the machines.

There are several ways to attach templates or models to the layout drawing. Tacks or staples can be used, but the preferred way is to use Scotch or masking tape. If one quarter inch or larger holes are punched in the paper templates and a small piece of tape placed over the hole, the template may be fixed in place by pressing the tape through the hole onto the cross-section paper. The tape may also be made into a hinge and fastened to the rear side of the template. This is also a good way to hold models on the layout drawing.

When the templates are ready to be placed on the outline drawing of the buildings, various possible arrangements may be photographed and a record made for future discussions and study. When placing the templates, keep in mind the necessary working space to be provided around each work station. Not only must there be room for a free movement of the machines and men, but also space must be provided for work banks of "before and after" parts or materials. It is sometimes well to make templates for these work banks. If skids are used, space must be allowed for moving them into and out of position.

In the case of conveyors or other moving parts of machines, it is well to show the direction of movement and the working position on the templates. Templates for all space-taking articles, rooms, benches, trucks, and the like, should be made and placed on the layout drawing. This avoids not allowing enough space at the work stations.

Aisles and the flow of materials can and should be shown on the drawings, too. Templates can be used for the aisles, and colored strings placed over tacks will show the flow of materials. It should be borne in mind that wide aisles are best even though they do take up space. It is also well to keep aisles straight with the fewest possible turns, offsets and angles. If power lift trucks are to be used, then the aisles must be wide enough for trucks to pass with their loads and to make a U turn. When the kind and size of handling equipment has been selected, the vendor will be glad to advise the maneuvering space required.

When the templates are in place and the aisles are indicated, the flow of materials from one operation to another can be shown by placing a colored string to represent each product. This technique will often bring to light "bottlenecks," backtracking or long moves which can be corrected. This flow of materials is well worth study, as many savings and reductions in process time can be made thereby.

The goal of all layouts is a straight line from one operation to the next in the fewest and shortest moves. If the processing shows that certain operations are not so fast as others, the solution may be more equipment for the slow operations, or a change of method or further breaking down of the operation. A smooth balance should be reached but not at the expense of slowing down operations. If some few operations are too fast, it may be possible to add more work for those operations. If this cannot be done, then the answer may be space for banking materials before and after the first operations so that they can work part time.

If the template layouts are to be photographed, it must be remembered that colors will only show as shades of gray, which are not too satisfactory. However, photography is now available which can reproduce prints in true color. If the plant layout is quite large, the camera can be placed on supports above the templates to make a scale photograph.

Where the operations are simple and the chances for different arrangements are few, photographing can be eliminated, and those concerned may be shown the actual template layouts. This may even be done for large plants, if the executive group is closely knit or small in size. However, there is then no record of the different arrangements, and much time may be lost in going over the same ground several times.

After the template layouts have been finally accepted, working drawings should be made showing all the data of the template layout along with the dimensions and specifications for the placing of the equipment. If the drawings are complicated, separate drawings should be made for the location of services such as electric power lines, water lines, and line shafting.

These drawings will show the codes that identify the equipment, lines of travel, service lines, and the like. Some layout engineers show these codes on separate sheets, but it will be advantageous if they are put on the same drawing. Thus, when prints are made, the identifying codes are reproduced at the same time.

After the rearrangements have been completed, the drawings should be brought up-to-date and kept up-to-date. Even with the very best planning, it will be found that little details have been overlooked and that changes will have to be made in the drawings. If these omissions are not corrected as found, confusion will develop in the future.

As a word of caution, those working on plant layout must be accurate in their work. The building space and the location of partitions, columns, doors, and windows must be carefully checked. If the architect's drawings are used, they should be checked as to accuracy, since buildings are not always erected as planned. The layout drawing itself must be true to scale, and the templates must be correct representations of the equipment. If accuracy in all details is not maintained, very serious troubles can ensue, even to the point where the equipment will not go in the space provided for it.

CHAPTER 28

PLANT MAINTENANCE

•

DEFINITION

What is plant maintenance? Many different conceptions of plant maintenance are prevalent, but from the viewpoint of good management the following definition applies:

Plant maintenance is the function of installing plant facilities and keeping buildings, machinery, and services in condition for ready and efficient use.

PURPOSE

The objectives of plant maintenance may include:

1. Correct installation of any and all plant property.
2. Prevention of breakdown, or loss to production, of plant property.
3. Proper care of buildings, yards, machinery, and services.
4. Correct and prompt repair and restoration of equipment to service in case of a breakdown.
5. Keeping of maintenance costs under control.
6. Recording of data concerning plant equipment.

There is a natural human tendency to neglect inanimate things such as the machines, buildings, and other facilities of a plant. To a large extent, the venture capital of an enterprise is invested in such equipment and structures. Therefore, the safeguarding of money stored in this form would appear to be an obvious necessity, apparent even to an untrained management. Unfortunately the study and analysis of many plants, in many different industries, has revealed that plant equipment is too often grossly neglected, sometimes to the point of complete uselessness.

Although nearly every plant has a maintenance department, often it is either not properly used by management or considered of minor importance. Frequently it is located in some out-of-the-way place. It may be undermanned with inexperienced help who do not make the best use of their time. Management does not always provide it with ways and means for properly performing its work.

Many times repairs, hastily made, prove only temporary. Some executives think that patchwork and baling wire repairs are ingenious and accomplish all that is necessary; but this practice has been discredited. It is now axiomatic that production is increased and costs are lowered by thorough and expert repair workmanship.

The remedy for maintenance problems is the same as for any production problem; a plan that anticipates the requirements and provides facilities to meet them.

PREVENTIVE MAINTENANCE PLAN

The importance of providing a planned preventive maintenance program cannot be emphasized too strongly, regardless of whether the kind of equipment used to produce the output of the plant be fine and delicate instruments or heavy and rugged presses. The best manufacturing methods, plant layout, and production schedules will not maintain a high standard of operation, unless all processing equipment, tools, jigs, fixtures, and gages are maintained in good condition, with a minimum of interruption and delay to production and personnel.

Organization

It is possible, practical, and profitable to plan, schedule, and control maintenance work and its cost, so that the continuity of factory operations is undisturbed.

Management must realize the importance of preventive maintenance. It must make up its mind to have a correct program and insist on its performance, if the full benefits of preventive maintenance are to be enjoyed. The size and kind of organization required for preventive maintenance depends on the type of industry, the size of the plant, the quantity and kind of its equipment, and the complexity of the manufacturing operation.

The department should be built along the lines of general procedure for organization as discussed in Chapter 25, "Organization," of this section. The organization under a plant engineer, as indicated in this chapter, can perhaps be considered a staff function, although the maintenance within the plant engineering is certainly a line function and should so be set up.

The departments of maintenance required to service the plant should be selected once the line of authority has been established; the responsibilities, duties, and authority should be written in manual form as outlined in Chapter 25. Inasmuch as the work and direction are of an engineering and tradescraft nature, the maintenance personnel should have adequate engineering background and education, or experience in craftsmanship.

Ordinarily the divisions of a preventive maintenance department are:

(a) Supervisor's office, including:
 1. Draftsmen.
 2. Stenographers and clerks.
 3. Records and reports.
 4. Maintenance inspection.
 5. Maintenance scheduling.
 6. Maintenance performance.
(b) Electrical maintenance.
(c) Millwrights.
(d) Machine shop.
(e) Carpenters.
(f) Masons and bricklayers.
(g) Steamfitting and plumbing.
(h) Lubrication.
(i) Belt and drive repair.
(j) Janitors, window washers, cleaners.
(k) Riggers and laborers.
(l) Gardeners and yardmen.
(m) Fire prevention.

(*n*) Guards and watchmen.
(*o*) Painters.
(*p*) Tinsmiths and welders.
(*q*) Maintenance stores.

If the plant is small, however, many of these services can be combined or furnished by outside contractors as required.

The success or failure of any preventive maintenance program depends on the type of individual selected as its head and on the amount of understanding and administration by top management.

It is much more difficult to supervise maintenance work than to supervise direct workers whose established standards of quantity and quality of output are easily determined. Maintenance work is spread over the entire plant, and a clear understanding of all the production department's functions as well as a wide variety of skills, knowledge, and efforts, is required.

The supervisor must have the required technical knowledge and executive ability to see that orders are properly given and promptly carried out. He must also have the energy and stamina to follow a large variety of tasks over a wide area. He must have the ability to gain the loyal co-operation of his group, which must perform many difficult and sometimes unpleasant tasks at odd hours when others are relaxing. He must train his people to be on the alert to make minor repairs, before major repairs become necessary.

Of course, the more efficient the maintenance worker, the less work there is for him to do. This does not apply to a supervisor who must be able to handle a large volume of work and to assimilate many details. Careful consideration should be given by management to its choice of a maintenance supervisor.

Care should also be exercised in selection of other personnel for this department. Emphasis should be not only on the requisite aptitudes, but also on ability "to get along with others."

Procedures

A preventive maintenance plan is simple, and the amount of paper work is not very great. To make it work, however, requires intensive application to details and a close follow-up by management. Certainly, preventive maintenance is well worth the application and follow-up effort. Substantial savings in time, material, and actual depreciation may be made by preventing loss of productive time, due to breakdown of the equipment most needed to meet some critical delivery date.

A planned maintenance program is of inestimable value. A definite program, estimates, standards, and schedule for the performance of the actual work of the maintenance department will tend to increase individual effort and to reduce lost time to a minimum.

Book depreciation of equipment is, of course, a matter of time, but actual deterioration is caused by wear and neglect of upkeep. Hence, if wear is minimized and equipment is kept in good condition, the equipment will last longer and produce at maximum over an increased span of years. A word of warning is apropos at this point: *When the productive life of equipment is prolonged beyond its normal life by preventive maintenance, there is risk of obsolescence by reason of the development of modern and improved equipment.* Management and maintenance departments must be on the alert to adopt the new when analysis proves the advisability of change, even though the old is in good condition.

The amount of paper work required to service a good preventive maintenance program will vary with particular industries and companies. The following list represents the basic requirements:

1. Register of equipment numbers.
2. Machine data record.
3. Inspection data for machines.
4. Inspection data for buildings.
5. Oiling schedule.
6. Requisition for maintenance work.
7. Register of job orders.
8. Approved maintenance job order.
9. Inventory record of maintenance material.
10. Maintenance time card.

11. Maintenance work schedule.

12. Report of maintenance for management.

This list includes only the forms pertinent to the maintenance department. It is assumed that use will be made of other plant forms, such as purchasing requisitions, material requisitions, in-and-out time cards, and passes. Certain of the listed forms may be common to other departments and yet serve the purpose of the preventive maintenance plan.

Numbering System

If machines and equipment are not already numbered for ready identification, reference, and convenient recording of data, they should be. It is customary to have all machines numbered, and most plants have instituted this practice, if only for accounting purposes. Various types of code systems are in use, but, generally, they become very complicated and require extra effort to keep up-to-date, owing to changes and moving of equipment from place to place.

It is found that serial numbering of equipment adequately serves the purpose, avoids confusion, and is easily perpetuated. Whether a code system or straight serial numbering of equipment is adopted, the numbers should be plainly visible and affixed permanently. In some cases numbers painted on the equipment may be required, but a metal tag bearing the number is usually most convenient. Tags are easily seen and quickly attached and may be numbered in advance.

The "register of equipment numbers" is merely the means of identifying equipment and of assigning correct numbers to new equipment. It may be kept in any convenient form—a bound book will serve. Because of the importance of this record and the ease with which a book may be misplaced or lost, particular care must be taken not to permit the book to be removed from its designated location.

Responsibility for the register should be placed with a competent clerk, preferably in the accounting, purchasing, or maintenance department. It is an excellent idea to have a clerk in the maintenance department responsible for the register, and for furnishing copies of all entries made therein to the accounting and purchasing departments. This assures duplicate records in the event of misplacement of the original register.

Machine Record

The "machine data record," Figure 36, is best kept on cards filed according to equipment name and number. A card should be prepared for each piece of equipment and should record all data relating thereto. This card record not only serves as a complete inventory of equipment but also builds up a complete history useful to management when upkeep becomes too costly and replacement is indicated. It should be the duty of the clerk handling this file to watch the cards as postings are made and to report to the proper official any excessive charges.

Objectives of the "machine data record" are:

1. To furnish name, equipment number, complete description, installation date, location, value, and accompanying part of each machine and piece of equipment, in and about the plant.

2. To provide a means of recording cost of material, labor, and burden expended for each machine and piece of equipment, that is, cost of maintenance.

3. To guide management in questions of replacement or obsolescence.

4. To provide an authentic inventory of all machinery and equipment.

The responsibility for the "machine data record" can be assigned to a clerk in the maintenance department, where there is most need for this. However, the record will be of importance to the accounting department also, and the work might equally well be assigned to a clerk in that department.

Inspection Record

The forms "inspection data for machines," Figure 37; "inspection data for buildings," Figure 38; and "oiling schedule," Figure 39, serve the same purpose for all three functions. They systematically direct attention to the important points to be in-

MACHINE DATA RECORD					
Description		Depreciation—Location			
		Date	Value	Dept.	
Mfgr. Serial No. Model No.					
Date Installed HP RPM					

Date	Job Order	Replacement	Cause	Material Cost	Labor Cost

Machine Name   Equipment Number

(Use Other Side for Additional Data)

Fig. 36

INSPECTION DATA					FOR MACHINES							
Location	Name of Mach.					Machine No.						
Inspection Points & Periods	By	1	2	3	5	26	27	28	29	30	31	

CODE

A—Daily.
B—Weekly.
C—Semimonthly.
D—Monthly.
E—Semiannually.

J—Operator.
K—Foreman.
L—Maintenance Man.
M—Maintenance Engineer.
N—Master Mechanic.
O—Superintendent.

FIG. 37

		Jan.	Feb.	M	Sept.	Oct.	Nov.	Dec.
	INSPECTION DATA FOR				BUILDINGS			
	Building Name Bldg. No.				Year			
1	Roof							
2	Gutters, Down Spouts							
3	Skylights							
4	Windows							
5	Doors							
6	Aisles							
7	Floors							
8	Lights							
9	Stairways							
10	Fences							
11	Sprinkler							
12	Plumbing							
13	Laboratories							
14	Painting, outside							
15	Painting, inside							
16	Sidewalks							
17	Driveways							
18	Heating							
19	Ventilation							
20	Fire protection							
21	Housekeeping							
22	Fire hazard							
23	Safety hazard							
24								

CODE

G—Good.   B—Bad (repairs needed).   x Repairs ordered.
F—Fair.   xx Repairs made.

FIG. 38

OILING SCHEDULE										AND REPORT												
Month....										....												
Department			Equipment							Number												
										Dates												
			1	2	3	4	5	6	7	19	20	21	22	23	24	25	26	27	28	29	30	31

CODE

A—Daily.   J—Operator.
B—Weekly.   K—Foreman.
C—Semimonthly.   L—Maintenance Man.
D—Monthly.   M—Maintenance Engineer.
E—Semiannually.   N—Master Mechanic.
                                  O—Superintendent.

Note: Same type of form can be used for Inspection of Bldgs. & Equipment.

Fig. 39

spected, designate responsibility for the inspection, and record the fact that the inspection was actually made. In other words, the objectives of the three forms are:

1. To provide a record of those points and parts of machines, motors, and equipment to be inspected, oiled, and cared for.

2. To provide for scheduling such inspection, oiling, and up-keep.

3. To provide a means for finding weaknesses and making correction.

4. To provide a means of designating by whom inspections, oilings, and repairs are to be made.

5. To provide a means of delegating responsibilities for in-spections, oilings, and repairs.

Forms, of course, are only tools to be used skillfully and dili-gently in accomplishing a task. The inspection forms require very careful study of each machine, each tool, each building, each facility. Then determine the things that need attention to keep the plant in condition. After the data are recorded on the inspection forms, they are a means of follow-up to see that indi-viduals carry out their assignments. They become a schedule for regular and systematic preventive maintenance. Inspections can become routine, but not until personnel has been trained and has the knowledge to foresee and report expected trouble.

Maintenance Requisition

From regular inspections, a list of things necessary to keep the equipment in topnotch condition will be developed. One of the sources of the "requests for maintenance work," see Figure 40, is the inspection procedure. Any department head, foreman, or superintendent should have authority to originate a request for maintenance, when, as, and if needed. It should not be neces-sary for a regular inspection to develop the need for repair work. Also, most maintenance departments are required to do certain new work needed, such as building tables, benches, and cabinets. The departments should have the privilege of requesting such work, subject to the approval of superiors.

```
┌─────────────────────────────────────────────────────────┐
│            REQUEST FOR MAINTENANCE WORK                  │
│  To                              Date                    │
├──────────────────────────────────┬──────────────────────┤
│  Work to be done                 │  Dept.                │
│                                  ├──────────────────────┤
│                                  │  Equip.               │
│                                  │  No.                  │
│                                  ╞══════════════════════╡
│                                  │  ESTIMATED COST       │
│  Reason                          │  Labor      $         │
│                                  ├──────────────────────┤
│                                  │  Material             │
│                                  ├──────────────────────┤
│              Signed:             │  Total      $         │
├──────────────┬───────────────────┼──────────────────────┤
│  Approved    │  Work assigned to │  Checked by           │
│              │                   │                       │
│              ├───────────────────┤                       │
│              │  To be done, date │                       │
│  Date        │                   │                       │
└──────────────┴───────────────────┴──────────────────────┘
```

Fig. 40

A regular routine for handling "requests for maintenance work" should be established so that the proper authorities may be informed of the need for maintenance work easily and without delay. In the event of important breakdowns where delay means loss, the foreman should, of course, notify the proper authorities by telephone. The established routine of preparing the form should also be followed, for record purposes.

When a "request for maintenance work" is received in the maintenance office and has been properly approved, it should be analyzed. This may involve an actual visit to the location of the trouble. Analysis of the work to be done to assure the lowest possible cost is one of the important steps in the control of maintenance work.

Maintenance Orders

A form, which can be called "approved maintenance job order" (see Figure 41), is desirable, so that an established routine will require a thorough study of each job. On this form the work should be processed or broken down into the steps necessary to accomplish it, together with an estimate of the time required. Of course, ability to process the jobs and to estimate the time requires a practical knowledge of maintenance work. After the plan has been in operation for a sufficient period and data have been compiled, processing and estimating can become quite accurate. This should be an objective of the department.

In order to keep record of job orders, a register of jobs should be maintained. This can be a simple listing by numbers in chronological order and is merely a means of recording issued orders. By numbering the job orders and keeping a file in numerical order, the file will serve the purpose of a register. At least three copies of the job order should be made: one for the maintenance man doing the work (this should be accompanied by necessary blueprints and specifications), one for the maintenance office record, and one for the accounting department for costing purposes.

As mentioned before, all maintenance material should be kept in a locked storeroom. For large plants it is well to have a separate storeroom, under the direction of a storekeeper. Spare parts for all vital equipment should be properly stored, numbered, and controlled in the same manner as the direct materials discussed in Chapter 29. Card files showing a maximum and minimum quantity to be stored, together with information of "on order," "received," "disbursed," and a running balance of parts on hand, make an essential record for controlling maintenance materials.

Provision should be made, also, for a time card to record the labor expended for each job. Generally, the regular shop card is satisfactory. As a rule, maintenance men work on several jobs during a day, and it is well to have a time card designed for recording all data conveniently.

With a backlog of "approved maintenance job orders" and the necessary men, it is possible to plan and schedule the work of the

APPROVED MAINTENANCE JOB ORDER

Dept.	Job No.	Equip. No.

Requested by	Date requested

Approved by	Date approved

Assigned to	Date work to be done

| Work to be done | Estimated | |
	Time	Cost

Materials required	Quantity	Cost

Job checked by	Date

Job inspected by	Date

FIG. 41

department. For small departments it is better to schedule each man's daily work. For large departments it is better to schedule the jobs to be performed, keeping in mind the work load but permitting the foreman to assign the men to the jobs. Any one of several methods of handling the scheduling can be used. The simplest method is to place the job orders in pockets for the various divisions of the maintenance department, according to the day and hour the work is scheduled.

A check-up should be made of accomplishment and a comparison made with the estimates, both as to time and material. Periodic reports of accomplishment should be made to management. These will include data on the volume of work done, the amount of lost time due to breakdowns, and the ratio of maintenance hours to over-all plant hours. It should be borne in mind, however, that the ratio of maintenance hours to over-all plant hours may show wide variances. When the plant itself is shut down, that is usually the best time for maintenance work.

The practical application of the plan just described requires a knowledge of certain obvious practices, a few of which are detailed in the following pages.

CORRECT INSTALLATION

The very first requisite in keeping plant facilities in good working condition for their whole span of useful life is correct handling, from receipt at the plant to final installation. Equipment of a precision type can be so badly damaged in moving from the receiving platform to its proper location that it becomes useless for the purpose intended. In the case of heavy equipment, moving from place to place is an expensive and hazardous undertaking if suitable rigging is not available.

In handling and installing equipment, knowledge and experience are of the utmost importance, and management should be certain that these requirements arc mct in maintcnance personnel. Most equipment manufacturers furnish installation specifications and blueprints of foundations. These are frequently rigid, and an inexperienced maintenance man may think he knows a "better way." If installation specifications are disregarded, trouble is likely to result, and the life of the equipment may be materially reduced.

One of the most common errors in an initial installation is made in connecting the motor—there is a tendency to make the belt too tight, with resultant damage to the motor, belt, and equipment. Thus, the first requisite for preventive maintenance is to install all facilities, equipment, and services in accordance with standard practices.

PREVENTING BREAKDOWNS

The primary objective of a plant maintenance department is to prevent breakdowns and loss of productive time. To prevent breakdowns, all required and deserved care must be given to the equipment. It is a scientific fact that friction causes wear, costly damage, and loss of power. Advances in control of friction have been tremendous; nonetheless, wherever there is a moving part there is friction. Therefore all bearings, whether slide, annular, or thrust, require attention. This attention should include regular and periodic inspection, proper lubrication, the elimination of overloading, and the exclusion of dust and foreign matter.

Many thousands of dollars are lost yearly owing to failure of motors, and in most cases it is not the fault of the motor. The electric motor is one of industry's most faithful servants, but because it is so reliable it is too often forgotten. Whenever a motor burns out and requires rewinding, the motor has been overheated. Although overheating of a motor might be caused by an "electrical condition," this is rare.

Nearly all overheating of motors is caused by overloading, improper lubrication, or dirt. These can be avoided by intelligent diligent care and watchfulness. Overloading caused by running the motor with the belt too tight can be avoided by careful inspection, or by properly locking the adjusting base and providing a new drive if necessary. Of course, overloading can also be caused by the use of too small a motor for the energy requirements, in which case the remedy is obvious.

The elimination of dirt and dust may be difficult. One solution to the problem is to seek a better location for the motor.

Under any circumstances, provision should always be made for blowing out the motors regularly, thus preventing accumulation of foreign matter around the coils.

Lubrication

Lubrication of motors is a simple operation. Oiling is most frequently neglected from carelessness, or because of inaccessibility. Carelessness can be overcome by a program that places responsibility on and provides a regular schedule of attention by specific maintenance men. If the motor is difficult or dangerous to service, provision should be made for use of one of the many automatic oiling devices.

The use of the wrong lubricant is perhaps as bad as no lubrication. Each type of bearing and each condition of motor design require a specific kind of lubricant. Oil companies and equipment companies have determined the best lubrication for nearly every condition, by extensive research, and make recommendations accordingly. Therefore, to reduce motor trouble and repair to a minimum:

(a) Use the right motor for the work to be done.
(b) Install it correctly.
(c) Do not overload it.
(d) Keep it clean and properly oiled.

A similar code of service applies to all other types of equipment. The maintenance department must install equipment properly, know its characteristics, and plan to avoid expected trouble.

Building

Another important function of a plant maintenance department is the care of buildings, yards, and services. The average factory building is of substantial construction and will last for years. Regular attention to a few specific things avoids extensive repairs in the years to come. All exposed woodwork and metal surfaces should be painted at regular intervals and inspection for deterioration made between painting periods. When inspection reveals places where paint is worn or damaged, these should be touched up without waiting for any regular over-all painting.

Roofs of all buildings should be periodically inspected to detect and repair minor worn places. This prevents serious leaks and resultant damage to the interior and contents of the buildings. Any leaks noticed after storms should be repaired immediately.

Floors of most plants require constant attention from the maintenance department. Factory floors, especially aisles, are subject to considerable wear from heavy traffic. In nearly every plant there are locations where wear is so excessive that keeping the floors in proper repair seems to be an almost impossible undertaking. Too many times men struggle with a loaded truck because of holes in the floor. If a wear-resistant type of flooring is laid at these points much trouble and expense can be avoided. The extra cost of a good floor surface is soon offset by the elimination of the delays just described.

While we are on the subject of floor wear, the necessity of exercising care in selection of truck castors should be mentioned. Truck wheels should be appropriate for the floor over which they roll. Wheels should be chosen that are of the correct size for the load, for the floor, and for distance of travel. Care in this alone will effect large savings.

To summarize: *Proper care of buildings involves regular inspection of all parts of the buildings and the making of necessary repairs before real damage occurs.*

YARD

Proper care of yards is also one of the functions of the maintenance department. If yards are used for storage, or as productive work areas, their cleanliness and orderliness are properly the responsibility of the department using them; but their upkeep is properly the function of the maintenance department. All roads, walks, fences, ditches, and the like should be regularly inspected, and needed repairs should be made immediately. Fences should be painted and kept tight, with special attention to the posts and gates.

If yards are landscaped, lawns should be cut regularly, shrubbery trimmed, and growth kept under control. Weeds and tall grass should be cut down, not only for appearance but also to eliminate fire hazard. Well-kept buildings and landscaped yards help to build community good will and a feeling of pride on the part of the employees.

Machinery

Care of departmental machinery is frequently the duty of the department foreman, and it is good policy to charge him with that responsibility. Nevertheless, every piece of machinery and equipment should appear on the schedule of the maintenance department for periodic inspection. The department should make certain that all oil cups are in place and properly filled with the right kind of lubricant, that all joints are correctly tight, and that all adjustable parts are kept in adjustment. All points where wear might occur should be carefully examined and corrections made as needed. Parts that take strain and stress require particularly close examination to prevent serious accidents. Flywheels, grinding wheels, and high-speed moving parts should be kept in proper balance.

Painting

Included under the care of machinery and equipment are cleaning and painting. It is definitely the duty of the operator to keep his own work station clean and in order, but there are many parts of the machinery which the operator cannot and should not touch. For example, operators should not clean sump pumps, grinders, automatic machines, gears, large machine frames, and similar equipment. They should not be permitted to clean inaccessible parts, where it is necessary to move guards or parts of the machine.

The maintenance department should be charged with the periodic cleaning of all machinery and equipment. Regular schedules should be set up and thorough cleaning given when machines are shut down. The need of keeping all machinery painted is again emphasized. A standard color, selected from the painting codes developed for this purpose, should be adopted and adhered to.

SERVICE EQUIPMENT

The proper care of services is still another important duty of the maintenance department. By services are meant such things as air and hydraulic supply, water, vacuum systems, electric light and power supply, gas and steam supply, sprinkler and fire protection, plumbing, heating and ventilation, conveyors and transportation equipment.

Regular inspections are again necessary to prevent failures of service which, if they occurred, might even result in major catastrophes and cause shutdowns for indefinite periods. These various services are for the most part so reliable and so taken for granted that they are often neglected until trouble occurs. Regular inspection and prompt repairs will prevent trouble.

Admittedly, much of the work required of the maintenance department in connection with these services is occasioned by changes in production technique and layout. Scale drawings should be made of all the services and adequately detailed to permit easy interpretation. One employee, or even several, may know where all the piping and electric lines are located, where switches and valves are placed, and the location of underground lines; but this information should be a matter of record in case of future changes in personnel. It is generally helpful to have a distinguishing color for each branch of the services, using the standard color identification code.

REPAIRS

Notwithstanding inspection and all plans for prevention of breakdown, part of the time of the maintenance department will be devoted to emergency repairs. Many repairs of a temporary nature will be made. Such repairs should be recognized as temporary and replaced by permanent and expert repair work at the earliest possible date. The old adage, "If a job is worth doing at all, it is worth doing well," applies to all maintenance work. Whenever there are machine guards hanging by pieces of wires, boards nailed over holes in the floor, window lights broken, temporary and makeshift lighting, steam and water leaks, flywheels out of balance, belts flapping, or other evidences of lack of interest, careless and poor workmanship can be expected from the workmen.

CONTROL OF COST

Maintenance work is important; yet the cost must be kept under control. Methods for accomplishing this are discussed in earlier paragraphs. It is mentioned here to emphasize the fact that, when maintenance work is planned and repairs made before they become serious, the cost of maintaining the plant will be kept at a minimum. Furthermore, if maintenance work is planned and performed according to standard practices, the man-hours of the department can be controlled.

In any event, maintenance costs are in most cases justified by assurance that the productive departments will operate at capacity and without shutdowns.

SUMMARY

A history should be kept of each and every piece of plant equipment and of all facilities. For this purpose each piece should be tagged with an identifying number. A card record should be kept of all pertinent data, such as the name, maker, price, date of installation, nature of each repair and its cost, and any moves. If the equipment record indicates increasing costs and frequency of repairs, consideration should be given to replacement. Management should review the equipment record periodically for ready comparison of maintenance costs with results obtained. Other valuable records are discussed earlier in the chapter under the plan for preventive maintenance.

It is emphasized again that, if management is to enjoy the benefits of preventive maintenance, it must plan for maintenance. It must also supply the tools with which to do the work and follow through to make certain the work is performed in accordance with plans.

CHAPTER 29

PRODUCTION CONTROL

•

IMPORTANCE

Production control is one of the fundamental requirements for effective management of a company. There is no influence that so completely affects the production factors of material, labor, equipment, and product, as does production control.

Secondary in importance, but only slightly, to the physical requirements for such control is the requirement of proper *attitude* towards it, from top management down to the lowliest worker in the company. This intangible—the proper spirit, the desire to make the control work—is vital to the success of production control. Unless it can be instilled and maintained in the organization, any attempt to install this control will be foredoomed to failure before it starts.

DEFINITION

Production control is defined as that method or system which, over a period of time, regulates the order of movement of the elements of a manufacturing program in relation to each other and to the whole. It offers a choice of two distinct procedures:

1. Accurate advance planning of every operation and movement in manufacture, or

2. Constant follow-up of the product as it progresses through the factory, and the application of pressure to lagging items.

Although the *follow-up* method is quite common in industry, it requires greater expense and effort than *preplanning* to accomplish the same result.

For this reason *production control* as described in later pages is concerned only with that method of control which is based on careful preplanning for the manufacture of the product. It is concerned primarily with the *time* aspect of manufacture, although it also must concern itself with the *place* aspect, in combination with the *quantity* aspect of the product.

Production control therefore may be precisely defined as the control of all the processes of converting raw material into a product ready for delivery to purchasers. Usually, although not always, this includes the purchase of raw material. Usually, although not always, it includes the storage and the inventory of raw materials, semifinished, and finished products. These are always included, however, when they influence in any way the continuity of actual manufacture necessary to accomplish a given result in a given time.

Production control consists of three major phases, which are defined as follows:

1. Control of the use of facilities. This is accomplished by the following three steps:
   (a) *Planning*—which lays out in advance the essential elements to be controlled and co-ordinates them into an attainable performance or program.
   (b) *Routing*—which prescribes the path of travel of production through the manufacturing facilities. This is an endeavor to find the shortest path of travel to the most efficient equipment. In some cases routing may be a part of the current production control and a daily duty. Except in the case of "jobbing-type" manufacture, it is usually a nonrepetitive element that, once established, serves until some basic change is made in the product, process method, or production control itself.
   (c) *Scheduling*—which lists the parts to be made, usually in a prescribed sequence and within a specified period. This is a listing of what shall be done. In itself, scheduling does *not* provide production control. It is merely a static function, to which must be added the act of performance.

2. Control of inventory. This regulates the flow of raw and finished materials into the plant and into stock, so that the quantity requirements of the schedule are met.

3. Dispatching. This is the required act of performance and "follow-up" which starts something on its way and gives it movement towards its destination. Scheduling usually implies the method or process of assigning work to definite stations and, where necessary, accelerating or retarding its progress from point to point. It is the "breath of life" to production control, co-ordinating the factors of planning, routing, and scheduling, but must never be expected to do the entire job of controlling production.

PURPOSE

The basic purposes of production control are:

1. To give the best possible service to customers.

2. To secure the lowest possible costs in manufacture.

Within the limitations of available capacity, it endeavors to balance these two factors. The first must not be accomplished at the expense of the second, and vice versa.

Production control secures lowest possible costs by:

1. Using plant equipment to its utmost capacity on work it can produce most economically.

2. Using plant space to its utmost capacity, without congestion in the flow of material.

3. Providing and using labor with the greatest effectiveness by supplying proper tools and facilities and by setting equitable performance standards.

4. Putting work through in the most economical lot size.

5. Providing raw material at the right time, in the right place, and in the right quantity.

6. Moving work promptly and systematically in the sequence proper to the operation requirements.

7. Requiring finished product of the proper quality and in the proper quantity.

Proper application of these control elements creates a smooth and steady flow of production, conforming to requirements of quantity and quality. It results in adequate customer service and its lowest possible production costs. If these elements are not correctly applied and co-ordinated, the result will be:

1. Losses due to improper use of facilities.
2. Losses due to interruptions in the flow of production.
3. Losses due to excessive or unbalanced inventories, either in raw materials, work in process, or finished stocks.

These losses are the responsibility of production control, except when general policy dictates some other control in the operation of the plant or the procurement of materials.

ESSENTIALS FOR COMPLETE CONTROL

The three conditions essential to the application of effective production control are:

1. *The control should cover every factor.* Control of details is not enough; the general plan of production for the company must be fully developed first. Then the general production schedule and the departmental schedules should be developed and programmed, with sufficient flexibility to provide for changing demands. Finally the order itself must be analyzed and its component elements established in the proper place, at the proper time, and in the proper manner. Nor is it enough merely to control the manufacturing operations. Facilities used in manufacture (whether jigs, fixtures, blueprints, or instructions) must be related to the flow of production in such a manner as to secure the objectives of low cost and service to the customer.
2. *The right kind of system must be used.* This requires forms and routines that will give:
    (*a*) Adequate detailed information for planning.
    (*b*) Complete instructions for processing the work.
    (*c*) Accurate records of current and past performance.
   The system must be prompt in effect, adequate in intent, and usable in operation. It must never be considered in any other light than as a *tool* of control.
3. *Control must be administered by competent personnel, properly authorized.* The personnel should be so placed in the organization that their authority in their own field will never be questioned. On the other hand, they need not be

given authority beyond proper scope. How much personnel is needed will depend largely upon the size of operations. But in the last analysis their number must be justified by possible returns. Finally personnel must be properly trained, otherwise incompetence or lack of conviction (proper attitude and spirit) will defeat the purpose of the entire plan.

APPLICATION OF PRODUCTION CONTROL TO CLASSES OF MANUFACTURE

Basically manufacturing is divided into two major classes:

1. Manufacturing for stock, or own specifications.
2. Manufacturing to order, or customer's specifications.

Each of these classes may be divided into the following types of manufacture:

1. *Continuous manufacturing*—the conversion of materials by continuous processes, such as paper making, cloth making, grain milling, sheet-steel manufacture, chemical processes. Production control in this type of manufacture is chiefly concerned that expensive units work steadily on what is needed most, that raw material be available, that proper inventories be maintained, and that the maintenance and repair divisions allow manufacture to continue effectively and economically.

2. *Repetitive manufacture*—repeat orders at uniform intervals for many pieces of the product, usually for stock. All phases of production control, covering every detail of labor, material and equipment, are required in this type of industry.

3. *Made-to-order manufacture*—repeat orders at uniform intervals for one or a few pieces of the product, usually not for stock. These vary in size, design, and quantity, rather than in kind of product, material used, or operation. Production control is here concerned primarily with the preplanning of orders in the manufacturing schedule, working back from the required delivery dates. Emphasis should be placed on raw material stock control, to avoid surpluses which may not be disposable.

4. *Jobbing manufacture*—orders for one or a few pieces that may or may not ever be reproduced, which vary in every par-

ticular except the kind of material. Jobbing foundries, carpenter shops, and sheet-metal shops are typical of this class. Here, again, production control is concerned primarily with the order, with emphasis on the utilization of labor rather than on material or equipment.

5. *Other special classes are engineering manufacture, standing-order manufacture, warehousing and shipping*—these usually involve only some one particular phase of production control, often the preplanning phase. No matter how small a business, if it is big enough to operate, it is big enough to use and respond to production control.

This does not mean that the control must be elaborate, requiring a large staff of clerks. Production control may boil down to a simple order schedule, a proper material control, and effective use of labor. These can be handled through a simple routine by a regular member of the office or shop.

INSTALLATION

The General Plan

Every business, to be successful, must be run according to a plan. It may be an unwritten plan and not easily recognized as such. It may be carefully laid out in written form as the absolute law of the company. In some businesses it may be a very simple plan; in others a very complex one.

Somewhere between these extremes are found the majority of manufacturing companies. The general plan will usually consist of data or procedures covering (*a*) company policies on what to make, and when, and of what quality, (*b*) estimates of productive capacity, in some form, and (*c*) some knowledge of how much to make, from orders or sales quotas.

Organization

More than any other phase of a business, production control depends for its effectiveness on co-operation from all other departments. It usually has no line authority. Its very nature requires that other departments and people do work of a service nature for it or be guided by the policies and procedures established by it.

The production control department must be properly placed in the organization so that its influence will not be questioned, and it must be supervised by competent personnel with proper authority. To gain the co-operation and the respect required, the production control staff must show tact and deference to the judgment of others. Intensive application to its own job of securing compliance with approved requirements will then prove to all other functions that it is considerate of them, that it is competent to do its own job, and that it insists on being permitted to do it.

Management must define the lines of authority and responsibility and in turn must take the lead in observing them. Too often production control is a failure because of the chief executives of a company. With their years of experience in the business, they by-pass the organization channels which they themselves have created and give direct orders to manufacturing without either consulting with production control or notifying it that they have done so.

The number of functions to be supervised by the production control manager will vary according to the size of the business and the products produced. In some instances, for example, the shipping department will be supervised by sales; in others by production control. However, when management has established the policy to be followed, the first essential is the preparation of an organization chart and manual.

A typical production control organization chart is shown as Figure 42. This chart is expanded to show the essential functions. In a large company each of these may be handled by one or more individuals. In a small company it may be perfectly possible to staff the entire functional chart with two individuals.

It can be seen from the chart that much of the production control routine is handled by clerks. It is the mistaken concept of many people that production control is an expensive luxury. It is not; it is an economical essential. Analysis of the functions it performs will show that they are performed in every business, whether or not that business has good production control. The transition from bad to good is made when the people performing the functions are properly placed in the organization, given the necessary tools to properly perform their function, and then controlled.

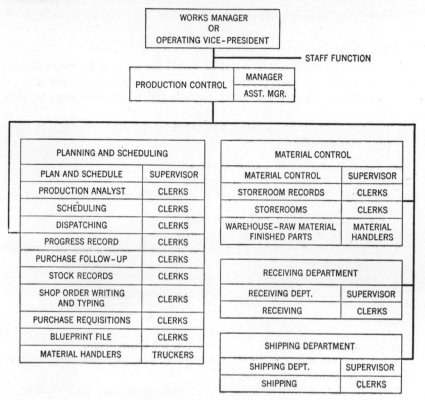

FIG. 42. Production Control Organization Chart

The organization chart should be supported by an organization manual. Outlines of the responsibilities and duties of the production control manager and his assistant follow:

Title: Production control manager
Responsible to: Works manager or operating vice-president
Responsibility: The production control manager is responsible to the works manager or operating vice-president for:

1. The general supervision and direction of:
    (a) Planning, scheduling, and dispatching.
    (b) Control of production materials and tools.

    (c) Factory order and procurement control.
    (d) Maintenance of records and files.
    (e) Material control.
    (f) Receiving and shipping departments.
2. Development and maintenance of systematic methods and procedures essential to orderly performance.

Duties:

1. To supervise and direct all activities within the range of his responsibility.
2. To eliminate methods, procedures, and records that are not essential.
3. To strive to improve established controls and recommend steps for simplification and improved effectiveness.
4. To perform the various duties designated by the works manager or operating vice-president.

Title: Assistant production control manager
Responsible to: Production control manager
Responsibility: The assistant manager is responsible to the manager for:

1. Planning, scheduling, and dispatching.
2. Factory order and procurement control.
3. Maintenance of records and files pertaining to orders and performance against orders.
4. Production analysis and follow-up.
5. Material control, receiving and shipping departments.

Duties:

1. To supervise and direct all activities in the department.
2. To see that shipping orders are handled promptly and in accordance with prescribed procedures.
3. To be familiar with shipping order requirements and their status.
4. To see that orders are scheduled for completion at the earliest possible dates consistent with shop capacity and load.
5. To see that work is dispatched in accordance with schedules, economically and with consideration of workers' skill and the adaptability of equipment.
6. To handle and expedite special cases of emergency requirement, with minimum disturbance of existing schedules.
7. To see that specified production control records are kept up-to-date and that files are maintained in orderly condition.
8. To refer all difficulties encountered with orders, schedules, or dispatching to the production control manager for decision and action.
9. To investigate cases of reported errors, and to take the necessary steps to eliminate them.
10. To perform other duties designated by the production control manager.

It should be noted that the production control department does not, in itself, provide all the factors of production control. It must be strongly supplemented by other departments. For example, the most obvious function missing from the chart is that of routing or processing as it is also called. Without it there can be no production control. Management must clearly define the place of this methods engineering function in the over-all organization picture. It must tie the various allied functions together with standard practice procedures and then administer the over-all plan to secure the desired results.

Sales Forecast

Production control for any industry must start with advance planning. In repetitive manufacture the period of advance planning can be in terms of months. In the case of jobbing manufacture, it is usually in terms of days or weeks. There is always, however, an opportunity for advance planning. Management should never take the attitude that "my company is different" in this respect.

Advance planning can best start with a sales forecast. Before the start of each new year, it should be the duty of the sales department to prepare a sales forecast, by months, showing the anticipated sales of each product manufactured or scheduled to be manufactured by the company. When this has been completed, it should be reviewed in a meeting of all chief executives, and tempered and adjusted to a realistic projection of future business.

Each key executive can materially contribute to this meeting and should be encouraged to do so. The chief engineer, for example, may advise that an engineering difficulty on the new model will release it to production two months after the date originally planned. The president of the company may advise that a large competitor was withdrawing his salesmen from a particular territory, enhancing the possibilities of sales in that area.

The completed forecast is of value not only to the production control department, but also to the sales manager for sales con-

trol, to the treasurer as a basis for a cash forecast, and to other
department heads as a similar guide and road map.

Every company should make a sales forecast, even if the
business is of the most erratic jobbing type. If the forecast is
no more than a projection of expected dollars of sales, it has
value. Few companies are required to generalize to this extent.
Analysis of old customers' orders, review of stock record cards,
a careful canvass of the knowledge in the heads of salesmen or
sales representatives will yield surprising results.

If the forecast is not perfect it still serves as a guide in charting the course. A sales forecast is not made once and forgotten;
it must be revised monthly to reflect actual experience and changing conditions. A realistic forecast is the first and most essential
step in production control.

Master Schedule

The sales forecast develops the requirements of the customer,
as far as these are known. It covers manufactured units and
service parts, where applicable. It normally shows the seasonal
buying habits of the ultimate consumer, or the distributing
agency, or both. Few industries have the facilities to attempt
to produce, each month, the items to be sold that month. Fewer
still can do so economically. It therefore becomes a basic and
very important job to convert the sales forecast into a monthly
production master schedule (Figure 43).

The master schedule is normally developed by a committee
made up of representatives of management, sales, finance, and
production. The size of the business will determine the title of
the individual who represents each of these functions on the committee. As a general rule, in all but very large companies, management should be represented by the active operating head of
the business—the president, the executive vice-president, or the
general manager. Sales should be represented by the vice-president in charge of sales or by the sales manager. Finance should
be represented by the treasurer or comptroller; and production
by the operating vice-president, the works manager, or whoever
the manufacturing head may be. In addition to these indi-

				MASTER SCHEDULE									
Item	Total Open Orders	Shipped through May	Total to Ship	June	July	Aug.	Sept.	Oct.	Nov.	Dec.	Jan.	Feb.	Mar.
0000 4/5-2/3	3,498	1,258	2,240	471	444	525	440	360					
5/5-2/3	859	303	556	279	198	79							
4/5-2/2	1,246	0	1,246	175	176	175	175	200	345				
4/2-2/3	4,044	0	4,044		182	400	500	500	500	500	600	462	400
5/2-2/5	3,088	0	3,088							1,000	1,000	800	288
1/0-0/0	500	0	500				100	200	200				
1/5-0/0	200	0	200				50	50	50	50			
1/2-0/0	720	0	720				100	200	200	200	20		
Total	14,155	1,561	12,594	925	1,000	1,179	1,365	1,510	1,295	1,750	1,620	1,262	688
0001	1,520	300	1,220	250	250	275	275	170					
0002	12,000	7,500	4,500	1,000	1,000	1,000	1,000	500					
0003	3,805	1,055	2,750	400	400	400	400	400	400	350			
0004	1,100	0	1,100						50	100	350	400	200
0005	1,000	0	1,000					25	200	500	200	75	
0006	2,000	0	2,000						25	450	800	725	
0007	10,500	6,100	4,400	600	600	600	600	800	800	400			
0008	4,150	400	3,750	200	250	500	500	850	650	700	100		
0009	2,400	100	2,300	300	500	500	500	500					

Fig. 43

viduals, the head of the production control department should also be present.

The committee correlates sales requirements, production capacities, and finance into a master schedule which satisfies the requirements of each function represented. The importance of this cannot be too strongly emphasized.

The sales department, for example, may want to sell a very

large proportion of the year's production in a very short period of time. Production may be unable to manufacture in this limited period. It may not wish to do so because of seasonal employment with its obvious inefficiencies. It may suggest that it be permitted to produce for stock on a uniform monthly schedule basis.

Finance should then make a cash forecast to determine the financial requirements of a production and warehousing plan. It may be found that additional financing is necessary, that money will have to be borrowed for three or four months of the year, that warehouse receipts may have to be used as collateral.

Sales plans may then have to be revised; the schedule may have to be revised a dozen times; a large or small financial reorganization may be necessary. When completed, the company will have not only a master schedule but also a master plan for its business for the following year. The problems encountered by the committee will be repaid a hundredfold. Increased profits can be realized by embarking on the year's production program with a sound master schedule to chart the course.

The master schedule will normally stipulate finishing dates only for the completion of an order or a group of orders. It can and may also designate finish dates in departments as a general guide. Every single order, no matter how small, should be given consideration and a definite place on the master schedule. This will avoid disturbance and loss occasioned by the interjection of unscheduled small orders into the regular flow of production.

When production is for stock, the master schedule should take into consideration the economical lot size and the profitable turnover of the entire inventory.

The design of the master schedule must be simple and flexible to accommodate requested changes and unavoidable delays. It must also be able to give effect to additional demands. It is good practice, after experience has been gained, to allow a definite percentage for expected changes in or additions to the schedule.

It is hopeless to try to schedule a complex production program without some type of easily read and quickly adjustable record. On the other hand, it is a waste of time and money to use an elaborate production board when a simple ruled form will do. No single design is best for all cases. Simplicity is the keynote for such control mechanisms.

Bill of Material

It is a primary function of production control to tell the producing departments *what* to make. Therefore, it must have a complete listing of every part that goes to make up the finished product. This listing is usually called a bill of material, and no production control plan can be effective without it. It is surprising today to find companies, both large and small, which still have no formalized bill of material.

The bill of material (Figure 44) is prepared by the engineering department from design and development drawings. It can take many forms, depending on the complexity of the end product. If the product has relatively few parts, it can be set up on a single piece of paper; if it is complicated, the bill of material may be an entire book.

Regardless of the physical form, it is essential that it show every part, every subassembly, and every assembly necessary to make a finished unit. It is common practice to have each main assembly and its detail separated from every other main assembly. This can best be described by comparing it to an outline. A bill of material for a desk, for example, would show:

```
 1 Center drawer:
 1    Drawer front.
 1       Panel.
 1       Lock.
 2       Drawer pulls.
 1    Left-side member.
 1    Right-side member.
 1    Drawer back.
 1    Bottom.
 4    Corner braces.
14    Nails.
 6    Glue blocks.
 1 Top left drawer:
      Etc.
```

Project No.	Name		Page
			1
Product No.	Name	Quantity required	
Assembly No. 24562	Name Transmitter	Req'd. per Product 1	of 3
Made by R.W.R.	Approved by H.G.S.	Date 8–4–47	

Item Number (1)	Part No. (2)	Part Name (3)	Quan. Parts per Unit (4)	P M SM or SP (5)
		Raw Material Specification		
1	22505	Electrode (Fixed)	1	M
2	34956	Body	1	M
	2¼″ Round H.H. Brass Rod		818⌗	P
3	24564	Lava Cup	1	M
	Unfinished 24564		1	P
4	24565	Plate	1	M
	16 (0.050″) H.H. Brass		18⌗	P
5	22496	Cover	1	M
	⌗26 (0.016″) Soft Sheet Brass		46.3⌗	P
6	22497	Ring	1	M
	2³⁄₁₆″ ± .010 O.D. × 2¹⁄₃₂″ ± ¹⁄₆₄″ I.D. Brass Tubing, F.C. Seamless		28⌗	P
7	22498	Diaphragm, Large	1	M
	0.003″ ⌗17 S O Duraluminum		1.75⌗	P
8	22500	Diaphragm, Small	1	M
	⌗200 (0.002″) White Pigmented Kodapak		6.25 sq ft or ²⁹⁄₃₂ sht.	

FIG. 44.   Bill of Material

It is important that each part, assembly, and subassembly, as well as the finished product, be numbered so that changes can be readily recorded and identified. In the illustration just given, a more expensive desk might be different only in the quality of the hardware used. A different type of drawer pull, therefore, would have a different number. This would change the drawer front subassembly number and also the center drawer assembly number. Proper identification by number will eliminate many manufacturing and order-filling errors. It is a definite aid to both the producer and the consumer in the ordering of spare or replacement parts.

In general a bill of material will show:

1. The product name and identification number.
2. The assembly name and identification number.
3. The subassembly name and identification number.
4. The item number.
5. The part number.
6. The part name.
7. The quantity of parts per unit.
8. The quantity of subassemblies or assemblies per unit.
9. Whether the part is purchased or made.
10. The raw material specification.
11. Who the bill was made by.
12. Who approved the bill.
13. The date.
14. The date of last change.

The Operation Sheet

The operation or routing sheet and the bill of material are the two most important tools of the production control department. Although their completion and use has already been described in Chapter 26 of this section, in connection with manufacturing methods and the processing of parts, they are here outlined again because of their basic importance. Management must insist that they be furnished to production control promptly, accurately, and in adequate detail.

The operation sheet (Figure 45) prescribes the path of travel

OPERATION & ROUTING SHEET

Form No.

Part or Assembly Name............... No............ Used on Model Nos...........

Drawing No................ Date........ Product......... Pcs. req'd............

Customer................. Prepared by............ Date........ App'v'd.....

Material............ Kind............ Form............ Rough Size........

Sheet...... of ....

Oper. No.	Operation Description	Equipment	Dept. No.	Machine Size & No. or Station No.	Patterns, Tools, Jigs, Fixtures, Gage Nos.	Lot Size	Set-up Time	Mach.-Hrs. per .. pcs.	Pcs./hr. and T.S. No.	No. of Workers Req'd.	Man-hrs./ .. pcs.	Labor Rate	Std. Cost

FIG. 45

of every part, subassembly, and assembly through the plant. It is a record of the shortest route to the most efficient equipment. For each operation, listed in its proper sequence, it shows:

1. The operation number.
2. A description of the operation.
3. The department number.
4. The machine the operation is performed on, along with its size and number.
5. The tools and gages required to perform the operation.
6. The setup time for the operation.
7. The standard time required to perform the operation, usually in hours per hundred pieces.

There is usually a separate operation sheet for each part. The heading of each sheet should show:

1. The part name.
2. The part number.
3. The drawing number.
4. The material specification.
5. The customer name (where necessary).
6. Who wrote the sheet.
7. Who approved the sheet.
8. The date.

Many companies find it desirable to show additional information on the operation sheet, in order that it may also serve the accounting department as a basis for standard costs. This is done by adding three columns to the sheet, which show the hourly rate for each operation, the standard cost, and the accumulative cost by operation.

The operation sheet is prepared for the production control department by the methods department. It is usually a repetitive form which, when once established, serves until some basic change is made in the product or in the equipment used to manufacture the product.

Wherever the preparation of operation sheets is placed in the organization, it must be performed by men with complete knowledge of the facilities and both technical and practical manufacturing experience. Each part must be processed with consideration for economy, machine utilization, material use, machine capacity, and the practicability of all methods employed.

Where possible, the processes should be worked out in conjunction with the departmental foremen. They will then understand why certain decisions were made and strive to accomplish the standard times set up for guidance and measurement. The operations must be interpreted into process layouts for tooling. They must describe in detail the exact fabricating or inspection operations, their position, and the sequence required to complete the part, subassembly, or assembled product satisfactorily.

Preferably, the time elements shown on the operation sheet are furnished by the standards department. These can and should be developed synthetically and, when properly established, can serve as a basis for incentive payment to the workers.

Where no standards department exists (and its importance is explained elsewhere in this book), times should be estimated by the methods engineer, the foremen, the superintendent, or the production manager, or by all as a group. Needless to say, the better the time standard, the better will be the production control.

The completed operation sheet serves three primary purposes:

1. It furnishes the tool division a complete summary of the tools and gages required to fabricate the part economically, within established standards.

2. It establishes time standards for use by the production control department in preplanning and scheduling the requirements.

3. It supplies the accounting division with a standard labor cost information.

Preliminary Scheduling

When the production control department receives the operation sheets, it is then and only then in a position to break down the master schedule into monthly and weekly departmental schedules.

Preliminary scheduling is a step-by-step procedure which requires consideration of many details, but it is fundamentally nothing more than the application of logical reasoning. It consists, primarily, of working backwards from the finish dates established by the master schedule, illustrated diagrammatically in Figure 46.

To use a simple illustration, the master schedule may call for completion of 100 refrigerators in June. The assembly time for the major assemblies, consisting of the case, compressor unit, freezing unit, controls, and interior accessories, may be one month. This, then, means that each of the major assemblies must be completed in May.

The major assembly, the compressor unit, is made up of two subassemblies—the motor and the compressor. If the operation sheet shows that it takes one week to assemble 100 compressor units, then both the motor and the compressor must be completed by the end of the third week in May.

The compressor may be purchased complete from an outside vendor. Production control must then see that it is received, inspected, and ready for assembly by the end of the third week in May. The electric motor which drives the compressor may, however, be made in the plant. Again it must be determined from the operation sheet whether or not this subassembly has sub-subassemblies, and, if so, the assembly time for the motor. If the motor assembly time for 100 units is three weeks, then the base, armature, field, and bells, and frame must be complete by the end of April.

This procedure is continued until each part, purchased or manufactured, is scheduled for its completion date. The individual parts are scheduled to departments and equipment in exactly the same manner.

The illustration just given has been oversimplified to indicate the general procedure which must be followed. In actual practice it is necessary to include inspection times where required, to give consideration to the maintenance of banks of material between operations, and to allow for reasonable expected failures and emergencies. It is also essential that management establish clear and detailed policies on the maintenance of work in process and on finished inventories, so that these factors, too, can be taken into consideration in the preparation of schedules.

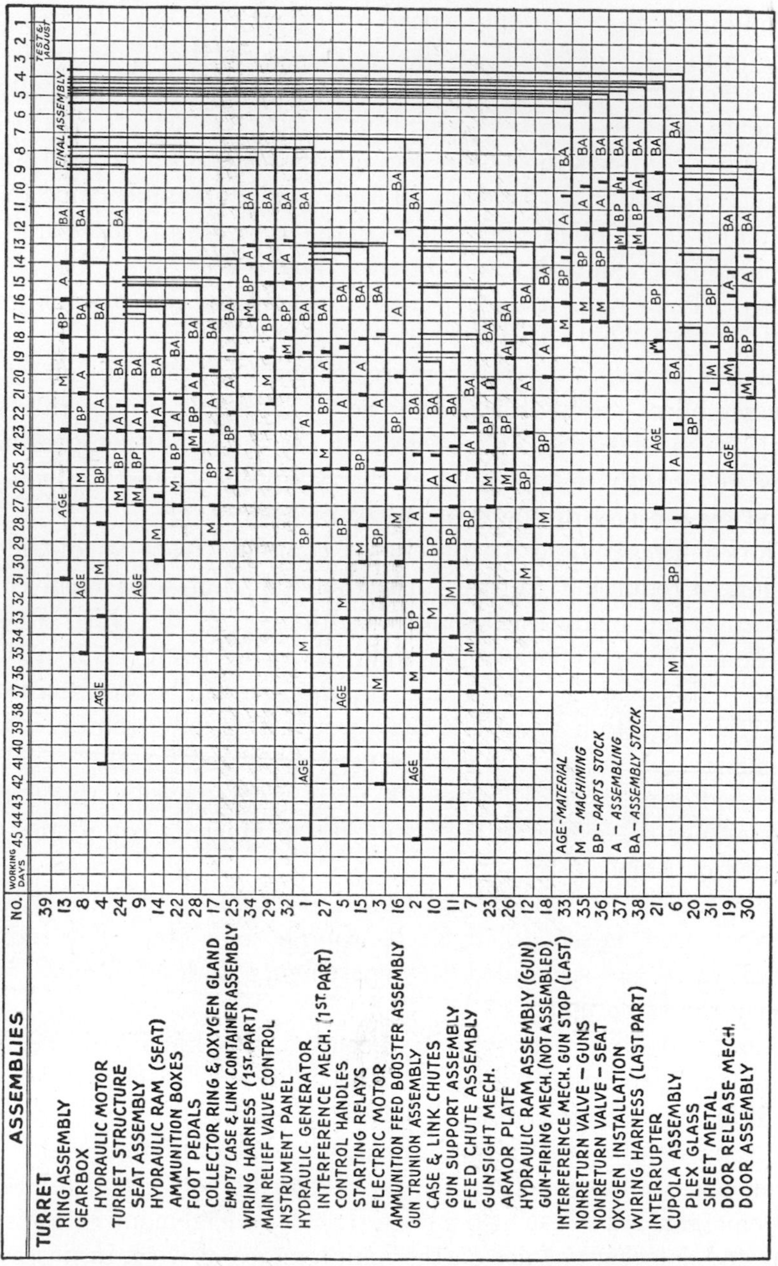

Fig. 46.   Preliminary Scheduling of Lead Time

Use of the Bill of Material

The operation sheet, as just explained, is the basis for preliminary scheduling of manufacturing operations within the plant, and for establishing the time periods in which materials are required. It can be readily seen that the operation sheet, in itself, is not adequate to complete the preliminary scheduling function. The bill of material must be used in order to accomplish the step-by-step breakdown from finished product, to major assembly, to subassemblies, and ultimately to individual parts.

On completion of preliminary scheduling, production control has available the quantity of raw materials and purchased parts. It knows the times when they must be available in order to meet the requirements of the master schedule.

Up to this point, however, no consideration has been given either to the amount of material which must be added to take care of scrap losses, or to the amount of material and parts which are available in stock and need not be purchased or manufactured.

The Stock Record Card

These cards are the basic material control record. They are most potent tools available to management for keeping inventories to a minimum. The card must be so designed that it will provide an auditable record of sales requirements, purchases, receipts, work in process, and disbursements. It must cover every item required to produce the finished product (see Figure 47). Good material control requires that the stock record file shall show, in detail, all transactions pertaining to any phase of material movement.

The size and design of the stock record card depends primarily on the type of equipment used for filing. A permanent visible file is almost an essential and may be obtained in a wide variety of styles, sizes, and prices.

The stock record file has several major divisions, depending on the methods employed to fabricate the parts. In general, the file will be divided into:

For Tub File

STOCK RECORD CARD

Part No.	Name		Location	Order Point
	Matl. Spec.			Quan. to Order

	Disbursements			
	Date	Order No.	Quan.	Balance

	Receipts			
Date	Order No.	Quan.	Cum. Total

	Procurement			
Date	Order No.	Quan.	Cum. Total

	Requirements		
Date	Order No.	Quan.	Cum. Total

Part No.	Matl. Spec.		Location	Order Point
	Name			Quan. to Order

For Visible Index File

FIG. 47

1. Raw Materials. The cards in this division cover all raw materials necessary in the manufacturing operation, such as bar stock, sheet stock, castings, and forgings.

2. Work in Process. In this division is the record of all shop orders issued to cover schedule requirements. In many instances semifinished parts are shipped to another factory for one or more operations and then returned for finishing operations. It is desirable to set up another separate record for these items, in order to remove any chance for confusion.

3. Finished Parts. This division is a record of individual parts, subassemblies, or assemblies, either purchased from vendors or processed by the company.

4. Finished Product. When completely finished units are stocked at the factory, a finished product record should be maintained. The quantity of the finished product to be maintained should be established by management, with any excess inventories deducted from requirements when the product is other than a seasonal item. When the product is warehoused throughout the country, the finished product file can be more effectively maintained by the sales department.

The stock record card can be designed to show the essential information in several different ways. The information given here has been found to be easily understood, quickly analyzed, and sufficiently detailed:

1. *Visible portion of card.* This portion of the card should serve to completely identify the item. This requires:
   (a) The part number.
   (b) The name.
   (c) The material specification.
   There is usually room on the visible portion of the card to show:
   (d) The order point.
   (e) The quantity to order.
   (f) The economic lot size.
2. *Balance of card.* This portion of the card furnishes the medium for recording all material transactions. It shows:
   (a) Requirements
       (1) Date.
       (2) Order number.
       (3) Quantity.
       (4) Cumulative total.

(b) Procurement
    (1) Date.
    (2) Order number (purchase or shop).
    (3) Quantity.
    (4) Cumulative total.
(c) Receipts
    (1) Date.
    (2) Order number (purchase or shop).
    (3) Quantity.
    (4) Cumulative total.
(d) Disbursements
    (1) Date.
    (2) Order number.
    (3) Quantity.
    (4) Balance.

Where space on the stock record card permits, it is helpful to show the source for each entry. It is also good practice to note quantity differential and standard package data on the cards, to aid in establishing maximum and minimum stocks and in requisitioning in proper multiples.

Many companies, wishing to centralize the shop clerical work, extend the use of the stock record cards to include perishable tools and supplies. When this is done, it is advisable to have someone from engineering, preferably the process engineer, establish the quantities of all new items required. Current item quantities can be based on past performance and adjusted to current usage.

Use of the Stock Record Card

When preliminary scheduling has been completed, all materials and parts required to meet the master schedule must flow across the stock record cards. The information on the stock record card has been previously described. To illustrate its use, the procedure followed will first be described. It assumes that the master schedule will exactly meet the sales requirements, that there will be no complications caused by receipt of additional orders beyond the master schedule, and that no cancellation of orders will be contemplated.

1. *Sales Requirements.* The master schedule specifies the total number of items which must be made available to meet the sales

requirements. This quantity must then be posted to the stock record card under sales requirements, in order to establish the goal to be met.

2. Procurements. This section of the card shows all previous purchase commitments, along with a cumulative total. In the case of a work in process, finished item, or finished product card, it shows all shop orders which have been previously issued for manufacture of parts, subassemblies, or assemblies.

3. Receipts. This section of the card records the quantity of purchased parts received. On cards coming under the other divisions, it shows the number of items which have been completed in the manufacturing departments on shop orders issued under the procurement section of the card.

The difference between the total quantity shown on the procurement section of the card and the total quantity shown on the receipt section of the card furnishes the balance due either from the vendor or from the manufacturing departments.

4. Disbursements. When an item is received from the vendor or completed by the manufacturing departments, it is added to the current balance on the disbursement section of the card. When a part is taken out of stock or moves from a finished stores location to an assembly operation, it is subtracted from the current balance on the disbursement section of the card.

The balance column in the disbursement section of the card, therefore, shows the current quantity on hand.

The master schedule quantity, which is posted to the stock record card, sets the goal. If it is 10,000 units, for example, and the card shows that 8,000 are due and 5,000 are on hand, there is then no necessity for ordering additional quantities from the vendor (or from the manufacturing department, as the case may be). It is important under such conditions, however, to check the actual order. This will assure that receipt, or completion, will meet the requirements set by the preliminary schedule. This check can readily be made, since the stock record card provides for posting of the order number in every case. Delivery or completion dates can be determined by reference to this order.

The master schedule in the previous illustration may call for 50,000 units. In this case, with 8,000 due and 5,000 on hand, it can be seen that 37,000 are required to meet the master schedule.

This 37,000 must then be compared with the monthly schedule dates shown on the preliminary schedule. If the preliminary schedule shows 10,000 scheduled for January, 10,000 for February, 10,000 for March, and 10,000 for April, it can be seen that the 13,000 due or on hand will last only through January and a short time into February. At least 7,000 should be delivered or made by the first of February.

5. Sales Requirements. In addition to the quantities obtained from the master schedule, this section of the stock record card will also record needs arising from sales orders in excess of the master schedule requirements.

This may be handled by having sales orders which exceed the master schedule posted directly when received within a specified time period within the month, or by having the sales department hold such orders throughout the month and give consideration to them in the revised master schedule.

The master schedule should be revised monthly in either case. The method followed should be determined by the length of time normally allowed for delivery and by the company policy on size of finished inventory to be carried.

The sales requirements column is also used to record cancellation adjustments which may be encountered.

If the business under consideration is of a job shop nature, it may be found impractical to work closely to a master schedule. In this case requirements only will be posted from sales orders, with no master scheduling information ever shown on the stock record card. In a jobbing operation it may also be found desirable to stock many parts on a maximum–minimum basis, to cover service and sales requirements. In some instances, as with electrical equipment, only a portion of the product is standard. Such items can best be handled on a maximum–minimum basis, whereas nonstandard parts are handled on a sales order basis.

Save for the exceptions in the sales requirements column, the stock record card usage presents no major variations from the procedure used for illustrative purposes.

6. Handling of Service Parts. Where service parts requirements are large in relation to the normal parts requirements, it may be necessary to separate these records, or even to have them maintained by the service department. This procedure will make possible an easier analysis of past requirements, and will supply a basis for future planning of service parts production. It will also eliminate confusion which might result if they were carried in the regular stock records.

If this is done, a high degree of co-ordination must obtain between the service and production control departments, in order to assure the necessary quantities of parts for both the service and manufacturing requirements.

Establishing Gross Requirements

When all sales requirement information is passed across the stock record cards, production control knows the status of stocks on hand or on order. It is informed as to the quantities of parts which must be purchased or produced to meet master schedule requirements. It must then add to the net figures a percentage allowance, which will take care of the normal scrap to be expected.

These percentages are normally based on experience, and variations from the percentages allowed are to be expected. It is important that accurate scrap records be maintained and made available to production control, in order that it may adjust its records to reflect actual experience. Large quantities of obsolete materials and parts can accumulate quickly if attention is not given to this factor.

The Manufacturing Schedule

The manufacturing schedule is the first realistic schedule to be developed insofar as the manufacturing departments are concerned. It is, in effect, the same as the preliminary schedule with the stock on hand deducted, plus a slight increase to take care of normal scrap. To go only this far, however, is not to assure efficient operation. It is necessary to refine the schedule in order to give effect to economical lot quantities and to smooth out the production rate over the available time.

Much has been written about economical lot quantities. Although most authorities agree as to the factors which should be considered, few agree as to either the weighting of the factors or the method of using them. The factors generally considered in establishing economic lots are:

1. The cost of one piece.
2. The setup cost.
3. The number of pieces required per year.
4. The cost of carrying inventory.

The latter factor requires consideration of many other factors and is in itself quite complicated. It is important to point out, however, that a conservative estimate of the cost of carrying inventory is 15 per cent of its value per year. This should be given due weight.

Few companies give effect to economical lot quantities, because the formulas used to determine them are, in themselves, so formidable as to be a strong deterrent to their use. The work involved in going through the formalized procedure does not, in many cases, justify the time and cost required. It is here that rule-of-thumb procedures, coupled with good common sense, contribute greatly to reduced manufacturing costs.

Often products and parts do not change materially during the year, or from year to year. In this case production control, assisted by the manufacturing and cost departments, should review the parts to be manufactured and empirically determine the economical lot sizes. It is not necessary or desirable to make the determination for all parts. As a general guide it can be stated that economical lot sizes should be determined only where:

1. The setup time is long in relation to the production time per piece, or
2. The time required to produce the entire year's requirements is quite short, or
3. The cost per unit is high, or
4. The storage space required per unit is large in relation to its value, or
5. The production quantity is very high and continuous.

After consideration has been given to the economical lot sizes, and to the desirability of producing at a uniform rate throughout the year, the manufacturing schedule can be established on a monthly basis.

Purchasing

When the production control department has completed the manufacturing schedule, it is then in a position to requisition the raw material and purchased parts requirements from the purchasing department. When a company has become experienced in the operation of a complete production control plan, it is usually advisable for production control to give purchasing advance material and parts requirements before going through all of the detailed steps previously outlined. This is essential in the case of some materials which require months to procure. Then, when the manufacturing schedule has been completed, the quantities ordered can be accurately revised and delivery dates clearly and positively specified.

Before finally determining the manufacturing schedule, the production control department establishes economical lot quantities in order to assure most economical manufacture. Similarly, it is important that production control give thorough consideration to economical ordering quantities. The purchasing department can then buy economically, consistent with the maintenance of low material and parts inventories.

It should be the responsibility of the purchasing department to furnish the production control department with lot differential quantity information and with data on standard packaged items and quantities. This will assist production control in establishing "ordering quantities" which permit the best possible prices. It will also serve to keep to a minimum the need for purchasing excess quantities, merely because the vendor does not have standard packages of the size requisitioned.

The factors to be considered in establishing economical ordering quantities are almost identical with those noted in establishing economical lot quantities. It is not necessary to use an overly formalized system, nor to make the determination for all parts. As a general rule, economical ordering quantities should be determined for those raw materials and purchased parts where:

1. The time required to use the entire year's requirement of the part is quite short, or
2. The cost per unit is high, or
3. The storage space required per unit is large in relation to its value, or
4. The quantity is very large.

In making the determination it is desirable that the production control, purchasing, and cost departments be represented. It is not enough to make the decision once and then to use the established figure year after year. The decision will be strongly influenced by the projected yearly requirements. The ordering quantities should be reviewed at least yearly, and oftener if there is a major change in the projected volume requirements, either up or down.

Procurement Forms

The physical form used by the production control department to advise the purchasing department of requirements is the purchase requisition (Figure 48). It is important that this form allow complete and accurate descriptions of the items requested, along with specific delivery dates. It is a common error for production control to furnish abbreviated and inaccurate descriptions and to expect purchasing to interpret these into correct items. It is equally undesirable for production control to call for indefinite generalized delivery dates such as, "first quarter," or "June."

The method of transmitting the information from the production control to the purchasing department depends on the type of manufacture and the type of purchased product. It has been found that for jobbing manufacture, or for similar types where the products vary with each sales order, it is advantageous to use an individual purchase requisition for each item. These should be numbered serially for identification purposes.

Where manufacturing is for stock, or to the company's own specifications, considerable clerical work can be saved by using a copy of the bill of material. This may be widened and can then also be used as a work paper in determining the manufac-

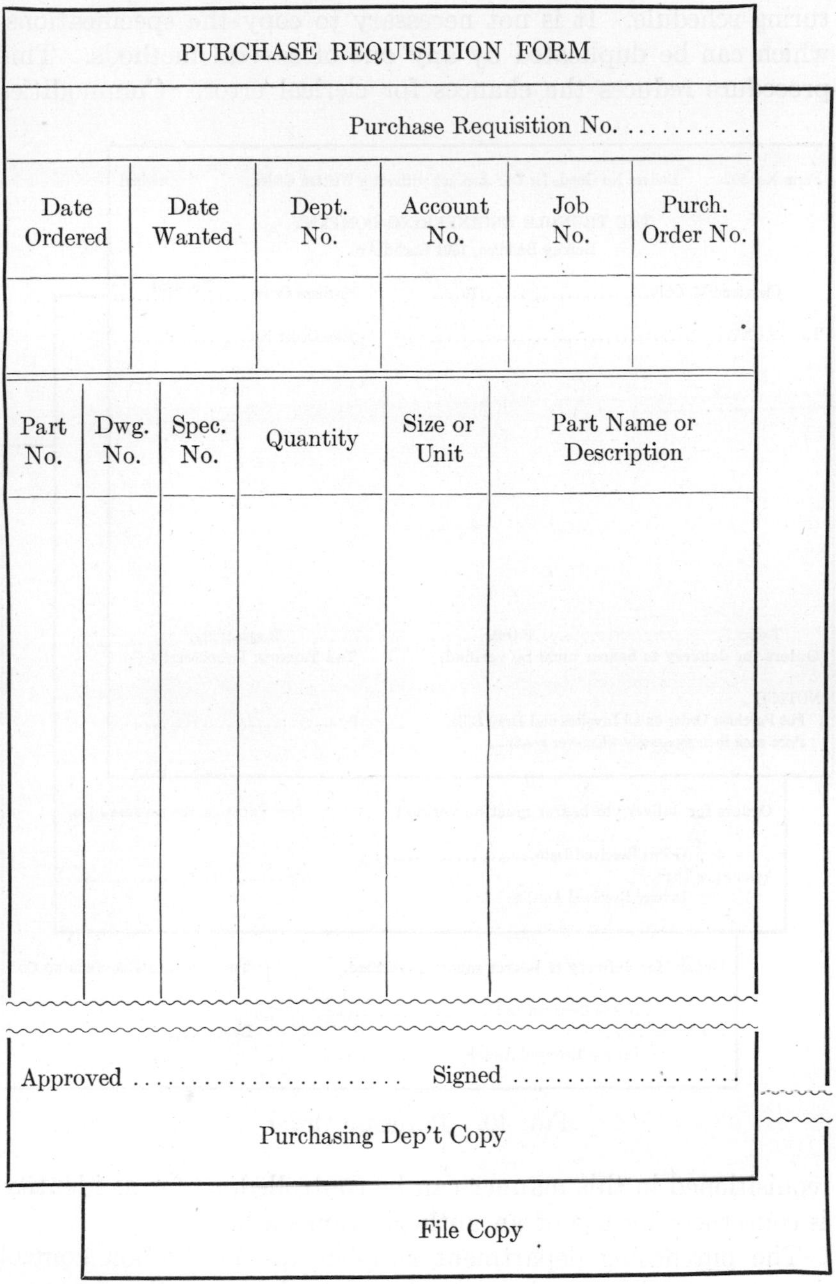

PURCHASE REQUISITION FORM

Purchase Requisition No. . . . .

Date Ordered	Date Wanted	Dept. No.	Account No.	Job No.	Purch. Order No.

Part No.	Dwg. No.	Spec. No.	Quantity	Size or Unit	Part Name or Description

Approved . . . .   Signed . . . .

Purchasing Dep't Copy

File Copy

Fig. 48

turing schedule. It is not necessary to copy the specifications, which can be duplicated by any one of several methods. This procedure reduces the chances for clerical error. Commodities

Form No. 502   Deliver No Goods for Our Account without a Written Order   Original

THE TRUNDLE ENGINEERING COMPANY
Bulkley Building, 1501 Euchd Ave.

Cleveland 15, Ohio......................19....   Purchase Order .... No. 4951 ....

To...   Sales Order No................

Terms..........................F.O.B........   Respectfully,
Orders for delivery to bearer must be verified.   THE TRUNDLE ENGINEERING CO.

NOTICE
Put Purchase Order on all Invoices and Dray Bills.   By...........................
Price each item separately whenever possible.

Orders for delivery to bearer must be verified.   THE TRUNDLE ENGINEERING CO.

Goods Received Date...................
Accounting Dept.   By...........................
Invoice Received Amt. $................

Orders for delivery to bearer must be verified.   THE TRUNDLE ENGINEERING CO.

Goods Received Date....................
Purchasing Dept.   By...........................
Invoice Received Amt. $.................

FIG. 49. Purchase Order

requisitioned in this manner can be controlled, as far as identity is concerned, by use of an authorization number.

The purchasing department supplies the production control department with one important and basic form, the purchase order (Figure 49). The number of copies required by production control varies with the particular business, but a minimum of two is recommended.

One is used to verify the quantity ordered, and normally changes the information on the stock record card from a pencil notation to an ink figure. This copy is also used by production control for follow-up purposes. The other copy is used by the receiving department as identification of and authorization to receive material.

Production control follow-up should only be internal. The purchasing department should be the sole contact with the supplier on delivery of raw materials, semifinished and finished parts, and supplies. This rule will avoid duplication of effort and insure a smoother flow of commodities.

Close co-operation among the production control department, the purchasing department, and the engineering department is essential to maximum factory output and to the maintenance of low economical inventories.

Receiving of Raw Materials and Parts

Among the production control department functions shown on the organization chart is included that of the receiving department. Certain types of industries do not follow this practice for very logical reasons. The following discussion will, therefore, treat the subject as though receiving and production control were distinct and separate departments.

Good receiving procedures are extremely important to good production and material control. Few companies fail to inform the accounts payable department of the receipt of material, in order that the vendors may be promptly paid; but many overlook the important tie-in with production control. It would be facetious to say that the payment of the vendor is an incidental function, but too much emphasis cannot be put on the urgent necessity for giving production control prompt, complete, and accurate information in this matter.

The basic receiving department informative form is the receiving report (Figure 50). It is this form which furnishes a complete detailed record of what is received and its condi-

RECEIVING NOTICE FORM

Shipper..

Shipping Point......................................

Carrier...

　　　　　　　　　　Prepaid ....　　Weight

Charges $................　Collect ....　　..............

Way Bill No...

Purch. Order No.....................................

Quan.	Container	Contents
	Barrels	
	Boxes	
	Cartons	
	Bundles	
	Crates	
	Kegs	
	Sacks	
	Loose	

Rec'd by......................... Date............

PLATFORM RECEIPT

To Accounting Dept.

To Production Control Dept.

To Other Depts. as Required

Fig. 50

tion and authorizes the accounting department to pay for such material.

The receiving report carries the same information as the purchase order and is often duplicated from it. Duplicating methods which permit blocking out of the price information can be used if desired. Columns may be added for recording quantities received, inspection results, stores receipt, and cost information.

The receiving report is made up in several copies, depending on the requirements of the particular company under consideration. The use of the copies and their minimum desirable distribution would be:

1. *Purchasing.* To notify purchasing that the material has been received in the plant and that further expediting, if previously initiated, is no longer required. This serves to clear the purchasing department's open order records.

2. *Production control.* To notify production control of the receipt of the material and to show that internal follow-up, if previously initiated, is no longer required. The received quantities are posted to the stock record cards, but only as a preliminary pencil posting.

3. *Inspection.* To notify inspection that the material is in and requires their service. They usually receive two copies, one to serve as a traveler to identify the material. The traveler copy follows the material through inspection and into stores. It is then sent to the production control department for notification of the good pieces, approved by inspection, and placed in stores. At this time production control makes its formal stock card entry in ink and is ready to prepare and issue manufacturing orders to the shop.

Purchasing Department

Organization

To attain an effective co-ordination of the purchasing department with production control and other departments of a company requires a systematic organization of the purchasing function itself.

Procurement consists of several important steps:

1. Selection of proper material sources.
2. Actual buying of materials and services.
3. Follow-up of deliveries, prices, and so on.
4. Record keeping.

If the purchasing department is very small and occupies a subordinate place in the organization plan, these separate steps frequently cannot be specialized and assigned to separate individuals. On the other hand, if the purchasing activities involve a complex and large operation, the department staff may consist of a great many people, having specialized functions; namely:

Purchasing agent—Supervision, selection of vendors, major contract commitments, etc.
Buyers—Order placement for classes of commodities.
Expediters—Follow-up on deliveries.
Clerks—Price record keeping, invoice checking, filing, etc.

Whether large or small, the activities of a purchasing department should be carefully defined and properly related to the other functions of the company (see Figures 4, 9, 10, and 42).

Basic Policies

There are several basic policies in the procurement of materials that are important to the effective operation of a purchasing department. They may be stated briefly as follows:

1. Purchases are to be made only from requisitions issued by specifically authorized individuals (see Figures 48 and 49).

2. All purchases must require adherence to specifications determined by those departments officially authorized to issue them (see Figure 44).

3. Whenever possible purchase orders are to be placed as a result of competitive bidding.

4. More than one source of supply should be available for the placement of purchase orders.

5. No payment for goods ordered should be authorized without proof and record of its actual receipt and quality (see Figure 50).

Record

The efficient operation of a purchasing department requires certain basic records for control. The more common ones are:

1. Purchase order files—These files contain copies of all purchase orders issued, one file by vendor's name and the other file by purchase order serial number. Frequently, these files are subdivided into open orders and closed orders (see Figure 49).

2. Price record file—This is usually a card record, showing the name of the commodity, the specification number if any, the vendors furnishing same, the orders that were placed, and the prices quoted or paid.

3. Specification file—This may be a part of the price record card. If not, it can take the form of a loose-leaf book, each sheet carrying the commodity name, the specification serial number, and the engineering or other details comprising the specification (see Figure 44).

4. Catalog file—This record consists of vendor's catalogs, bulletins, and the like, filed by vendor's name and card-indexed by commodity.

5. Correspondence files—Letters and communications to and from vendors and others.

Other records for the follow-up of purchases and similar data are sometimes maintained in the purchasing department. Their variety and scope will depend on the range of activity and the complexity of the company operation. The afore-mentioned records, however, if adequately designed and manualized, will usually be adequate for all requirements.

Purchased materials and parts may suffer partial or complete rejection by inspection after receipt. If the quantity is large, it should be the inspection department's responsibility to contact the production control department immediately, and to learn whether or not there is an urgent need for the material.

If so, a qualified inspection representative, together with production control and manufacturing representatives, should promptly analyze the rejected items for possibilities of rework and salvage, and initiate the steps for accomplishing it.

Some rejected items must be replaced. This is done through the medium of an invoice and replacement order. Copies of this order, which carries the same basic information as the purchase order, are sent to the purchasing department as a notification of rejections, to the accounts payable department for holding or adjusting payment, to the shipping department (in duplicate) to authorize return shipment of the item, and to serve as a packing slip, and to the production control department as a notification that reordering has been accomplished.

In those cases where there is an urgent need for the items and where rework and salvage are decided upon, a somewhat different form is used. It must carry adequate information for purchasing use in establishing an equitable price adjustment. Copies of this form may be used for recording actual rework and salvage cost information, if desired. The distribution follows that of the invoice and replacement order.

Instructions to the Manufacturing and Assembling Departments

The production control department, having prepared the manufacturing schedule and knowing the status of all materials, is ready to instruct the manufacturing departments to start producing. The time factor seldom permits the release of monthly schedules, although in some industries with few but standardized products this is possible.

It should be kept in mind that the manufacturing schedule sets the standard to be used for control. If this standard is on a monthly basis, then a large part of the month must elapse before actual production can be compared with standard, or variations controlled. For this reason manufacturing instructions are most effective when on a daily or weekly basis. It is the usual practice to use weekly schedules.

There is wide variation in the forms and procedures commonly used to issue manufacturing instructions. The two basic methods will be described, since most variations lie between the two.

1. *Repetitive or Stock Manufacturing.* Where the product is to the company's own specification, well standardized, and does not change materially over an extended period of time, manufacturing and assembly instructions are issued on a weekly schedule (Figure 51). Such a schedule is made for each department and usually shows:

(a) The part number.

WEEKLY PRODUCTION SCHEDULE

Department ....   For Week of .... 19......

Part Num- ber	Order Num- ber	Part Name & Description	Quantity Sched- uled	Sunday	Monday	Tuesday	Wednes- day	Thurs- day	Friday	Satur- day	Total

Fig. 51

(*b*) The order number.

(*c*) The part name and description.

(*d*) The total quantity scheduled for the week.

(*e*) The schedule for each day of the week.

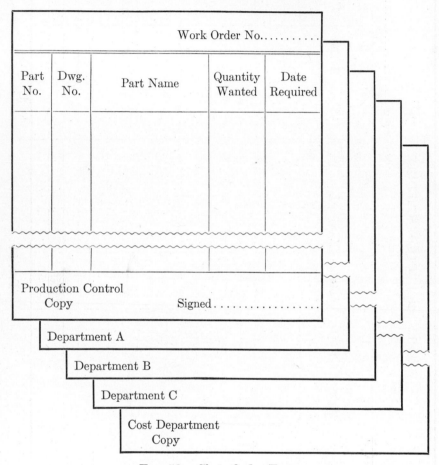

Fig. 52.   Shop Order Form

The weekly schedule is released early enough to give the departmental supervisor a day or two to study it, plan his work, and determine his labor requirements and assignments.

2. *Jobbing Manufacturing.* Where production is of the jobbing type, manufacturing and assembly instructions are usually issued by means of a shop order (Figure 52). The shop order is designed to show:

(*a*) The customer's name.

(b) The sequence date.

(c) The part name and number.

(d) The department and machine or machine group.

(e) The operation number and description.

(f) The material required.

(g) The time standard information.

(h) Space designed to be used as a time record.

(i) A space for remarks and special instructions.

When the shop order form is used, it is possible to design it so that it can be used as a master duplicating medium from which to run off the raw material release, progress record, and cost record forms.

The main difference between the two methods is that the weekly schedule is a separate item for each department, whereas the shop order goes from department to department. For ease of control, it is considered good practice to project the shop orders into departmental schedules, where this type of scheduling is used.

The production control department should never release any manufacturing instructions until the required material is available for use, or until completely satisfactory assurance that it will be available when required has been received.

It is the responsibility of production control to see that the manufacturing departments have available blueprints, operation sheets, and material releases. Many companies with standard products allow manufacturing departments to maintain blueprint and operation sheet files within the department. Except in unusual cases, it has been found more satisfactory to have these files maintained by production control and released with the manufacturing order. This greatly simplifies the job of keeping them up-to-date and reduces the possibility that manufacturing departments will use obsolete information.

An important function of the production control department is to "machine-load" equipment. The master schedule is a rough form of machine loading, since it must be realistic. However, conditions beyond management control can easily create bottlenecks, and careful machine loading should be done concurrently with preparation of the weekly schedule. In the case of shop orders, machine loads should be developed while these are being projected into the weekly schedules to be used for control purposes.

Accurate machine loading has not, in the past, received adequate consideration. The primary deterrent has been the absence of time standards for the various operations. It is certain that all companies will come to realize the importance of these essential tools and that no company will attempt to operate a production control plan without them.

Machine loading consists of determining the available time on every piece of operating equipment, whether it be a machine or an assembly working unit, and then adding up the time required for each part which must be made on it. By so doing, no equipment will be assigned more work than it is capable of doing in the time allowed, and sufficient time can be left open on the various pieces of equipment for emergency orders or failures.

Machine loading may show the desirability of changing the operation to another less efficient piece of equipment. Production control and methods and manufacturing can then weigh this loss in efficiency against the added expense of working overtime or extra shifts, thus meeting the schedule in the most economical manner.

When scheduling, production control should compare the actual accomplishment of the shop with the standard times being used. In those companies having wage payment plans which are adapted to daily and weekly measurements of performance, this is a relatively simple job. In those which have no time standards or performance measurements, judgment must be based on past experience. If manufacturing performance consistently shows activity at an 80 per cent level, for example, it would be very foolish for production control to schedule based on an activity level of 100 per cent.

When the weekly schedules or shop orders are released to manufacturing departments, production control also releases the materials required by these schedules. This is done with a material release form, usually in duplicate, which authorizes the storeroom to release the material and serves to identify the material as it progresses.

The duplicate copy is returned to production control as notification that the material has been taken out of stores. It is then posted to the stock record card as a disbursement. In some cases it is advisable to have the storerooms maintain bin cards for each item. When the storeroom disburses material, these not only indicate the quantity disbursed, but also the amount remaining in stock. This serves as a check on the stock record cards.

A good method for releasing materials to assembly departments uses a bill of material covering that particular assembly. In cases where the master bill of material can be duplicated, this method saves considerable clerical work.

In many instances the company has a cost plan which carries both raw material and process accounts. When this is the practice, the raw material release form can be routed from production control to the cost department for the accumulating of monthly transfers from the raw material account to the work in process account.

Dispatching the Work

The production control department does not release manufacturing instructions directly to the manufacturing departments, except in the case of a very small operation. These are released to dispatchers located in the manufacturing departments. Usually there is one dispatcher for each department, although department size and physical location may make it possible for a dispatcher to handle more than one.

The dispatcher is a member of the production control department, and it is his function to activate and control the manufacturing activities. Since he must co-operate completely with the manufacturing foremen, he and his dispatch racks are located as close to the foremen as possible. The dispatcher must maintain work assignments within schedule requirements and maintain records of all time used and work accomplished. It is, therefore, essential that he be furnished an adequate work space and facilities.

The dispatcher will receive the weekly schedules or shop orders, operation sheets, blueprints and material releases several days before the beginning of the work week. If shop time cards are preprinted, these will also be furnished him. If not, he will prepare them. Then, in co-operation with the foreman, the dispatcher will preplan the daily sequence of jobs to each machine and designate the worker who is to perform the operation. The dispatcher must know the schedule requirements thoroughly.

He is not expected to know the various skills of the departmental personnel, or the technical aspects of the various operations, although he will develop considerable familiarity with both. For these he is dependent on the foreman, as the foreman is dependent on him. Therefore, a mutual understanding and respect should be encouraged and, if necessary, insisted on.

The dispatch rack is the physical means employed for the preassignment of work. It has a pocket for each machine, in which are placed notes of all the jobs ahead for that machine and a pocket for the job actually being run. Attached to each work station is a pocket to hold the worker's time card and instructions.

Before the beginning of each shift the dispatcher will place all information in the pocket on the machine. This will save confusion around the dispatch rack at the beginning of the shift. The workers merely punch their job time cards in and start work.

It is essential that production control receive an accurate count of good pieces produced. In many companies this count is received from the inspection department. This is good practice and is usually justified where quality requirements make in-process inspection desirable.

Where inspection count is not warranted, a count can be obtained from the material move men or from the dispatcher himself. In cases involving many operations on the same part, the worker's count is accepted with periodic checks. The amounts reported by preceding operators will serve as a check on subsequent operators.

Handling Scrap

When raw material, semifinished or finished parts, are scrapped and must be replaced, this should be done only by means of a material requisition because of the importance of accounting for the usage of all material. This allows production control to operate more effectively, and accounting records will be more accurate. In a jobbing type of operation, when rejections exceed the normal scrap allowance, it is important that prompt decision be made as to whether or not to replace the lost items. Otherwise machine setups are torn down and have to be set up all over again. Production control should receive very close co-operation from inspection in this respect. It is best to obtain such decisions by telephone or in person and to let the paper work follow later.

In more standardized types of operation, the material requisition goes to the production control office, which ascertains its affect on the allocation of materials and parts for the lot in question, or for other units using the same raw materials or finished parts.

In either case the requisitions should be approved by the production control supervisor, or by his authorized assistant, and then be put across the stock record card as a pencil notation. When material is issued against them, an ink entry to the stock record card will be made.

Salvage

When a company has an established salvage procedure, it should be tied in very closely with production control, as any salvage operation will, as a rule, interfere with schedules.

Control

Planning, routing, and scheduling form the basis for control. Dispatching is the first step in control. Failure to complete any operation on time immediately warns the dispatcher that corrective steps are necessary. Where failures are nominal, the dispatcher and the foreman co-operate to bring conditions back to a scheduled normal. Where variations are large, the production control supervisor, alone or with one of the manufacturing executives in major cases, is called on to act. Actions may range from notification to the sales department that one particular order will

be several days late to complete revision of the manufacturing
schedule.

The dispatcher should make a daily report to production control, showing:

1. The jobs run that day.
2. The number of pieces reported made.
3. The number of rejects.
4. The number of pieces salvaged.

This will permit production control to make daily postings to the
weekly schedules and to determine trends which may cause future trouble if not corrected.

Inventory

In order to start out with accurate stock record cards, it is important that a complete and accurate inventory be taken before
initiating any production control plan. This inventory should
cover open purchase orders, work in process, open customers' orders, and all other factors affecting the production control plan.

Most companies today have acceptable techniques for taking
inventory, and no attempt will be made here to explain how it
should be done. It is to be noted, however, that the initiation of
a production or material control plan is a large undertaking. All
steps preliminary to taking the inventory should be carefully
planned. All records requiring posting from inventory information should be complete and ready to receive the information.
Last but extremely important, sufficient personnel to complete
all steps promptly should be trained and available. Failure in
this respect has often required that the job be done over again
at great and unnecessary expense.

CHAPTER 30

MATERIAL AND INVENTORY CONTROL

•

Purpose

There are many aspects of the subject of inventories: financial, quantitative, and merchandising; but all of them are related to one fundamental premise—the objective of any business enterprise is to make a profit. One of the many handmaidens to this queen of objectives is inventory, the purpose and control of which are discussed in this chapter. Technical aspects were covered in Chapter 29 of this section.

Development of Inventory Concepts

The origin of inventory preceded that of industry itself and dates back into antiquity. In the earliest age of barter the primitive trader or craftsman had to first harvest or fashion a stock of products before he could proceed to the marketplace to trade his goods.

As trading crept out of the handicraft and barter stage and into the industrial and merchandising age, business commenced to deal in surpluses of goods. This transformed inventory into the problem child of business.

Inventories originate in many ways:

1. *By premeditated plan,* to satisfy a proposed merchandising program, the requirements of which are greater than the normal producing capacity.

311

2. *By carelessness,* as a result of which too much is made through outright failure to control manufacturing facilities.

3. *By accident,* when conditions beyond management's control, such as technological advance, obsolete a product before the industry can readjust itself to the new conditions.

4. *By mistakes,* as when blunders in design or production make a product unsalable for reasons of undesirability or faulty workmanship.

As products become obsolete and unsalable, many concerns adopt the expedient of leaving them in the inventory rather than perform the painful operation of writing them off as so much scrap or junk. Others, in a desire to keep the plant operating and employees on the payroll, pile up inventory beyond any reasonable demand. "It's like money in the bank," they say, "and only costs us 6 per cent."

Review of Basic Principles

Many executives can tell the exact cost of selling a unit of product, of hiring and firing a man, of advertising in relation to each sale, and yet find it difficult to put down in black and white how much they are spending to keep a stock of goods on hand.

In some cases only two or three of the elements are taken into consideration, in spite of the fact that each is a definite factor in arriving at the total of inventory carrying costs. It has been found that total carrying costs vary from 12 to 35 per cent of the inventory value. Many are too high; an even greater number are too low.

Following are three estimates of the cost of carrying inventories, given by three concerns in reply to a questionnaire. Each is a long long way from the popular 6 per cent that is so often and so confidently referred to.

Cost of carrying inventory varies with the industry. For perfectly good reasons, there may be considerable differences even among companies in the same industry. However, in summarizing the results of this study, it was found that these costs totaled to 15 per cent for an average group of manufacturers. This figure represents a safe minimum for the cost of carrying inventory.

COSTS OF CARRYING INVENTORIES

Per Cent per Annum

	Concern A	Concern B	Concern C
Interest on capital invested	6.00	6.00	6.00
Taxes	2.50	0.55	2.00
Insurance	0.50	0.20	(Included above)
Housing	0.50	1.24	0.70
Keeping housing in repair	0.25	(Included above)	
Looking after inventory:			
Handling	2.00	3.16	(Included below)
Taking inventory	0.25	1.03	(Included below)
Clerical costs	1.00	2.58	4.60
Deterioration, spoilage	3.00		
Repairs	1.00		
Obsolescence	5.00	3.43	4.00
Total	22.00	18.19	17.30

The next basic principle states that inventory control is the foundation for operating control of any typical business. By that is meant not merely control of inventory amount, but control of the quantitative factors with which inventory is concerned. These are material procurement; production schedules; shipping schedules; the physical balances of raw, processed, and finished inventory; and the physical facilities for handling the inventory.

The final basic principle relates to the fiscal control of inventory. This is concerned with money or values, which become the basis for determining the profitable or nonprofitable operation of the company. The amount of capital required is established on this basis, as is the cash value and liquidity of the inventory itself.

CURRENT TRENDS

Without adequate control it is only too easy for materials to be transformed into more of one kind of finished parts than is actually required by the market demand and less of another. Customers are lost, orders are lost, and profits "gone with the wind."

It will thus be seen that the control of inventories is fundamental, not only to a steady progress of the production program,
but also to the satisfactory attainment of a sales plan. Inventory control, therefore, must be all-inclusive. It must embrace
not only raw material, work in process, and stores, but also finished goods in the plant and on consignment.

The ideal inventory condition would be one wherein the turnover of raw materials matched the time needed to procure them,
wherein finished parts were assembled into salable finished stock
which moved off the stockroom shelves within the period required to process more.

It has been often said that an enterprise, including its facilities
and organization, is merely the extended shadow of the man or
men at its head. By the same token, the efficiency of a plant
and of its management is frequently revealed by the size and condition of its inventories. There is the constant tug of war between the sales and manufacturing departments—both of whom
believe that their programs can only be attained with large reserves of finished stocks and raw materials—and the financial
department, which views money tied up in inventories as a sterile
sequestration of cash and unrealized profits that should be in the
company's surplus.

Modern recording practices in inventory control lean towards
visibility, such as perpetual inventory systems of the loose-leaf or
visible card types. In these the item balances are continuously
checked, and a book balance is drawn off at the close of each
accounting period. This is opposed to the traditional method of
a detailed physical count at stated periods to determine the inventory position of the company.

However, this modern streamlined practice is applicable only
where raw and finished inventories are very large in comparison
with process inventories. In industries where work in process
constitutes the bulk of the inventory, there is probably no better
method of control than the time-honored one of inventory taking
at the close of each fiscal period.

"Perpetual inventory" is a phrase that dates back many years,
but unfortunately it is a condition too infrequently found.

In spite of the preachments of executives and consultants in the accounting phases of business, the custody of inventory still remains in an embryonic stage. It is still not unusual to enter a plant and find valuable materials and products left unguarded, subject to theft or destruction.

It is bromidic to say that inventory represents cash (sometimes in a negotiable form). Yet management still does not fully realize that inventory should have the same safeguards as the cash and bank account of the company.

Owing to changes in costs, the trend in accounting is toward relating the profit and loss statements to inventory through standard costing. To measure the cost variances in operation, data on which is necessary to effective management control, there is also a definite trend towards cost control as an *operating* function, rather than as a financial function. Standard costs of labor and material and factory overhead only are carried into the inventory, in order to tie it directly to the profit and loss position of the company.

The first development resolves itself into measuring labor, material, and expense at the point of operation. This bases the variances on activity rather than on units of product.

Another development advocates the charge-off of all overhead as a current monthly expense on the profit and loss statement, relieving inventory of any overhead whatsoever.

This method treats factory overhead in the same manner as selling and administrative overhead, and finds most favor in the processing and similar industries. Federal income tax requirements, however, restrict the possible application of this practice to very limited fields. There are other practical objections, concerned with the interior operation of a business, which make the method unacceptable to most plants.

Because inventory control has achieved a recognized status in business, its purpose and usefulness are not challenged so frequently as they used to be. Nevertheless, the question is occasionally asked by executives, "What *is* the purpose of inventory control?"

Fundamentally, its financial purpose is to enable management to determine its cost of sales, so that the profit or loss on sales can be determined. The only type of business where inventory control is not needed is that which has no inventory, such as a professional service or brokerage operation.   Profit and loss statements *can* be produced by the ratio method, that is, by proportioning the costs in terms of the sales dollar.   This method does not, however, provide for a proof of the costing used, nor does it expose the actual application of working capital in the balance sheet items.

Accountants have argued at length over the relative merits of the two methods.   One group holds that, unless standard costing of sales is worked through the cost of production into inventory, and out again, the profit and loss statement is an interesting statistical exercise without fiscal significance.   The other group claims the same accuracy of result by the standard cost ratio method, if the basic standards for labor, material, and overhead have been precisely and correctly determined, and the variances have been accurately measured.

The argument is somewhat abstract, because, in the final accounting, the United States Treasury Department requires annual profit and loss determinations by the inventory method.   Therefore, for managerial control, any reasonably accurate interim statement is satisfactory.   As long as the apparent variance in the inventory balance is small (2 per cent or less), the ratio method is sufficiently accurate for control in the average enterprise.

OPERATING ASPECTS

The operating aspects of inventory control involve four basic functions, namely:

1. The material procurement relationship.
2. The application of inventory control to process methods.
3. The physical mechanism for inventory control.
4. The organization for inventory control.

In the function of *material procurement,* the relationship required is that the right quantity and quality of materials shall be available at all times.   Without inventory control, the purchasing department functions on hunch and price differentials and usually buys from the standpoint of expediency or persuasive price salesmanship.

In the application of inventory control to process methods, three important functions stand out clearly. The first is to care for materials awaiting use, through proper custody and placement. The second is to determine the material requirements by proper correlation with the production and sales programs. Finally, the cost of materials and supplies used in factory operation must be furnished, so that there is a complete realization of the value involved in processing these materials.

With proper application of inventory control to process methods, it is actually possible to reduce costs and to improve labor's efficiency. The right kind of material must be available at the right time. Hurried substitutions, requiring additional labor, or facilities other than those which would ordinarily be used in that particular operation, are costly.

Who should have jurisdiction over inventory control? This question can be answered by saying that circumstances alter cases. But not to dodge the question, it can be maintained that inventory control *must* come under the jurisdiction of the *operating* division of a business—*not* the financial. There are some exceptions, of course, which only prove the rule.

Within the operating division, there will be some question as to whether the purchasing, production, or manufacturing departments should have jurisdiction over the inventory. Except for very special circumstances concerned with the internal administration of the business, the most satisfactory place for inventory control is in the production department.

In considering this placement of inventory control, it must be remembered that the quantity aspects of inventory (and possibly its detailed costing) are important, rather than its financial aspects. From that point on, the effects of inventory control will naturally travel through the financial division of the company for such uses as may be required of it.

FINANCIAL ASPECTS

Perhaps the most interesting aspects of inventory control lie in the financial side of a business. There are two important considerations here, which may be summarized briefly as:

1. The effect of inventory control on profit and loss.
2. The relation of inventory control to working capital or cash position.

In any consideration of the effect of inventory control on profit and loss, the basic concern is with the salability of the inventory. Inventory control presumes that only salable inventory is produced. Consequently, if the inventory produced is not salable, profit or loss become directly related to this particular factor.

It follows, therefore, that management must know at all times the salability of its inventory. The method of determining this is rather simple if an unprejudiced approach is made. The first step is to classify (to *age*) the inventory into its logical rate-of-turnover groups. It becomes obvious, for example, that, if the average turnover rate is once a year, and a large part of the inventory turns only once every five or six years, management has been remiss. It has not correlated its production and sales program and has automatically prevented itself from realizing the profit it should expect from the business.

It is remarkable to find in examining the inventory accounts of many companies that comparatively few of them have been aged. Not many companies would think of neglecting to age their accounts receivables; yet inventory is only one step removed from receivables. It is goods remaining in the hands of the manufacturer instead of in the hands of its customer, and conditions relating to the age of the invested capital and to the profit in inventories and receivables are identical.

It may be stated, therefore, that the aging of the various divisions of an inventory is one of the prime requirements in interpreting the profit and loss picture of a company. As pointed out earlier, this involves not only its salability but also the actual cost of keeping the inventory on the property. Inventory is not a static item on the books of the company, to be regarded as a temporary diversion of working capital. It must be considered in the same light with accounts receivable.

The second important financial aspect of inventory control is concerned entirely with its relation to the cash or working capital position of the company. A comprehensive survey, made by one of the largest credit agencies in the United States, reveals the fact that certain industries are blessed with extremely high rates of inventory turnover and that others have extremely low rates.

It has been found that the heavy capital goods industries operate on approximately 4 turns of inventory per year. The consumer goods industries, such as textiles, average close to 24 turns per year. Industry as a whole, excluding these two extremes, averages between 6 and 12 turns per year.

Oddly enough, industry fares much better in its turnover rate than does distribution. If a few of the lines that reach the consumer through retail outlets are taken, the following comparison is interesting:

INVENTORY TURNS ANNUALLY

Product	Manufacturer	Wholesaler	Retailer
Clothing	7.0	4.0	3.5
Furniture	6.0	6.0	5.5
Hardware and Tools	6.0	4.0	3.5
Shoes	9.0	7.5	3.0

These figures point out that, although the manufacturer has a hard enough time, there are worse financial hazards in the retail business. The annual reports of failures among retail establishments are significant in this respect.

It is easy to see the effect of slow inventory turnover on the cash position of a company, particularly if the rate of turn is low. This condition becomes more complicated if, with a low rate of turnover, the sales program results in an increasing volume of sales. The cash requirement for inventory purposes can then easily pyramid to a point which will reduce the company to insolvency.

From the financial officer's viewpoint, inventory should never be more than the net working capital. Good practice requires that it should not exceed 75 per cent of the capital figure. If this ratio is exceeded, management should examine most carefully its sales and production policies.

Inventory control seeks to reduce this financial hazard and *will* do so if aggressively and consistently applied to the operating plan of the business.

Managerial Aspects

The managerial aspect of inventory control is a tender subject in most companies, since it touches on management's judgment and ability. The three most important phases of the subject may be listed as:

1. Speculation in materials.
2. Determination of sales policies.
3. Determination of production policies.

There still exists a too large school of managers who are confused about the real objective of business—which is to make profits. They believe that they can outguess the laws of supply and demand. They think they can either enhance operating profits or mitigate operating losses by speculating in the raw materials from which their products are made.

In the second managerial aspect of inventory control, it seems obvious that inventories should not be created for sales program until there is assurance that the program will be realized. Yet there are enthusiastic sales managers, convinced of their own powers of accomplishment, who are willing to set the course of a business directly against the stream of a general business trend. They demand an inventory position that will cover their most optimistic quotas. It is at this point that management must step in and exercise the function of inventory control, tempering the enthusiasm of the sales department with the realities of cash and capacity.

The final factor in this trio of managerial aspects is determination of production policy. Although this is closely allied to sales policy, there are several interesting points of divergence. First of all, management must be concerned to maintain its operating facilities, which means its organization and plant, as a "going" business. This sometimes requires the manufacture of inventory contrary to the immediate sales picture. Or it may mean a reduction in the operating rate of the plant, contrary to the current sales picture. Again, the product itself may be of such a nature that it is better to keep it in finished form than in raw material form; in this case the production policy will have no immediate relation to sales activity.

But the most prevalent reason for unbalanced and extravagant inventories is that too many manufacturers are without an adequate system of production control coupled with an accurate business forecast.

CHAPTER 31

LABOR
COMPENSATION
AND CONTROL

•

DEFINITION

Labor compensation and control may be defined as the regulation of direct and indirect labor in such a manner as to secure the highest possible earnings for employees and the lowest possible costs for the company.

There are three types of labor, each generally considered as separate and distinct. These are direct labor, indirect labor, and nonproductive labor.

There is, however, no universally applied definition for each. Many companies consider the two latter types as one and the same. The widening use of wage incentive plans in industry makes it desirable to separate the three, as is explained later in this chapter. For this reason they are here defined as:

1. Direct Labor. That labor which works directly on the product being manufactured and whose efforts tend to change the size, appearance, or condition of the product.

2. Indirect Labor. That labor which closely assists direct labor, actually handling the product, but not changing its size, shape, appearance, or condition. This group would include setup men, material handlers, and inspectors. If these activities can be directly measured to specific units of the product, they are frequently considered as direct labor.

3. Nonproductive Labor. That labor which serves direct labor, but only remotely. In this group would be maintenance men, storeroom keepers, factory clerks, watchmen, janitors. They do not, as a rule, handle the product being manufactured.

No effort is made to point out all the possible exceptions to these definitions. The subject has been argued for many years by the accounting fraternity without satisfactory solution, and it is not important that we attempt an all-inclusive definition here.

Basic Labor Compensation and Control Considerations

It is a general misconception that direct labor forms a very large percentage of the sales dollar. Studies of many industries have shown that the average amount of direct labor in the sales dollar is 17 cents.

It is an equally general misconception that the amount of direct labor in the sales dollar depends on the amount paid to labor. Such a viewpoint seems almost unworthy of mention; yet almost every industrial enterprise has a rather rigid limit to its base rate structure in localized areas of the country.

Except in isolated instances, base labor rates for a given occupation will not vary materially from one plant to another. This is especially true today because of equalization and stabilization by both the Government and labor unions during the war years. In the same plants, however, the labor *cost* of the same identical item per unit produced will vary as much as plus or minus 50 per cent.

Labor control, which really deals with labor cost, must concern itself with the services rendered by labor for a given amount of money, not with the rate paid to labor for a given period of time.

The second basic consideration regarding labor compensation and control is that "Labor is only as efficient as management's plans for it and the tools with which it is expected to work." None of the various compensation controls and techniques, later to be described, will work if management does not have a good organization plan, a good plant layout, a good production control plan, adequate equipment, or the other tools which it is management's responsibility to provide.

The Basis of Control

In order to obtain a control of any kind, it is necessary to establish an accurate standard and to measure results against that standard. Any variations from the standard must be traced and corrective action promptly taken, to hold variations to a minimum.

The basis for labor control is the careful determination of direct, indirect, and nonproductive labor standards.

Direct Labor Standards

Direct labor standards should be set by time study or based on time study standard data and should always be expressed in terms of time. When this is done, they need never be changed, except with a change in methods.

A timekeeping procedure must be set up for reporting the number of pieces produced or the production of each operator or each group of operators. With time standards set at so many minutes per piece, or minutes per hundred pieces, the operator's production can be multiplied by it to determine the standard time for the work he has produced.

When the standard time is divided by the actual time taken by the operator to produce the pieces, the result, expressed as a percentage figure, will give the performance of the operator. For example, if the operator works eight hours in the day or 480 minutes, and turns out 100 pieces having a standard time of 360 minutes per 100 pieces, then his performance is $360 \div 480 \times 100 = 75\%$.

The time standard should be so set that an average operator, doing a fair and honest day's work, without undue fatigue, will perform at 100 per cent.

The timekeeping procedure should be so set up that each worker's performance is computed by 10:00 o'clock of the day following. When a performance under 100 per cent is found, as illustrated previously, immediate corrective steps can be taken.

It is possible to determine the performance of each department or of the factory as a whole, by adding the standard hours of work of all direct labor in the department or factory, and dividing it by the total actual hours worked. This figure, when multiplied by 100, will give the departmental or factory performance.

The control is accomplished by having each foreman receive promptly a report of the performance of each employee in his department as well as of the departmental total. The plant superintendent, or works manager, should receive a daily report showing the performance of each department and the plant total. Where a departmental performance is below 100 per cent, he should immediately investigate that department to determine and correct the weakness. The chief executive of the company should receive a daily report of the plant total performance and at least a weekly report showing the performance by departments.

The Time Study

The technique of making time studies has been described in the many excellent books on the subject. No attempt will be made here to give a detailed explanation of how a time study should be taken; there are, however, certain basic principles which should be followed. If they are not observed, the most painstaking application of accepted techniques will fail.

Every employee who is required to perform against a standard should know how a time study is made and what factors are taken into consideration. He must be assured that it is a fair and equitable method for measuring his activity. This can and should be done by the following methods:

1. Post all time standards on a bulletin board convenient to each department. In addition each individual operator should be furnished with the time standard for each job he works on.

2. Post on the plant bulletin board an abbreviated description of the method of establishing the time study and standards.

3. Prepare a complete and detailed time study manual. Insist that all time study men follow it. Make a copy available to any

employee desiring it for study. A time study manual, easily understood by the average worker, will of itself aid in improving time study procedures.

4. Publish periodical articles on time study in the company house organ. These should be made both interesting and informative.

5. Explain, to each worker being time-studied, what is being done and how it is being done. Enlist his active co-operation.

6. If the employees of the company are organized, train several respected union leaders in time study techniques. Their knowledge of the subject will prove most helpful to management in any grievance involving time study. It has been found that union men selected from the plant and thus familiar with the operations make excellent time study men. It is good practice to train time study men from within the plant rather than to hire them from outside.

Before a time study is taken, the time study observer should advise the foreman and the union steward in the department, if the employees are represented by a union. It is the responsibility of the foreman to see that the operation is properly set up, that the speeds and feeds on the equipment are properly adjusted, that materials and supplies are available, and that the method employed by the worker is in accordance with the operation sheet. All this should be checked with the methods engineer before starting the study.

Time study consists of a study of elements. By this is meant that the operation being performed is broken down into small steps, and the time taken for each step is measured and recorded. For example, a typical sequence of elements would be:

Element 1. Pick up piece and place in jig.

Element 2. Drill one hole.

Element 3. Drill second hole.

Element 4. Remove from jig.

Element 5. Blow out chips.

Element 6. Place in tote box.

By this method it is possible, merely by selecting the proper elements, to build up "synthetic" standards which can be used to create a final standard. For example, the element "pick up piece and place in jig" can, when properly timed, be used for any other operation calling for a similar piece and a similar jig. The time required to drill the same size hole, to the same depth, in the same kind of material, will be the same for any part.

By plotting numerous drilling operations, charts can be built up from which the correct time for drilling any size hole to any depth in any type of material can be selected. The benefit from such standards, when used for estimating, is of obvious importance.

Leveling

Every time study taken should be leveled, or normalized. This means that the time study observer determines whether the operator is fast, normal, or slow. He then adjusts the study so that it will be applicable to an average operator working at a fair speed. It is not unusual for a company to take the most meticulous time studies and then fail to level them. The result is that, where the time study was taken on a fast operator, the standard is very tight. If taken on a slow operator, it is very loose.

Leveling is perhaps the least scientific step in the development of a time study into a time standard. Yet, if leveling techniques are intelligently developed and consistently applied, their effectiveness cannot be questioned.

The time study can be leveled in total, without consideration of elemental times, or consideration can be given to the rate of speed of each element. Neither method, applied exclusively, has been found to be entirely satisfactory. It is not practical to attempt to level each and every element. When the worker's performance on one element is obviously inconsistent with the over-all rating, then this particular element should be separately leveled.

For example, an operation may require that an operator walk 30 feet during each cycle. When working on the part and performing the machining operations, he may be normal and leveled at 100 per cent. However, it may be found that he is an unusually slow walker. In that case the element of walking 30 feet might be leveled at 70 per cent.

The process of leveling also considers the selection of the elemental times. This is required because a number of cycles are always taken, and, as a rule, five or more different times for each element will result. Many methods are used for selecting element times. They all agree on one thing, namely, that any elemental times which are unusually long or short should be eliminated.

The method of selecting elements which can be most readily supported and most easily justified to employees, or to their representatives, is that of eliminating the unusually long or short elemental times and averaging the remainder. It would not be advisable to attempt to explain how long or how short an elemental time should be, to justify its elimination. Conditions alter cases, but there is usually a reason for such variation. The alert time study observer will note them, and they will be taken into consideration in determining whether or not that particular time should remain.

There are several ways to improve the leveling of time studies. The first step is, of course, to train the time study observer carefully and continuously. This can be done most effectively by having him rate the pace of another employee who performs certain standardized operations at varying rates of speed.

For example, it has been determined that for an average person a fair time in which to deal a deck of cards into four piles is 0.38 minute. One time study man, while timing another on this operation, should note his pace and attempt to estimate the proper leveling percentage. The actual time taken to deal the cards can then be compared with the correct time of 0.38 minute to determine the accuracy of the leveling.

Demonstration operations can be worked out and the correct time for the operation developed by an experienced time study observer and checked carefully by one or more others. Trainees can then practice on these demonstration operations. As they become more skilled, they can study operations in the plant which have been well standardized and validated. With a great deal of practice they can then become both accurate and consistent.

The skilled observer must constantly check himself to be sure that, in the course of time, he does not change his idea of an average operator. There are several ways in which this check can be made. He can study two or more operators performing the same operation and compare the results. If the difference between the two leveled percentages is seven or less, the results are considered to be satisfactory. He and another operator can check each other by occasionally studying the same job at the same time. Their leveled percentages should not have a difference greater than seven, to insure approximately the same idea of the skill and effort expended by the average operator.

As an example, if one operator rates a job at 105 per cent and the other 98 per cent, the result is considered satisfactory. If, however, one rates the job at 105 per cent and the other at 97 per cent, one or the other is wrong. Both should go back to the standardized times and check themselves to regain their accuracy and consistency.

The time study observer will become quite skilled in leveling, but it is a good general rule to eliminate any time studies wherein the operator is rated at less than 75 per cent or more than 125 per cent. The more nearly normal the operator, the smaller the chance for error.

It should be remembered that no matter how much effort and skill is exerted by an operator, or how little, an element which is controlled by the speed or rate of feed of a machine is not effected by his activity. This is often overlooked, with resultant loose standards. A machine-limited element, in other words, is always leveled at 100 per cent.

Personal Allowance.

It is obvious that the leveled cycle time cannot be used as the time standard. Every employee requires a certain amount of personal time for going to the washroom, getting a drink of water, and so forth. Additional time is allowed for these personal requirements, and this time is expressed as a percentage adjustment of the cycle time.

It is standard practice for companies to expect the workers to be at their machines at starting time, ready to go to work. It is, however, becoming common to allow time at the end of the day for the workers to wash up preparatory to going home. This is normally considered in the personal allowance time.

The usual personal time allowance is between 5 and 10 per cent. It is usually standard throughout a particular plant, and is determined primarily by the accessibility of the washrooms and the location of the drinking fountains. It is not desirable to vary the allowance with the seasons, but rather to take the conditions which will be met into consideration when setting the standard.

Fatigue Allowance

The fatigue allowance is another time allowance which must be added to the cycle time. No universally acceptable definition of fatigue has ever come to the author's attention. It is the consensus of authorities that the fatigue allowance is the time allowed for the operator to recoup the energies expended in the performance of his particular job. For example, parts which must be examined under a magnifying glass, in order to detect minute defects, will be more fatiguing to the eyes than parts which require only checking with snap gages. Similarly, parts weighing 90 pounds are physically more fatiguing to handle than the same number of parts weighing only 10 pounds. Parts weighing 10 pounds handled in a cool well-ventilated room will be less fatiguing than the same number of parts weighing the same amount but handled in a hot humid room.

In addition, frequency of effort is an important factor in fatigue. A small part weighing 1 pound that must be handled once a minute all day long will be extremely fatiguing.

It is possible to establish the proper allowance for fatigue by time-studying the same operator, on the same job, at various times during the day, and for several successive days. The varying rates of output obtained from these studies can be tabulated and the fatigue thus derived. This method is acceptable where an entire plant, or a large department of a plant, do approximately the same type of work under approximately the same conditions.

As a rule, however, this method is too slow and expensive, and the time study observer uses his own judgment as a basis for establishing the percentage allowance. The establishment of fatigue allowances by judgment is certainly not scientific and is seldom consistent. The best method is to use the fatigue allowance developed in job evaluation and to convert this into a percentage figure by means of a formula, table, or chart. This method cannot be termed "scientific," but it is the most consistent and accurate method yet developed.

The job evaluation fatigue allowance takes into consideration mental effort, physical effort, and surroundings. For illustrative purposes, in one plant the maximum possible job evaluation points for fatigue allowance were 50, and the minimum 11. Since the generally accepted fatigue percentage range is from 5 to 40, the formula:

$$\text{Per cent allowance} = [(F - 10)\tfrac{7}{8}] + 5$$

was used. The symbol F stands for "fatigue points." By this means a range was established consistent with allowances which had been used but which had not been uniformly or systematically established.

It is best, when using this method, to record the fatigue factors on the back of the job evaluation sheet. If the company has job evaluation, the information is already established for all jobs in the plant. If not, the time study department can, if it wishes, make a separate study of all jobs to determine fatigue allowances. When this is done, procedures should be set up to assure that the information is kept up-to-date at all times.

Machine and Tool Allowance

The time study observer must be very careful that all noncyclic elements are included in the study. A noncyclic element is one which does not occur every time a part is produced or an operation completed. For example, an operator who is performing a grinding operation will have to dress his grinding wheel occasionally. Cutting tools will have to be sharpened, empty tote boxes will have to be replaced with full boxes of parts, and so on.

The time required for these noncyclic elements is usually considered as machine and tool allowance. In the past, these intervals were added to the cyclic time as a percentage factor. It is better practice to determine their frequency and to add them as a time element. Thus, if a grinding wheel must be dressed at the completion of every 10 parts, and the time taken to dress the wheel is 1 minute, then the element time per piece is $1 \div 10$ or 0.1 minute per piece.

Completing the Time Study

When the time study has been completed, the leveling factors determined, and all allowances established, the time study can then be converted into a standard time. The first step is to analyze the time study. This is done by selecting the elemental times as previously described, and comparing each elemental time with selected standard elemental times as a check on their accuracy.

Take the same illustration previously given. A chart has been developed for synthetic determination of the time it takes to drill certain size holes to certain depths in various kinds of material. If there is an element "drill one hole" in the time study, then the recorded time should be compared with the charted time. If there is appreciable variation, an investigation should immediately be made to determine why. It may be caused by a dull drill, or the quality of the drill may be below standard, or the observer may have erred.

If the recorded time can be justified by a condition which will always occur on that particular operation, the recorded time should be used. If it cannot be so justified, the job should be restudied. If the check does not bring out the error, the job should be timed by another observer. The answer must be found and a correct time determined.

If the recorded elemental time varies only slightly from the selected standard time, selected standard time should be used. This statement may be disputed by some who have had unfortunate experiences with poorly developed synthetic standards or who have seen them abused. However, failure to follow this procedure will result in numerous standards with identical elements, each of which is allowed a different time.

Selected standard time elements should not be used unless they are uniformly described. The time study observer or analyst must be sure that they start and stop at the same point. Although very few time study men do so, it is a good practice to record on the time study sheet the exact division point between elements. By so doing, the accuracy of selected standard times can be greatly improved.

No attempt has been made to describe the procedure for studying and improving the methods employed on a job before time study. It has been presumed that this has been done. The procedure is called methodizing and is most important. Many companies leave this to the time study observer. Because so few time study observers have the experience and qualifications for this type of work, it is believed that it should be done by the methods department. The subject is covered in Chapter 26 of this section, rather than here.

Whether or not methodizing has been accomplished as part of the analysis function, the observer or analyst should carefully review the time study for possible elimination or combination of elements. This will result in greater productivity.

After analysis of the study has been completed, and the elemental times have been established and totaled, the next step is to apply the personal and fatigue allowances. The almost universal method of doing this is to add the two percentages together. This percentage, multiplied by the total cycle time, is then added to the total cycle time, thus:

Cycle time	= 10.00 minutes
Personal allowance	= 10%
Fatigue allowance	= 30%
Total allowance	= 40%
10 minutes × 0.40	= 4.00 minutes allowance
10.00 minutes + 4.00 minutes	= 14.00 minutes per piece standard

This method, although generally used, does not give a correct time standard. If the operator takes the time allowed for personal and fatigue and performs each cycle in accordance with the time standard for that cycle during the remainder of the time, he will not produce 100 per cent performance at the end of the day. A more accurate method is to deduct the personal and fatigue allowances from 100 per cent and to divide the remainder into the standard cycle time. For example:

Cycle time	= 10.00 minutes
Personal allowance	= 10%
Fatigue allowance	= 30%
Total allowance	= 40%
100% − 40%	= 60% (or decimally 0.60)

10.00 minutes ÷ 0.60 = 16.67 minutes per piece standard

The standard for the operation should be converted into terms of "hours per piece" or "hours per 100 pieces," to simplify performance computations. This will serve as an aid to the accounting and estimating departments.

Use of the Standard in Controlling Direct Labor

The method used to measure performance by means of the time study standard has been explained. Mere measurement, however, will not establish a direct labor control. This can only be accomplished by immediately detecting variations from standard and by taking prompt corrective action.

It is in this respect that most control fails. Attempts to intimidate the worker who does not perform up to standard by reprimanding him or threatening discharge are not substitutes for control. They will usually fail to secure the results desired. Management then has no recourse but to accept low performance or to install a wage incentive plan.

It will be remembered that at the beginning of this chapter it was said that "Labor is only as efficient as management's plans for it and the tools with which it is expected to work." It may also be said that "A wage incentive is an attempted substitute for good management." A wage incentive is not a good substitute for good management. Its use does, however, quickly bring to management's attention failures which directly affect the worker's pocketbook and performance.

For example, if a worker has to wait for material, he will, with a wage incentive plan in effect, quickly and effectively call the delay to the attention of his foreman or the material move men. It is management's responsibility to get the material to the worker, but, unless failure to get material adversely affects him personally, the worker as a rule will be quite content to wait all day for it. Performance will thereby suffer.

In the control of direct labor one thing should be remembered. When a performance record shows that a man has failed to produce at 100 per cent for one day, it is not necessarily a measure of that man. He may not be feeling well; he may have serious family difficulties which affect his work; there may be other handicaps. If a man fails to make 100 per cent performance for several days in a row, there may be many other possible reasons for his failure. For example:

1. He may have been improperly selected for the job, not having the aptitudes required.
2. He may not be properly trained in the correct methods of doing the job.
3. He may not have had enough materials to work on over the full working period.
4. He may not have had the correct tools for the job, or any tools at all.
5. His equipment may not have been working properly.
6. He may have been working at less than a normal pace.

It can be seen that, out of these six reasons for failure, five of them are factors over which the worker has little or no influence. They are the primary responsibility of management. Thus the odds are 5 to 1 against management and with the worker. Consequently, it is management's job first to check into each of the factors which are their responsibility and to see that they are corrected. Management can make very effective use of time study observers by having them check the operators who perform at lower than 100 per cent. They can very quickly determine the reason and call it to the attention of the responsible department.

Direct labor control measures more than activity of the workers themselves. It also gives management a measure of its production control, its material control, its tool control, its inspection, and, in short, all its other manufacturing controls. When all is said and done, *this is management itself.*

Indirect Labor Standards

There are relatively few indirect labor jobs for which standards can be set by time study and economically used for control purposes. The difficulty lies not so much in establishing the standard, but rather in measuring the activity.

A craneman, for example, might serve one group of direct operators and handle only one type of product. The standard time for picking up the material and transporting it for varying distances could quite easily be determined by time study. However, to record each piece handled by him would be tedious. To measure the distance that he transported it, or even to estimate it, would be hard. Computations to determine the standard time allowance for the work he did during the day would take more time than could be saved by exercising the most rigid control.

Since indirect labor is an overhead expense, the method of controlling it must be different from that of the control of direct labor. Its importance should not be overlooked merely because it cannot be so readily measured. Indirect labor expense is always a considerable per cent of the direct labor amount and may be several times the direct labor amount.

As with any other control, indirect labor control requires that standards of performance be established. Certain classes of indirect labor, such as routine inspection and specialized material handling operations, can all be set by time study standards. They may be controlled exactly as though they were direct labor, as described in preceding paragraphs. This can also be done by expressing them in terms of direct labor.

However, when the latter method is used, provision must be

made for an element of fixed expense that occurs in a certain proportion of indirect labor work. Some personnel are retained permanently, regardless of the volume of production, in order that the organization may be held intact. There is always difficulty in replacing certain key individuals, who must be kept on. The work of certain employees has little relation to plant activity; yet they are required to perform their functions, regardless of the volume of production.

The various indirect operations should be analyzed just as carefully as the direct operations. In many cases the various classes of work performed may even be time-studied. The standards, however, should be expressed in terms of a fixed and variable factor and related to direct labor.

That is, the crane operator's standard may be established at 24 hours per day, plus zero per cent variable. The standard for internal trucking may be expressed as zero hours per day fixed, plus 2 per cent of the standard direct labor hours. The inspection department standard may be expressed as 100 hours per day, plus 2 per cent of the total direct labor standard hours.

The method of determining standards on a fixed and variable basis by means of charting, is explained in Chapter 15, Section 2. This chapter explanation treats the subject in terms of dollars, but exactly the same procedure is used when working with hours.

The over-all executive control of indirect labor treats it as one element of overhead expense. It is exercised through the use of a budgetary control, which expresses its standard as a fixed and variable and relates it to direct labor. For factory management control there is not sufficient detail, nor can it be obtained rapidly enough, for maximum effectiveness. Factory management control bases its standards on direct labor and uses the fixed and variable method also but does it departmentally or even by groups within a department.

Knowing the scheduled direct labor hours, factory management can pretermine the indirect labor hours required and control their actual usage promptly and effectively. The determination is accomplished by applying the indirect labor formula to the standard direct labor hours. This determines the indirect labor standard.

The control consists of finding the reason for adverse variations and correcting the causes. It should be remembered that, when this method is used, the indirect labor standard is determined from the direct labor standard. Poor performance on the part of the direct labor may necessitate greater amounts of indirect labor than standard.

The indirect labor control should be closely associated with other budgetary control activities, because the balance of the other overhead expenses should be controlled in the same manner as described for indirect labor. That is, standards should be expressed in terms of fixed and variable factors related to productive labor. In order to obtain a complete control, it should be possible to add the indirect labor standard with the other overhead standards in order that a complete overhead factor may be determined.

Care should also be taken in breaking the over-all control down into departmental control factors. Detail control must be consistent with the over-all control, and the same accounts must be considered in reaching a total. For example, the same functions considered as indirect labor in the budgetary control must be considered as indirect labor in the factory control and in the departmental detail controls. In addition the sum of the detail standards must equal the budgetary control standard.

Nonproductive Labor Standards

Nonproductive labor standards are determined in the same manner as indirect labor standards. There are, however, more opportunities to set direct time study standards for nonproductive labor than for indirect labor.

A toolroom, for example, will do no productive work. But standards from time study standard data can be set for each job done in the toolroom, and a control exactly like the direct labor control can be set up. Direct nonproductive standards have not received the acceptance they deserve in industry. There are a great many nonproductive operations that can be put on direct standards accurately and economically, such as window washing and painting.

WAGE INCENTIVE PLANS

Wage incentives are defined as extra compensation earned for extra effort or for effort above normal.

Incentives may be generally classified into two broad divisions: those that are financial in nature, and those that are not. The two most commonly used financial incentives are the piecework plan and the standard hour premium plan. Nonfinancial incentives are seldom formalized and rarely used, although the measured day work plan is quite economical to operate. It has advantages which will be shown later.

Piecework

Piecework is a financial incentive which provides for direct compensation of the workman on the basis of what he produces in physical pieces. The piecework incentive is constructed by multiplying the labor standard by the employee's hourly rate, which gives the piecework price. In other words, the piecework rate represents the number of cents or the number of dollars that the workman will be paid for each good piece that he produces. He can calculate his own earnings by multiplying the number of good pieces he has produced by the piecework rate.

Originally, piecework plans were operated as follows: If the employee's piecework earnings were less than what he would have earned had he been paid his hourly rate for the time worked, he would receive only his piecework earnings. This, of course, penalized him severely for a poor day's production. Today, however, the employer is compelled by law to pay at least a minimum hourly rate. In addition, very few plants that have been organized pay less than the base hourly rate for the hours worked.

In order to have adequate control, the labor control previously described should be established, even though the piecework method of compensation is employed. If piecework is used without the labor control, it will be possible for many employees to perform at less than a normal rate of effectiveness.

This makes for excessive costs not only in the improper utilization of machinery or facilities but also in direct labor dollars. The base rate should be the correct rate for an average man doing a fair and honest day's work. If an operator performs at less than 100 per cent and is paid for 100 per cent, then the direct labor cost is directly increased.

Piecework plans have been abused in the past and are not always so acceptable to labor as the standard hour premium plan. When both are properly established, there is no difference between the two, but too often piecework rates are set without regard to base rate or time. This practice is most ill advised and can lead only to trouble, not only with labor, but also with regard to profitable operation of the business.

A proper piecework plan will establish base rates by job evaluation or classification. These rates will be high enough to attract and hold labor if paid only on a day work basis. The time for each job will then be determined by time study and the piece price determined by multiplying one by the other. The worker will be guaranteed his base pay for the hours worked and will be expected to produce 100 per cent performance.

The time standard, of course, will be so set that an average operator doing a fair and honest day's work will perform at 100 per cent. It is considered bad practice to have a separate base rate and guaranteed rate for a job. It is even worse to have, in addition to these two, a third rate on which the piece price is based.

Premium Plans

Premium plans, including the standard hour premium plan, calculate the total standard time allowed for the operator's daily production. This is then converted into dollars.

In other words, the standards given to the various operators are expressed in time. The number of pieces that the operator has produced for the day are multiplied by the time standards. The result is the total standard hours produced and earned by the operator. A comparison between this standard time and the actual time will give his performance.

In order to convert the total standard earned time into money, it is only necessary to multiply the total earned time by the operator's established base rate. This will give his earnings for that day. The result will be the same as if piecework were used, but will have the added advantage of constantly stressing time.

Examples of the computations involved in the standard hour premium plan for a standard work week of 40 hours are:

Without Overtime

	Over 100%		Under 100% (guaranteed)
Hours actually worked	40		40
Earned hours	50		30
Base rate	$1.00		$1.00
Pay = $1.00 × 50 =	$50.00	$1.00 × 40 =	$40.00
Performance = $\frac{50}{40}$ × 100 =	125%	$\frac{30}{40}$ × 100 =	75%

With Overtime

Hours actually worked	48		48
Earned hours	60		40
Base rate	$1.00		$1.00
Pay = (48 + 4) × $\frac{60}{48}$ × $1.00 = $65.00		(48 + 4) × $1.00 =	$52.00
Performance = $\frac{60}{48}$ × 100 =	125%	$\frac{40}{48}$ × 100 =	83.33%

With Day Work Included

Hours actually worked	8
Day work hours	2
Earned incentive hours	7
Base rate	$1.00
Pay = (2 × $1.00) + (7 × $1.00) = $9.00	
Performance = $\frac{7}{6}$ × 100 =	116.67%

Under other forms of premium, the operator may receive his base earnings plus only a part of the saving in time. In other words, if the operator saves 2 hours' time, he may be given only 75 per cent of that saving, multiplied by his base rate, as an incentive earning. The other 25 per cent sometimes is used as incentive payment to foreman and indirect labor.

There is little justification for giving the operator only part of the saving he has been able to accomplish. This merely results in a constantly declining piecework rate, or standard dollar cost, as the operator increases his productivity. This method also has the added disadvantage of complicating the cost accounting procedure. It makes it difficult to determine what to establish as the standard dollar labor cost.

The type of incentive just described is called a *split incentive*. It is generally used where management does not trust the standards which have been set and fears that labor will "run away with them." The split incentive is extremely unpopular with labor, needless to say. Unless standards are accurately set and management has confidence in them, they should not be used in the payment of incentives. Split incentives should not be considered unless unusual conditions make them necessary; such as critical quality in the product or processes that involve very little man effort.

Measured Day Work

One other frequently found type of wage incentive is measured day work. This is used to control all labor, both direct and indirect, whether paid on an hourly or salary basis.

The incentive for the workmen lies in:

1. A high base rate.
2. The requirement to produce to standard to hold his job.
3. The possibility of advancement to a higher rated job for continued high performance.
4. Job security as a result of high performance, when reduction in plant forces becomes necessary.

The advantages of this form of labor control are:

1. A high guaranteed rate for employees for all time spent in the plant.

2. A method which permits management to determine the performance of the worker.

3. Simplified costing and payroll procedures.

4. Standards that can be used for estimating, planning, and layout purposes.

5. Assurance that equipment and facilities will be used to the greatest advantage. For example, a worker on piecework might

be satisfied with low earnings, thus tying up machines or floor space because of his low production rate.

6. A management requirement to replace poor equipment, correct poor working conditions, improve unbalanced operations, train foremen and workmen, and plan better, in order to secure good performance.

7. The facility with which changes in methods or improvements in equipment can be made without labor's acquiescence. The changes in standards thus resulting do not directly affect the employee's pay. This is most important.

As in all other incentive plans, the basis for measured day work is sound standards. These require the same facilities for time study and the like that other types of incentive plans demand.

Standards for indirect labor are again expressed in terms of time but usually consist of fixed and variable factors. Generally, the variable factors will be expressed as a ratio or percentage of direct labor. For example, the standard for supervision may be: 12 hours per day plus 5 per cent of direct labor hours supervised.

After all jobs are classified according to skill, responsibility, and the like, an hourly rate should be established for each job classification which conforms with any labor agreement and with trade or industry levels. Every workman can then be assigned to the proper job classification and receive the hourly rate established for this classification.

Measured day work provides for no additional compensation to workers beyond their hourly rate. If a worker consistently fails to perform within reach of the standard time set, he may be replaced or transferred to a job more suitable to his qualifications. It should first be established that the low performance is his fault and not due to management's failure to provide proper training, proper material, tools, or equipment.

The mechanics for securing control through a measured day work plan are as follows:

1. A performance sheet will be prepared and posted daily, showing each worker's performance in percentage of standard. This is obtained by dividing the standard hours by the actual hours.

2. In addition, a daily performance sheet will be prepared for each department. This will show total standard direct hours, total standard indirect hours, total actual direct hours, total actual indirect hours, performance per cent for direct labor, performance per cent for indirect labor, and total excess hours. These, in turn, should be consolidated into a performance sheet for the factory as a whole. All performance sheets should be available by 10 o'clock the following morning.

3. The standard average hourly rate for direct and indirect labor can be determined, in each department, by dividing the total earnings by the total number of standard hours produced. The actual average hourly rate for direct and indirect labor can also be determined by dividing the total earnings in the department by the actual hours worked. All costing and accounting should be done at the standard average hourly rate. The difference between the standard earnings and the actual earnings will give the performance variance.

Bonuses

One other form of incentive frequently used is that of a bonus award. The word "bonus" is, unfortunately, frequently used to describe incentive payments resulting from standard-hour or piecework earnings. Actually it is, as Webster defines it, a sum "given or paid over and above what is required or payable."

Since it is an extra payment above the amount actually earned, it is an individual and discretionary gift made to the employee for performance or other reasons for which the management decides that he has not been adequately rewarded.

Frequently it is given for reasons not related to individual performance, as to distribute more than expected company earnings in a good will gesture to the employees.

Bonuses usually reflect management's opinion of the individual's capacity, effectiveness, attitude, and personality. They are not scientific; usually they are not measured awards. If they are paid on a basis of measurement of effort, they are no longer bonuses, but fall into the class of incentive payments.

CHAPTER 32

QUALITY CONTROL

•

DEFINITION

In the long history of industry it is relatively only a few years since a rifle manufacturer developed and applied the principles of interchangeability to his product. In a comparatively short time these principles were adopted and applied to many products by other alert industrialists. Mass production was thus born. The two World Wars, the winning of which depended on the excellence and quantity of materials of war, caused American industry to make tremendous strides in quality control. The related functions of standardization and precision of measurement have also progressed very rapidly. In wartime production, the trend of industrial development was toward tremendous output of high precision, resulting in the manufacture of easily interchangeable products possessing long life and stability. Peacetime manufacture naturally followed this trend and took advantage of the techniques and procedures that were "mushroomed" for war. Certain of these techniques and procedures, governing the excellence of the product, are termed "quality control."

"Quality control" is therefore defined as establishing desired standards or regulations for a product, providing the means of meeting those standards, and assuring that the product conforms with the standards and regulations. When the causes of variations are controlled, product design and specification, production, and inspection can be controlled at a cost consistent with the selling price. Consequently, these several functions of quality control must be constantly checked in order to produce a desired quality.

Purpose

Quality control is without meaning, however, if the product lacks the qualitative aspect desired by the manufacturer. It should be an inherently good product that has been carefully engineered, carefully manufactured, and carefully sold. The purpose, then, of quality control is to produce and market a product whose cost is consistent with price. It is as much poor business to sell too good a product at a loss as it is to sell an inferior product at too great a profit. For instance, a company cannot long survive if it sells a $100 suit of clothes for $25.

The attainment of either result is dependent on quality control. It is the mortar that binds together the bricks of labor, material, and expense. Therefore, no manufacturing operation can be completely successful unless the product meets these three requirements:

1. It must be made at a cost that will yield a profit at current prices.

2. Sufficient quantities of good units must be produced to meet shipping requirements.

3. The condition of the product must satisfy the standards, set by management through design for manufacture, and by the customer for functional use.

Stated again, it is the purpose of quality control to safeguard effectively the quality of the product at a minimum cost. It must insure the interchangeability of parts for assembly operations in the plant and for service operations in the field.

Application

These objectives are attained as a result of competent inspection by the quality control unit of the organization. Inspection, however, must not be confused with quality control, which is a method of securing a good product. Inspection is merely the procedure used to check the result. In other words, inspection is a means to an end—quality control.

Quality control has been defined as the method or operation established by management in order to secure a good product. The character of that method will depend on the general policies which establish the competitive position of the company in relation to other companies in the industry. If leadership is desired, the quality of the product is most important as a factor in the endeavor to develop features for competitive advantage. There may be some penalty attached to this leadership, due to the added cost of research and development activities. If, after consideration of such extra costs, the management decides that a second or even lower place in the industry is best suited for its operation, the problem of quality control becomes less difficult. Modifications can then be made to meet competition with minimum expenditure.

Quality control is one of the important objectives of management. Its establishment and administration determine whether the enterprise will be satisfactory and profitable.

Quality control is also a function of the inspection department. It is basically a statistical function that provides the chief inspector with data on past and current operations and assists him in making decisions. Through inspection and quality control analyses, leads or tips may be developed for new specifications or changes in methods of inspection. If management is kept currently informed of such developments, it can determine when and to what degree to take advantage of them.

Quality control reveals the amount of inspection required on incoming materials and parts. Certain parts may require only spot or random check; a nominal percentage of others may be inspected to ascertain the quantity of rejects. If rejects are excessive, additional quantities must be inspected in order to insure usable production materials and parts. On still other materials and parts, inspection will start at 100 per cent and then can be reduced to a nominal percentage to insure uniform production. Quality control should designate which materials and parts are to be forwarded to the laboratory for tests which the inspection department is not equipped to make, such as:

1. Fatigue tests.
2. Mechanical analysis.

3. Life tests.

4. Laboratory tests.

For example, quality control in refineries is maintained in the laboratory by periodic check of the products sampled at specified stations.

The rebuilding of products to be sold as "rebuilts" presents another problem for quality control and inspection. For example, one or more parts may be remachined undersize to eliminate wear marks, and the corresponding parts may be machined oversize. In order to maintain quality standards, it is imperative that like limits be maintained on the smaller or larger dimensions.

The establishment of tolerances and limits should be the result of the combined efforts of the part and tool engineering, processing, and inspection departments. When this plan is followed, many costly operations can be eliminated; yet the quality standard established for the product can be maintained.

Quality control of a method or operation requires an organization for its administration. This is provided by the inspection force, which is discussed later in this chapter. Inspection consists of examination and decision. It is necessary because the human element in manufacturing introduces errors which preclude ideal results. Inspection is required to interpret quality rulings. By means of proper gages, inspection assures that all conditions of material specifications, performance of operations, and finished product conform with quality standards as established by management.

In turn, management must assure the quality of the gages themselves, by maintaining constant inspection of these tools. This is accomplished by:

1. Providing master gages for checking production and inspection gages. These will be maintained by the engineering or inspection department and kept under lock and key.

2. Establishing time limits for which gages can be used in production without being inspected for accuracy. The time limits will depend on the required tolerances and the frequency with which the gages are used.

When a quality control and inspection department is being organized, it is of utmost importance that the floor inspectors be instructed to maintain quality within the limits set forth by the engineering department. They should not be permitted to set up independent inspection standards, which in their thinking are "good enough." As a further check on quality, the quality control function should be furnished copies of all customers' complaints about quality. These will help ascertain how the products are received and how they are performing in the field and reveal possible weaknesses which may have been overlooked.

The organization of an adequate inspection force presents a real problem. In the endeavor to safeguard quality, the inspection effort can reach a point where the flow of production is impeded and the inspection cost may seriously impair profits. A distinction must be made between necessary examinations and those that may be dispensed with. Frequently, when new products are added to the existing line of products, there is a tendency to apply excessive inspection with the idea that it will be reduced when the necessity for it no longer exists. In actual practice such reduction does not occur, in many cases, and this avoidable cost continues as a part of the fixed expense.

Inspection is necessary, and it can be expensive. It should therefore be subject to continual examination, to improve its effectiveness and reduce its cost. Here the inspection records can be of considerable aid. These records, indicating as they do where and to what extent rejections are made and for what reason, constitute a valuable guide in determining what inspections should be strengthened or reduced.

Inspection cost can, in many instances, also be reduced by lessening the severity of standards that are unnecessarily stringent. Some inspections may be eliminated. Better inspection aids may be provided in the way of equipment for measurements and tests. Workmen may be made responsible for certain examinations and tests without interfering with production. Operation of automatic machines is a good example of the latter, where workmen are required to use gages to conform with quality requirements. Cutting boards to length in a wood mill is another illustrative example. Here the operator is required to cut each board to certain specified lengths to meet production and quality requirements and reduce waste. Every instance of such inspection by direct workers should, of course, be safeguarded by adequate inspection checks made by members of the inspection department.

SECURING QUALITY CONTROL

Control of quality is secured by four related steps:

1. Determining standards.
2. Measuring performance.
3. Providing organization.
4. Securing action.

Determination of standards of quality is the vital element of quality control and deserves the most serious consideration by management. Various departments of a business contribute to the determination of standards and are affected by them; consequently, top management must also correlate these activities.

In nearly every shop, especially those of long standing, "shop practice" develops. It, too, has a place in quality control. Too often, however, shop practice is the only control. Shop practice can perhaps be best expressed as an understanding between the engineering department and the shop as to tolerances that will be allowed. Many times these understandings are satisfactory but being "unwritten laws" are subject to individual interpretation and change. As a result the product will vary from time to time. If the product is made too well, with expensive materials or excessive labor, profits are imperiled; if the product is made inferior, with either poor material or poor workmanship, customers become dissatisfied and are lost to the company.

Standards

Clearly written specifications of quality that permit only one interpretation are of inestimable value to any company purchasing material and converting it into a salable product. It is well, therefore, that standards be clearly specified in writing and that a definite procedure be established for their maintenance. The design engineer is usually responsible for origination of standards of quality, but the sales department, purchasing department, methods department, shop foremen, production department, and inspection department should all have a voice in their setting. Each department has its own interest, but all must be subordinated to the best interest of the company. Oftentimes this is a matter for top management decision.

When standards of quality lend themselves to a numbering system, they are generally specific but are not always subject to the same interpretation. For example, 10″, 10.0″, 10.00″, and 10.000″ all appear to have the same meaning. In some shops, however, the figures to the right of the decimal point are significant and denote differences in precision.

When two or more parts are required to be assembled, the degree of "fit" required should always be specified and the mating parts dimensioned to tolerances that will produce the desired fit. The American Society of Mechanical Engineers' standards committee has made extensive studies of dimensional "fits" and has established standards which are a satisfactory guide. It has also defined and coded certain materials to a standard terminology.

It is well to give the maximum tolerance, or the difference between the high and low limits of a dimension, that will give the desired fit or size. In other words, the limits on dimensions can be as "loose" as possible to secure low costs, easy planning, producing, and inspecting. It is possible to read a micrometer consistently to the nearest 0.003″, a steel scale to 0.010″, and a steel tape to ¹⁄₆₄″. When the tolerance is wide, say ±0.010, then the operation to produce the dimension can be on old equipment with an ordinary operator and with few cuts. But if the tolerance is narrow, say ±0.002, then good equipment, a skilled operator, and extra cuts are required.

Another reason for having the widest possible tolerance is the cost of gage maintenance. Gages will wear with use, and it is common practice to make gages somewhat under the tolerance limits especially on "go" gages. If a tolerance is expressed as ±0.010″, then, the "go" gage could be made to a −0.007″ and have a 0.003″ wear before it would pass parts that were under the limit and materially affected the cost of the operation. When

the tolerance is ±0.001″, then the "go" gage could be made to a
−0.0008″ and only have 0.0002″ of wear before it would pass
parts that were too small.

The subject of gage wear brings up another problem and that
is the checking of gages and withdrawing them from service when
they are likely to pass bad work. In most cases it is necessary
to have three sets of gages to maintain adequate 100 per cent
inspection. One set of master gages should be made to the
limits. These would be used only for checking and be kept in a
locked gage room. A second set of working gages should be supplied to the operator for use at the machine. These gages should
be well within the limits to permit gage wear and a machine
setting that produces parts that are within the limits. The third
set of gages is for the inspector. These may be worn operator's
gages that are still within the limits. The theory of their use
is that they permit a slightly greater tolerance than those gages
to which the part was made.

If machines and humans could always produce identical work,
there would be no need for tolerances. Tools that cut, form,
shape, finish, and so on, gradually wear, so that no two pieces
are exactly alike. In addition, because of the method of holding,
play in moving parts, expansion or contraction, errors in construction, variances in material, or outside influences, no two
operations are ever performed exactly the same, whether by
machine or by hand. For these reasons it is frequently required
of the operator that he inspect his own work as it is being made
and thus avoid accumulation of a large amount of bad work.
If the limits of the operator's gages are slightly under the required tolerances, a longer gage life is permitted, and the chance
of off-tolerance work is reduced. Care and study must be given
to this problem, so as not to tighten the tolerance beyond the
scope of the operation.

The reason for a different set of gages for the inspector is to
catch any human failures on the part of the operator to use his
gages properly, and to detect worn operator gages. As a general
policy, this inspection should be made as concurrently as possible in the period that the part is produced. This reduces the

risk of a large quantity of inferior work—thus effecting immediate control.

The establishment of dimensional standards should be in the form of a written standard practice and kept up-to-date. In the early days of our industrial era nearly all dimensions were shown as a whole number and a common fraction. The introduction of better machine tools has made the use of decimals a common practice. Some engineers still use a combination of fractions and decimals on the same drawing and specify tolerances on the drawing as a whole in such statements as "$\pm \frac{1}{32}$ on all fractional dimensions and ± 0.005 on decimals except where shown." When fractions are used, it is generally necessary to convert them to decimals in computing processes and tools and even for adding and subtracting. Thus, fractions are time-wasting as well as confusing and if converted to decimals create added chance for error. The use of decimal dimensions, in practice, avoids these confusions and errors, and saves considerable time.

In the development of inspection standards for material, correct engineering specifications must be developed covering grade, size, and condition of raw material, process material, and finished material. Many of these specifications cannot be expressed as numbers; hence the problem of stating tolerances is difficult and requires much care and thought.

It has been said that the only sure way of getting people to agree on a problem is to reduce it to something which can be counted. This is not always possible when developing specifications. This is particularly true of requirements involving judgment of appearances such as color and smoothness. Other specifications involving the description of a process or trade practice can cause serious differences of judgment because of variance in interpretation. Written specifications should be as clear and complete as possible, but with due regard for brevity.

Many other inspection standards are required, such as standards for packing. These will specify the material to be used and the method of applying packing material to the product. Standards for the custody of material will specify the type and method of storage necessary to keep raw, in-process, and finished materials in proper condition throughout the process of manufacture. Standards are even required for the inspection department itself which will clearly define the procedures and the objectives required for successful prosecution of its effort.

Labor standards as described in Chapter 31 of this section are basic for quality control. They should be established for each direct operation by careful time studies and thoroughly analyzed by those selected to approve them. These standards should be expressed in terms of *good* units per hour and should represent attainable performance by an average worker, with average effort.

In the development of labor standards, proper allowances should be included for all factors relating to the performance of the operation, such as fatigue, personal requirements, the handling of material, and the *normal spoilage of material* incidental to the operation.

Normal spoilage of material is an important item in some operations and only slightly important in others. It must be recognized, however, in the development of every standard with whatever allowance may be necessary.

Allowances for normal spoilage of material require the exercise of sound judgment, with consideration of the character of the operation, as it is performed from day to day. For example, certain unavoidable spoilage of material occurs when tools are adjusted or changed in connection with the operation of automatic screw machines. This represents a considerable item of time, particularly with large machines cutting from rods of large diameter. Such normal material spoilages are usually established as allowances for tool adjustment and changes, which is satisfactory.

In a foundry, whether the operation is one of making cores or making molds, allowances must be made for the spoilage associated with the character and temper of the molding materials. Such allowances may assume large proportions with complex patterns. In some instances, with extremely large complex patterns requiring floor or pit molding, the hazard of spoilage may be so great as to necessitate a standard of pieces produced.

Whether good or bad, these are safeguarded by continual inspection as the making of the mold progresses toward completion.

In a woodworking mill some spoilage occurs in the performance of most of the operations. The rate of performance of these operations is so rapid that the allowance for spoilage, if any, is usually quite small. The degree of material spoilage for each operation should be recorded, however, for purposes of control.

In a rubber mill, the tire builder has an opportunity to examine each piece of material as he applies it to a tire and is expected to reject defective pieces. The allowance for rejected material found is therefore included in an allowance for handling material. Rejected pieces can then be considered in connection with the operation that produced them.

Spoilage of material, or waste, occurs with all manufacturing processes and falls into two broad classifications: avoidable waste and unavoidable waste. Waste can be a considerable factor affecting the operating profit. Every reasonable effort should be devoted to reducing waste to a minimum. The establishment of standards of unavoidable waste for each process operation will keep waste within proper limits, through the administration of quality control.

The proper time to establish unavoidable waste standards is during the course of time study. Considered from an economic viewpoint, the establishment of a normal material spoilage or unavoidable waste standard should be a further result of that study. This is considered good practice and should be the common practice. Many companies, however, consider waste sufficiently important to warrant the creation of a separate department for waste control.

Such departments are made responsible for the examination of waste and its causes, the establishment and revision of waste standards, and the control of waste, through various activities. These include publicity of waste production with reports and scoreboards, rewards for waste reduction or changes of design or methods of manufacture to reduce waste.

All these activities should be a part of the function of quality control, except the establishment of unavoidable waste standards. These standards should be established as a by-product of time study activities, in co-operation with engineering. The principle of "creeping change" should be applied to these as to other standards. One time study engineer may develop an acceptable standard or performance for a particular operation. Later another engineer, while studying the same operation, may discover an economical possibility completely overlooked by the first engineer, leading to the establishment of a new better standard. In like manner, new and better waste standards may supplant the existing ones.

In addition, the foregoing considerations affect other functions of the company. The spoilage of material and the resulting machine time lost are essential factors that affect the planning and scheduling of the production control department. The material spoilage factor must then be added to the unit requirement, in addition to the normal cutoff and chucking loss, as in bar stock uses. In other products, such as molded parts, spoilage allowances must be used to produce the desired quantities without additional setups.

Preparation for small lot quantities is expensive. It is necessary, therefore, that the production control department know the quantities to be added for spoilage of every nature so that a sufficient quantity of material can be furnished to yield the required quantity of *good* pieces.

The complete co-operation of the engineering (product and tool), time study, inspection, and manufacturing departments is required here.

Other allowances depend on the types of products made. For example, when abrasives are processed, more than one size of grit is produced from the lot at the grinding operation. When this is screened, several sizes are obtained. In order to produce the required quantity of a definite size, an analysis of the screening results (which is actually an inspection operation) will assist the production department. It can then schedule the proper quantities of raw material to obtain the required quantities of finished material.

This problem also applies to the food industry. For example, in canning sliced and chip beets, a definite quantity of sliced beets may be scheduled. This, in turn, requires the scheduling of facilities for chip beets.

Another need for inspection co-operation is found in grading products for size or quality. Production control can function more efficiently when constantly informed of the results and is then in position to provide the right containers in specified quantities.

In connection with the design of the product, it is a function of engineering to provide the essential specifications for its manufacture. These should state the grade, size, and condition of each kind of raw material to be used. When necessary, they should provide a description, with sufficient detail of the visual, physical, and chemical examinations and tests to which the materials must be subjected, and the characteristics required for their acceptance.

With clearly defined specifications affecting the acceptance or rejection of material received from vendors, quality control can be administered through inspection activities with intelligent decision.

In some cases material may be received which does not quite comply with all the specifications, thus presenting a problem as to its acceptance. When in doubt, engineering can always be consulted for advice, although the responsibility for decision remains with quality control. When such cases are of sufficient importance because of urgent need for the material, or because of reciprocal relations with the vendor, they may very properly be referred to management.

In similar fashion and for the same reasons, material that requires an expenditure of labor to make it usable should be referred to management for decision. Such cases are particularly important because of arrangements to charge the extra cost to the vendor, where this is possible.

Engineering advice and aid is essential in the form of specifications as to type and method of handling, transportation, and storage of material through all process operations. Various materials used in process may require specially designed containers at different stages. These, in turn, may determine the kind of transportation unit to be used and the size of the loads to be transported.

All essential processing specifications should be made available for each part and for each assembly, in accordance with an accepted formal arrangement. These should be provided by the methods engineering department, compiled on operation sheets which give complete manufacturing specifications.

Operation sheet instructions should cover all manufacturing requirements for the complete processing of the unit. These should include adequate descriptions of the material and operations, listed in the required sequence, indicating the machines and tools to be used, and showing the allowed time for each and the standard hourly rate of production, as described in an earlier chapter.

Each required inspection operation should be listed on the operation sheets, in the same manner as manufacturing operations. This applies regardless of whether the inspection is made during the processing of the part or during the withdrawal to an inspection room. Complete specifications show at what stage of the process the inspection should be made; the character of the inspection, whether partial or 100 per cent; the quality requirements; the allowable tolerances; and the gages, instruments, or equipment to be used for examinations and tests.

Thorough inspection of a part after a setup is not sufficient. It has been found that an inspector assigned continually to the production from a group of machines will materially assist in eliminating scrap losses or unnecessary salvage operations. Final room inspection is necessary for purchased commodities but is costly on production work. The error is found only *after* the lot has been finished, and 100 per cent inspection is then necessary to sort out the defective parts.

Reworking or salvage operations are a troublesome problem for the production department. In many instances they require a special setup for which tools and equipment are not readily available. The schedule clerk must delay some other urgent production order to perform the salvaging operation. This results in broken delivery promises and, if permitted to become chronic, will cause a complete breakdown of the scheduling plan.

In spite of every safeguard to maintain quality levels and thus secure interchangeability, unusual circumstances sometimes arise which challenge the validity of these principles. A classic example is that of typewriter assembly. The mass production of the modern typewriter, requiring the highest degree of interchangeability in parts for assembly and field service, has still failed to eliminate the special skills and techniques required of the workman who makes the final assembly.

Theoretically it should be possible to disassemble a group of new typewriters in perfect working condition, mix the parts, and reassemble the same number of working machines. Actually, few of them will function correctly until the deft touch of the skilled assembler has made the minor adjustments required.

This does not mean that quality control and inspection have failed in their function. It actually underlines their necessity, for without them each typewriter assembly would be a complete salvage operation.

The operation sheet should specify the inspection requirements to the utmost practicable extent. In some instances, because of the necessity to provide detailed precise instructions covering a series of complicated physical and chemical tests, or because the nature of these may be confidential, or for other reasons, they may be issued as separate instructions to the quality control department only.

Such inspections should, however, be designated with an identifying symbol, and reference made to them on the operation sheet, with an allowed time for performance. In connection with the latter, an allowed or standard time should be established and recorded for each inspection operation. Time standards are necessary, both for the control of inspection cost and for scheduling production.

Performance Measures

Without performance records to show the results of quality control, very little quality will result. Records are essential for developing the experience encountered and the source of such experience.

Such records must show, first of all, the responsibility for the quality observed; that is, whether it was the vendor's fault, or the operator's fault, or management's fault by reason of improper engineering or specifications. Performance records should show the costs accumulated at the point of loss so that the conditions creating the loss can be determined and suitable action taken.

Above all, performance records must be current and conducive to quick summarization. They should be built up from satisfactory lot or order reports into daily, weekly, and monthly accumulations. Cumulative records of rejections, classified by causes, is a positive requirement for quality control and an absolute necessity for improved quality standards.

The technique of statistical quality control may be used, under proper conditions, to supplement the regular procedures of inspection. As its name indicates, statistical control of quality is an analytical method of determining the *trend* of quality. It requires rather special techniques of analysis and refined methods of measuring quality deviations. It is particularly applicable to mass production of small items on automatic equipment, although it has been used successfully for more general conditions of manufacture. Under suitable conditions it can maintain a proper level of quality with a minimum inspection cost, but because of its special requirements it is not yet widely used in industry.

Where it can be employed, this type of inspection has the objective of using statistics to prevent the making of defective output. This, of course, reduces the amount of inspection, and produces fewer rejects, less salvage, less scrap, and fewer dissatisfied customers.

Statistics can be used to point out the conditions and operations that are causing trouble. If proper follow-up and investigation are made to correct the troubles, then the quality defects can be reduced or even eliminated entirely. Then, as spoilage is reduced to practically a minimum, control can be exercised to keep it at a minimum by using the regularly recorded inspection data. In other words, statistical quality control "locks the barn door before the horse is stolen," because when inspection data are charted they can disclose any "creeping" of the production operation toward the specification limits, before spoiled work is produced. This is the most important result of statistical control, which would justify the expense and trouble of preparing the data in chart form.

The application of statistical control must be made with careful judgment. Although it can be applied to every inspection item, if this were done the number of charts and recordings would, for almost any shop, run into unwieldy detail. When the chance for error is slight, or where the operations are not continuous, the benefits of this control do not justify the cost of securing them. But when the value of the piece is high and the chance for error great, or where the continuous flow of a large number of parts or volume is important, or where the inspection operations are difficult, then it might be worth while to bring the operations under statistical control.

Control chart technique as applied to inspection data will grow into a mere paperwork procedure, if there is a lack of use and interest on the part of the chief executive. It is his responsibility to take such corrective action that the charts disclose as being necessary. If action is not prompt and decisive, then it is better that the charts not be made in the first place.

Organization

Standards and records alone will not produce quality control. Like any other human activity, the proper application of such control requires organization. The organization for this purpose is usually called the "inspection department" (see Figure 53). The effective use of an inspection function in the manufacturing operation requires a careful definition of its two most important functions:

1. Authority.
2. Relationship to other departments.

Before quality control can become effective, it must be sold to the complete plant organization. Top management must be "quality-minded" and transmit this attitude to the secondary management, to the foremen, and to the workers themselves.

Frequently, the man at the bench or machine does not know the use or reason for the parts or operations that he is making. Through the use of moving pictures or working displays of the final product, an understanding of the functioning of parts can be given to the men and women who make the company's product. A sincere and continuous selling drive, always building on the pride of good workmanship, will develop an organization quality mindedness.

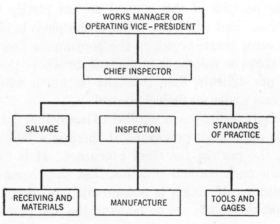

Fig. 53. Inspection Department Organization

If quality is desired in a plant, the lines of inspection authority must be properly and firmly defined to assure that quality. If the pressure for production is paramount in a plant, and if the department inspectors are subordinate to the department foreman, it is natural for the foreman to take a chance and overrule the inspectors. If this happens very often, the inspector will pass borderline cases rather than have an argument. Likewise, if the foremen and inspectors report to the same production superintendent, a similar condition is fostered.

Occasionally it is found in some plants that operational inspection is carried on by people who take instructions from two "bosses"—the chief inspector on techniques of inspection, and the foreman or superintendent on discipline, reporting, assignments, and shop rules. This basic violation of good organization practice renders inspection useless as far as control of quality is concerned.

Obviously, the inspectors should have their own functional chief. Normally, the chief inspector should have an organization rank equal to the shop executive whose work he is inspecting. Both should report to a common superior of management rank, but this may not always be desirable for reasons particular to the company or the manufacturing process.

The inspection department and individuals in it can create a difficult personnel and industrial relations problem if not carefully organized and administered. Favoritism to or collusion with operators by the inspectors can, under certain circumstances, become a real temptation. If such cases are ever disclosed, management must deal with them most severely. The inspection department is a judicial body; it must keep its judgments sound, and, like Caesar's wife, its integrity must be above reproach. If this is done, it will become the important element it should be in quality control.

Frequently, inspectors can and should do other work beyond the actual operation of inspection. The rule, "when a piece is picked up, do some work that enhances its value," finds a ready application in these cases. Such work for inspectors is: counting, wrapping, packing, certification of output, loading conveyors, and classifying.

Some regular functions of an inspection department and common to all of them are:

1. Development of inspection techniques.
2. Inspection of tools and gages.
3. Recording of scrap and good pieces.
4. Disposal of scrap.
5. Reduction of losses due to defectives.
6. Salvage and repair.
7. Care of gages and test equipment.
8. Inspection standards laboratory.
9. Consultation on quality standards.
10. Training of inspectors.
11. Control of inspection costs.
12. Development and maintenance of inspection procedures.

A variety of forms and procedures are necessary to implement the activities of an inspection department. Many of them must be closely co-ordinated with the activities of the production control and engineering departments. Reporting forms, particularly, must be designed to avoid duplication of other reporting media used by these two departments. Such forms vary widely for each specific type of manufacture and must be individually designed for each specific case.

Record forms, for interior use of the inspection department, are similar to the equipment record forms used for plant equipment. They are needed to provide a record of the location and condition of all inspection equipment. They, too, vary for each industry.

Other forms, for the collection of statistics on quality, scrap, salvage, and the like, may be required. Their individual design involves consideration of the same point made with regard to reporting forms.

Forms and procedures for inspection are a part of the general framework of control. Careful analysis of the media used in other departments is required, if a simple and effective system for quality control is desired.

Functional Relationships

The relationship of the inspection department to other departments must be clearly set up in the organization manual. As a staff function reporting to top management, it has responsibilities that frequently put it at loggerheads with other staff and operating departments.

Inspection is a referee function. It does not tell how or when the play should be made, but whether it is made correctly. If this relationship is clearly defined to the organization and thoroughly understood by it, the inspection department will be completely effective and successful.

A properly conceived inspection department will not only determine the degree of quality control being exercised but also determine the responsibility for observed deficiencies in the product. Such deficiencies may be caused by carelessness on the part of the operator, faulty design in the engineering department, defective material from the vendor, or any other of the many reasons for defective products. The responsibility becomes a matter of record.

ACTION REQUIREMENTS

The inspection department must have complete authority over the product, one from which there can be no appeal except to top management itself. This is necessary because a change in the ideal of quality usually becomes a change in company policy. This last is a matter for management decision only.

Therefore, the inspection department must have authority to:

1. Stop operation on a product when the quality standard is not being attained.
2. Designate the disposition of raw, processed, or finished material.
3. Prescribe the limitations under which work can be performed on the product.

Standards, records, and organization provide the necessary mechanism for quality control, but quality control will not result unless there is action. There are several channels through which action can be secured. For the operator, himself, incentives for good work can be established which will minimize defective workmanship at its very source. For the product, salvage work orders can be issued for reworking the defective units into a satisfactory condition, provided the cost of doing so is less than the cost of scrapping the piece.

Frequently, the action required goes even more deeply into the problem of poor quality and may require a revision of part or all of the standards incident to proper quality control. Other management devices can be used to secure necessary action in maintaining quality control. These may take the form of special committees to review the entire problem and may lead back into any one of the several channels from which defective products may issue.

Summary

Quality control is a definite management responsibility and should be exercised as directly as possible by management. Effective quality control requires an impartiality of viewpoint that will have only one objective, that of a good product. It must maintain this objective at all times, regardless of operating influences which may be brought to bear on the organization charged with this responsibility.

Consequently, the inspection division, which is management's tool for maintaining quality control, must be placed as close to the top as possible. There must be a clear understanding of the authority and responsibility of the inspection division throughout the organization. It must be supported actively and consistently by top management if it is to serve its purpose.

Quality control is achieved in five main steps:

1. Determine the quality desired, and then set up standards of quality, both in material specifications and limits for manufacture that will produce the desired quality.

2. Build an attitude of quality mindedness throughout the organization.

3. Install a properly organized and equipped inspection department that will enforce the quality standards set.

4. Provide records, charts, and reports that are simple and effective and that will give currently the "score" of the operating department.

5. Train the inspection personnel so they will know what they are doing, why they are doing it, and how to be fair and honest judges of workmanship.

CHAPTER 33

EXPENSE CONTROL

•

PURPOSE

In organizing the operation of a manufacturing plant for profitable results, many controls are required. These have been presented in other chapters of this manual. Of particular importance is the control of manufacturing expenses, commonly called factory burden or overhead, and designated hereinafter as expense control.

This subject has been dealt with in some detail in Chapter 15 and 17, Section 2. It is enlarged on in the following pages because it usually comprises the largest expense, both as to classification and amount, in any industrial enterprise.

Because of its importance to any industrial operation, management should insist on a satisfactory plan of expense control and particular attention to its effective application.

DEFINITION

Expense control is properly a subdivision of budgetary control and an integral part of cost control. It requires certain detailed but easily applied procedures. Special routines and techniques are necessary to its application, so that the operating executives responsible for manufacturing can make practical use of the data thus presented.

Expense control is defined as that subdivision of budgetary control and that part of cost control which contains all indirect expenses having a direct relationship to factory or manufacturing activity.

It does not include direct labor or direct material, nor general, administrative, or selling expense. Nor does it include expenditures made in behalf of the asset accounts of the company.

APPLICATION

The application of expense control to a manufacturing operation requires the following basic procedures:

1. *A chart of accounts,* which systematically classifies expenses. The customary and desirable form for this chart is shown in Figure 54. Such a chart is commonly called an "acrostic" chart of accounts. The simplicity, flexibility and adaptability of this form are so apparent that it has been widely adopted in practically every departmentalized business operating under modern accounting practices.
2. *An expense account record folio* for each account number, consisting of:
    (*a*) A graphic record of actual expense plotted against activity, as shown in Figure 12, Chapter 15, Section 2.
    (*b*) An account distribution sheet showing:
        1. Number and name of account.
        2. The formula for its fixed and variable content.
        3. A complete definition of the account. For example, if the account is "Oils and Greases," there should be listed, following the description, the different oils and greases and the places where they are used.
        4. A time schedule showing when payment must be made for the expense incurred. For example, if the account is "Taxes," each tax should be listed and the date of payment specified, even though the account is on an accrual basis.
        5. A correct expense distribution, indicating the apportionment of the total expense to different departments or products. Weight must be given, in prorating such expense, to the capacity, expected volume, value of equipment, and other physical attributes of the departments over which the expense is to be distributed.
    (*c*) A *labor payroll distribution,* properly recording and distributing direct and indirect labor. This record must match the departmental designations set up by the chart of accounts, and lend itself to ready use in relating labor and expense. Wherever possible such distribution should be made from actual time card charges which, if not available, should be provided for in the timekeeping system. Figure 55 illustrates a typical form for accumulating the payroll distribution.

Account Name	Account Number	Department Numbers					
		10	20	30	40	50	60
		Account Number Designation					
Salaries and other indirect payroll accounts	01	10–01		30–01			
	02		20–02	30–02	40–02		
	03						
	04 to 50						
Indirect material accounts	51 to 80						
Taxes, deprec., insurance, and other indirect accounts	81 to 99						

Department Legend

Number	Name
10	Foundry
20	Machine Shop
30	Inspection
etc.	

FIG. 54.   Chart of Accounts, Acrostic Form

In establishing the fixed and variable content of any expense account, the method for graphically analyzing an indirect labor account as described in Chapter 15, Section 2, can be used to great advantage. It gives a most accurate result.

Each expense account folio will therefore consist of a graphic chart and a distribution sheet. These should be on standard size sheets, preferably 8½x11, and arranged in a ring binder by department or account number or both.

Account	Number	Department				Total
		10	20	30	40	
Direct Labor		$	$	$	$	
Indirect Labor	01					
	02					
	03					
	04					
	05					
	06					
	etc.					

FIG. 55.   Payroll Distribution Sheet

PRESENTATION

To be of any value to the operating organization, expense control must lend itself to current and immediate use. For the best results this requires a *daily* record of the expenditures caused by the manufacturing operation.

This is not so difficult as it sounds. The elements of expense controllable within the factory are usually created in the factory. They are recorded on tangible media, such as requisitions for supplies and other indirect materials, and time cards for indirect labor and other nonproductive and service efforts.

The procedure assumes that stockrooms have been established in the factory for effective expense control and that all expense material is placed in stockrooms and issued on requisition, rather than delivered in bulk to the using department, which is then charged with the total invoice amount. Where requisitions are used, the daily accumulation can be easily made. It requires that requisitions and, in the case of labor, time cards be turned in and posted daily on a suitable columnar form.

In some cases, this work can all be done at the end of the month with some saving in time, provided there are many similar requisitions issued during the month which can be grouped. However, the additional work necessary to make such entries daily is negligible, compared with the value of keeping the information current. Moreover, immediate closing of the expense accounts can be effected at the end of the month.

Similarly, the indirect labor charges lend themselves admirably to the same procedure and use. As a rule, the daily accumulation of payroll charges is automatically required by established timekeeping and payroll procedures. The daily control in this case is merely rearrangement of the daily indirect labor charges by expense account classification, after such information has been entered on the payroll itself.

The control of expense labor, as a matter of fact, can be very closely related to the direct labor that makes it necessary. It can usually be expressed in the form of a standard of hours or persons, tying the expense labor directly to the direct labor it serves.

Departmental supplies and expense labor charges constitute a very large per cent of the expense items directly controllable in the factory. However, they may represent a rather small portion of the total expense chargeable to a factory, which would take into account such items as depreciation, insurance, rent, and other expenses created by virtue of the fact that the business is a going one.

These latter charges do not fluctuate from day to day and, for that reason, need not be considered in the daily controls to be established. However, they must be included in the expense control plan. The general factory management can then correctly relate the importance of and the effect of variances in the controllable items to the total expense necessary to run the plant.

Such daily expense controls are, of course, supplementary to the monthly expense control presented to the responsible executives in the usual budget form. By a correct adaptation of the detail thus shown (that is, by grouping and comparison with standard), the daily presentation can be used just as effectively as the required monthly summarization of all the various expenses, or more effectively.

If it is possible to present these figures to management in graphic form, much time and effort will be saved, and very prompt results can be attained.

This can be readily accomplished by plotting the data, monthly or otherwise, on chart paper (see Figure 12). This can be blueprinted and quickly distributed the same day. The advantages of this method are obvious, but require a chart mindedness on the part of the persons receiving such reports.

USING THE EXPENSE CONTROL

The mere presentation of complete and systematic data will not alone accomplish expense control. The executive responsible for the operation of the factory must take a critical attitude towards all such data. He must carefully analyze each expense by comparing the actual with the standard established for it. He must determine whether and where and, more particularly, how economies can be effected in the expenses he is scrutinizing.

This requires, additionally, that such information be given to the proper subordinate heads, particularly those responsible for creating the expense under review. The organization principles underlying this phase of control are described fully in Chapter 17, Section 2.

An organized procedure must therefore be established, in the form of reports and conferences, which will attain the objectives of expense control as required by management. Unless this is done, the "policing" of results will be lacking, and expense reduction will not be accomplished.

As stated earlier, expense control is a subdivision of the general budgetary control and an integral part of cost control. It is essential, therefore, that any applications to the control of factory expense be made to conform to the master plan of control. They must fit accounting-wise into the general accounting records and procedures. Unless this is provided for, there will be no assurance that the data presented for managerial action are valid or complete.

5

Industrial Relations

CHAPTER 34

PERSONNEL SELECTION, PLACEMENT, AND DEVELOPMENT

•

The problems of personnel selection, placement, and development have been with industry for many years. The attention these problems have received, however, has been at the best spasmodic. They receive active attention in periods of labor scarcity but are given little or no recognition when the labor supply is abundant.

Regardless of the availability of labor, the successful operation of any business is directly influenced by the manner in which management utilizes its men, materials, and facilities.

In selecting the materials used in a product, exhaustive tests are made covering physical characteristics, color, appearance, durability, and numerous other properties. Testing laboratories are established in order to guarantee the integrity of the product. Where the company itself does not maintain its own laboratory, it may have tests run, or it may purchase by certified specification.

Similarly, a new piece of equipment must be recommended by skilled engineers, and its success in other plants is investigated. A final decision to purchase is reached only after management is assured of the machine's performance, or its versatility, or its length of service.

Man, the most important element in successful business enterprise, should be selected and used with the same care given to material and equipment. The new employee should be tested. A final decision to purchase his services should be reached only after management is assured, insofar as this is possible, that he will be able to perform the job adequately.

It is generally true that every company in a competitive industry has an equal knowledge of the raw materials which can be used in the product and of the tools and processes by which those materials may be fabricated. It is logical to assume, then, that the company which selects and utilizes its men effectively has a marked advantage over others which do not.

The majority of industrialists agree that effective selection, placement, and development of employees is both desirable and profitable. It is reasonable to ask why they have not done more about these problems.

It has been only in relatively recent years that industry has utilized the services of the employment manager, or the personnel manager, or the industrial relations director. This specialization has improved the quality of personnel and has aided materially in placement, for example, by formally defining the job, by determining the requirements of the job, and so forth.

It is true that not all this has been done scientifically, but it has been done systematically. It is certainly a step in the right direction, but there is yet much to be desired. Results in personnel work have fallen far short of the degree of scientific precision found in other activities.

The most obvious opportunity for improvement lies in the field of testing; yet this possibility to date has barely been touched on. There are many reasons for this, the primary one being the fact that most existing tests are quite expensive. In some cases, the economics of the business make it impractical to utilize the existing testing tools at all.

It is also true that the majority of the tests available today have been developed and validated academically and are understood only by the trained psychologist. The profit motive has long since spurred investment in research and development of material testing equipment. Tangible products resulted which could be sold to industry at a profitable return.

Personnel tests, on the other hand, have not in the past had any great profit potential. The research and development work on these intangibles has been confined to our institutions of higher learning, and the effort expended has been primarily a "labor of love."

The cost of developing and validating industrial tests has been prohibitive to the universities. They have, therefore, confined their activities primarily to the academic field. In spite of this, the universities have developed tests which can be applied to industry. This will only be done well, however, when there is joint effort and acceptance by each of the knowledge and experience of the other.

Industrial Use of Tests

In order to use tests effectively, industry must first understand that they are only a few of the many tools of management. It is too often the case that a company that has never used tests will jump headlong into a testing program. It will completely ignore judgment and experience and base decisions only on test results.

Such procedures can only result in failure; but, because such practice has been common, industrial tests have received a "black eye" and are scoffed at by executives who have not taken the time to seek the reasons for failure.

Industry must learn to walk before it can run. It therefore behooves management to initiate testing programs on a small carefully controlled basis, giving simple basic tests at the beginning. Few companies operate time study programs successfully and thus are not ready for advanced motion study. Similarly, the average company must master the simple tests before undertaking the more advanced.

To illustrate this, there are a number of tests which have been carefully worked out to determine the vocational interests of an individual. By means of these tests, it can be accurately determined whether an individual is suited to sales work or engineering work, for example. By adding other tests and narrowing down the fields, it is surprising how neatly the skilled psychologist can place the "square peg" in the "square hole."

These tests, however, are relatively advanced for the average company. For a start, it is desirable to determine the vocational interest of an applicant only to the extent of whether he likes routine or variety work.

To carry on the illustration further, suppose management knows that a prospective employee likes routine work, as can quickly be determined by easily understood tests. Management has an intimate knowledge of the jobs in the plant and an application blank outlining the experience of the prospective employee, along with information which can be secured by interview and from references. A much better selection and placement can then be made than would be possible without the very elementary vocational interest test.

The illustration stresses the importance of using test information *along with* such other available information as can be secured. No test is 100 per cent valid, and all tests err sometimes. Conversely, however, tests are extremely useful in keeping the employer from making mistakes. They point the direction of the interview and often indicate the desirability of further specific information.

In general, industry wishes to know two things about an applicant or an employee:

1. His ability to perform an individual job.
2. His personality make-up.

If these two things can be accurately and economically determined, the initial step in industrial testing has been taken. Tests are available which will give this information; and for the average company, inexperienced in testing, this information is as much as can be absorbed. A test battery which would give this information would consist of:

1. A mechanical alertness test which would indicate the individual's mechanical aptitude and give some indication of his reasoning ability.

2. A test to determine the individual's background in mathematics and science. Most industrial jobs require some knowledge of these things and such a test also indicates the ability of the individual to absorb training along these lines.

3. A manual skill test to determine how well the individual can use his fingers, hands, and arms. Manual skill, to some degree, is required in almost every manufacturing operation.

4. A test to determine the personal characteristics of the individual, how well he gets along with others, how well they will co-operate with him. Average personal characteristics are satisfactory in most jobs of a manual type, but many can be much better accomplished by an individual with what is usually called a "nice personality."

5. A simple vocational interest test to show whether the individual likes routine or a variety of work. The use of such information is self-evident.

6. A test to measure the individual's susceptibility to emotional appeal. Such a test would show the stability desired in supervisory or in difficult trying work, as well as the high susceptibility to emotional appeal which can be most troublesome under adverse conditions.

7. A test to indicate the ambition of the individual and his attempts to improve himself on his own initiative.

Figure 56 illustrates a typical individual test by such a battery. This test records the answers mechanically and avoids the use of pencil and paper, which is often distasteful to factory employees.

The first three tests give information as to the person's ability to perform on the job. The last four give a picture of the personal make-up. A battery of tests can be economical enough to give to every employee as a part of the hiring procedure. They can be used not only for selection but also for placement, upgrading, training, and counseling.

When they have been absorbed into the personnel activities of

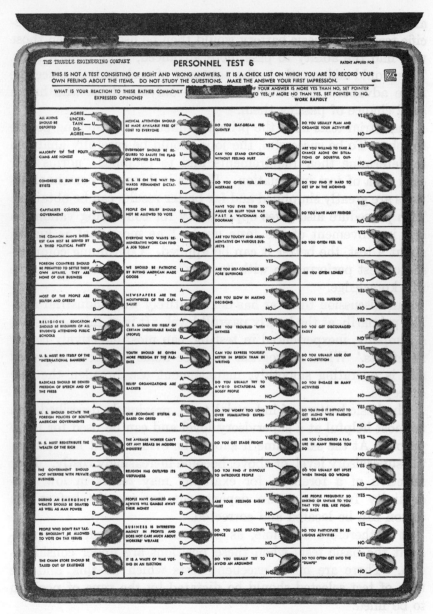

FIG. 56. Mechanical Test Panel

an organization, they may be supplemented by longer more specific tests. The basic battery would then be used to screen those who had the ability to pass more advanced, more refined tests. This would add greatly to the economy of such testing, since the more advanced tests would be given only to those who had a good chance of passing them.

Industrial tests have the primary function of matching people to jobs. To be successful, the jobs should be carefully analyzed to determine their requirements and to establish "norms" for each area of test information. If this is done, all personnel actions are greatly simplified and far better results can be obtained. This procedure also gives opportunity for continuing validation and improvement of the tests used. The more that is known about a test, the better it can be applied. Continuing comparison of test performance with "norms" serves excellently to give this knowledge.

Our discussion thus far has dealt entirely with industrial testing, primarily at the hourly payroll level. It is at this point that a company, inexperienced in testing, can most effectively center its efforts. When a program in these fields has been absorbed and is operating smoothly, management can broaden the test concepts.

The basic battery of industrial tests, previously described, can be most helpful at a supervisory level and can be used for these people. At the same time it should be evident that mistakes at the supervisory level, or above, become increasingly costly. Poor selection of a foreman, for example, may result in low productivity from an entire department for months before the reason can be located and corrected.

It is therefore desirable, as previously indicated, to supplement the basic tests when these positions are under consideration. There are many excellent tests which do this, and the type of test selected should be dictated by the type of position to be filled.

Tests very similar to the basic industrial battery are available for office positions. In most office jobs of a clerical nature, mechanical alertness has no particular value. Verbal alertness and arithmetic reasoning is of importance and can be substituted for mechanical alertness. Similarly, whereas backgrounds in mathematics and science are applicable to most factory jobs, backgrounds in grammar and arithmetic are useful in office jobs.

These supplementary tests are the same in principle but deal with problems more general to the office than to the factory. Instead of a manual dexterity test in the shop, the office testees may be given sorting tests, typing tests, shorthand tests, and so forth. In the case of the more important office positions, other supplementary tests can be added as previously described.

Tests are not expensive in themselves. The time required to give and interpret more advanced tests is expensive, however, but is justified by the savings which can be made. Business economics will not permit lengthy tests, difficult to interpret, for all employees. It should be realized, however, that in the supervisory, administrative, or executive group expensive testing is very often economical in the end.

When a company initiates a testing program, it gains concepts which are often rather startling because of their newness, although they would be self-evident if given previous consideration. Management quickly discovers from tests, for example, that the requirements of a good foreman are quite different from the requirements of a good operator.

This is so obvious that it seems elementary; but time after time industry will make a good operator into a foreman. He fails, and the company not only loses him as a foreman, but also loses the good worker, because pride seldom permits him to return to his old job.

In a like manner, channels of upgrading will open up where none were previously considered. Instead of basing promotion on exposure to or experience in a related job, management will see that a good carpenter's helper, for example, may not necessarily make a good carpenter. Knowing this, transfer and promotion may be made to entirely unrelated jobs. Agreeable surprises will result when it is seen how quickly a new incumbent grasps and gets on top of a job which, although foreign to his past experience, is nevertheless particularly suited to his physical and mental make-up.

This is one step in the development of the latent potential of the employee. It is supplemented by a wise counseling and training plan which can be custom-built around the knowledge gained from testing. Valuable employees result.

DANGERS IN TESTING

There are several ways in which tests are misused, and it is well to indicate a few of these.

It has already been pointed out that tests must not be used as final answers. This tendency can be overcome by understanding that tests are nothing more than a means of obtaining information from the person being tested. This same information could be obtained by interview or by a close relationship with the person over a long period of time. Seldom, however, can the necessary time be taken to secure the information by interview and, generally, employee turnover makes it difficult to have a long personal acquaintance with him. The test quickly secures in a systematic consistent usable form, information which could be obtained by other means. If testing is thus regarded, it becomes clear that test information is supplementary information and should be so used.

A second common danger in testing is that people using the test attempt to read into it something for which it was never intended. If the test is a good test, they become blindly confident of it. As their experience broadens, they begin to interpret the test more and more minutely. To illustrate this, it was found that an individual with broad experience in testing drew the entirely fallacious conclusion that anyone who made a specific score on a particular test would "fly off the handle" once every five weeks. Such interpretations are not uncommon and should be meticulously guarded against.

A third danger in testing is that the information thus secured is improperly used. Many people will advise against giving any test information to supervisors for fear of misuse. Yet how can the full benefits of testing be secured if the information is not given to those with a need for it? The answer, of course, lies in properly training the people who apply the information in both its interpretation and use. If this is not done, a testing program can be quickly ruined by turning down a request for a raise because, "You are emotionally unstable," or some equally thoughtless statement.

The fourth danger in testing results from applications by an individual who is not well-grounded in manufacturing operations. This danger can best be illustrated by an example that actually occurred. An attempt was being made to establish "norms" for a particular operation. The individual in charge tested all employees on the operation and then made a statistical determination of the operators' ability based on time study.

The result was the establishment of "norms" which seemed to be factual and were certainly based on an accurate measurement. However, they simply did not make sense to a person who understood manufacturing, as:

1. On a job which obviously required a high degree of manual skill, the best operators had very low manual skill.

2. In a group operation where monotony was relieved by conversation, the norms indicated the best operators rated low on personality.

3. In a job difficult to learn, but routine when once learned, the norms indicated the desirability of having individuals on the job who lacked the ability to learn and who were very susceptible to emotional appeal.

The particular group of operators had been a consistent trouble spot, and the turnover in the group was extremely high and costly. Investigation revealed:

1. The highest performer had only mediocre ability to perform, but, being a widow with children to support, she worked continually at a fatiguing pace, foregoing all personal time, to assure her continuation on a well-paying job. The tester did not know that a time study is leveled or normalized to an average operator and that a high performance can be secured by foregoing the personal and fatigue allowances which are added to the basic elemental time.

2. The company had a poor wage incentive plan which paid relatively little for quite a high performance above standard. The better operators, rather than exert themselves, took a very leisurely pace, received their guaranteed day rate, and worked

nights at other jobs to increase their compensation rather than to exert effort on their day job.

3. The material and production control was ineffective, and there was a continual shortage of materials. The old operators, by knowing the ropes, got the large part of the material. The newer operators could not have performed better if they wanted to, because they did not have the material to work on.

4. The old operators were extremely antisocial and unpleasant and picked on new girls so much that they quit their jobs rather than work with these individuals.

It can be seen that a theoretically validated conclusion can lead to very false conclusions unless tempered by knowledge and experience in industry.

BENEFITS

Sound personnel selection, placement, and development, like every other management function, cannot be installed and made operative overnight. The program must be slowly and soundly developed and administered by experienced personnel. Its results are reflected rapidly in earnings, however, since it is the only means whereby management can give man the same consideration and care that is given to material and equipment. It is the means by which maximum utilization of man power can be obtained and:

1. Determines the ability of applicants quickly.
2. Helps get the right man on the right job.
3. Eliminates the training of failures or hopeless cases.
4. Gives records useful in selecting old employees for promotion or transfer.
5. Helps to reorient dissatisfied employees.
6. Serves as a basis for counseling and training.

CHAPTER 35

JOB EVALUATION

•

INTRODUCTION

Good industrial relations result when properly placed employees are getting satisfactory production from jobs that have been clearly defined, systematically measured, and adequately compensated. The control of employee productivity and the fitness of the men for the jobs have been described fully in previous chapters.

The systematic measurement of the job itself, however, requires a different approach and a distinctive method of appraisal. This technique, called job evaluation, has as its purpose the determination of the relative importance of jobs, in order that a sound and equitable base rate structure, essential to any wage payment plan, can be established.

Job evaluation is a particularly pertinent subject because, in our complex and socialized economy, the workman at the bench, machine, or desk must be satisfactorily integrated into the production scheme if the gains thus far realized in the national economy are to be retained.

BASIC PRINCIPLES AND DEFINITIONS

Job evaluation (or "job rating" which is an alternate and infrequently used expression) is the process of describing the responsibilities, skill, experience, physical and mental effort, and the like, required to perform a given task. It is an appraisal of the task itself and not of the workman who is doing it. The performance of the task results from the applied effort of the worker and is described by the term Merit Rating, or personnel rating.

In other words, a worker's fitness for a job is quite apart from the requirements of that job. This distinction must be carefully borne in mind at all times when making a job evaluation. The measurement of the worker's fitness involves very different factors from those which determine the requirements of his job.

The basic theory of job evaluation is founded on the proved fact that certain specifications or requirements are inherent in, and common to, all operational processes. If properly identified and scaled, these can be used to determine the relative scale position of all jobs in any given process.

A good deal of trial and error has entered into this technique. Even today, differences of practice and philosophy exist among the practitioners of job evaluation. However, most authorities agree that the following job elements, usually called factors, may apply completely and properly to any operational process. Their use, therefore, defines the basic principles of job evaluation.

The major factors in any job are:

1. Responsibility.
2. Skill, or dexterity, or accuracy.
3. Mental effort.
4. Practical knowledge.
5. Working conditions.
6. Physical effort.
7. Fatigue.

In practice, these factors are frequently subdivided, in order to secure a more precise measurement of the job requirements. For instance, the factor of responsibility is frequently divided into responsibility for safety of others, responsibility for materials, and responsibility for tools and equipment. The factor of skill is subdivided into dexterity and accuracy; and the factor of working conditions into hazard and surroundings.

Consideration must next be given as to how the values for these factors are to be distributed over a job. That is, what value should be given each factor out of the total value given to all the factors?

Usually, the factors concerned with skill are the most important as they are basically inherent in the job requirement. Therefore a large proportion of the total values allotted to all factors, usually around 50 per cent, will be given to the skill and mental factors.

Next in importance will be the responsibility factors, and experience has shown that 25 per cent of the total values should be allotted to these. The effort factors come next, as is logical, because since time immemorial mere brawn has been the least essential requirement in the application of human effort to the production of goods. The value allotted to these factors usually approximates 15 per cent of the total. Factors such as working conditions and practical knowledge (being supplementary to the other job requirements) are allotted the remainder of the values, about 10 per cent.

In passing, it is of interest to note that these value allotments are considerably changed when applied to office occupations. Here it is found that great stress must be laid on the responsibility and the mental requirements of a job, with the result that only 50 per cent of the total values may be allotted to skill, effort, and other remaining factors.

TECHNIQUES

Many techniques have been devised to measure the relative position of jobs in a plant. Only a few have stood the test of practical application: those using comparison of rates as the method of positioning jobs on a scale, and those using points.

The comparison method divides the job wage rate over the various factors used, which are practically the same as those in the point system. It then determines by careful and tedious comparison of all jobs, factor by factor, the relative order of position between the highest paid job and the lowest paid job.

The Point System pays no attention to the wage rate paid. From an arbitrary scale of 100, 500, or 1000 points, it assigns to each factor its proper number of points. Each job is analyzed by factor and then given a selected number of points from the total points allotted to each factor.

In the course of job evaluation's application to industry, the point allocation has crystallized in the following ranges:

Responsibility	200–240
Skill, dexterity, accuracy	230–300
Mental effort	100
Practical knowledge	80–100
Experience	120–150
Working conditions	75–100
Physical effort	60
Fatigue	50

The various ways of applying these points require fairly complex manuals. However, all these techniques are fully described in a great number of publications and books which can be secured from any industrial library.

Basically, the points in each factor are allotted to a job by a system of degrees. These may vary from 3 to 8, depending on the nature and content of the factor. For example, the factor of practical knowledge (a term which is more satisfactory than the word education) is allocated 80 points and is divided into 8 degrees as follows:

Point Value	Degree	Description
10	1	*Minimum:* Ability to carry out *verbal orders*, comprehend safety regulations, and count up to 100.
20	2	*Very Low:* Ability to understand and carry out *written orders*, and to identify and mark material or product.
30	3	*Low:* Knowledge of simple mathematics; ability to add, subtract, multiply, and divide. Knowledge of elementary tools, ordinary materials, and common methods.
40	4	*Below Medium:* Ability to make calculations in fractions and decimals. General knowledge of process, procedure, and specifications within department.
50	5	*Medium:* Ability to use simple shop formulas and to work from sketches and plain mechanical drawings. Familiarity with chemical reaction, as involved in shop practice.

Point Value	Degree	Description
60	6	*Above Medium:* Ability to obtain solutions by use of trigonometry, algebra, and standard scientific formulas; and to prepare reports of nonroutine type such as analysis of personnel utilization, physical test of materials. Some knowledge of mechanical or electrical principles to maintain, adjust, or design equipment. Considerable working knowledge of manufacturing process specifications.
70	7	*High:* Ability to work from complex drawings, use complex formulas. Knowledge of technical developments, mechanical or electrical, scientific principles, physical and chemical properties of materials.
80	8	*Maximum:* Specialized ability obtained by technical training or equivalent industrial education in chemistry, metallurgy, processing, tool engineering, etc. Ability to formulate data effecting higher policy, planning and procedure.

The evaluator selects the degree which fits the job description, and assigns the points indicated for that factor of the job.

Each of the preceding plans has its ardent proponents, but the great majority of job evaluations in industry are made by the point system. This indicates its superior practicability.

INSTALLATION

Before installing a job evaluation plan, particularly in an organized shop, there are two essential requirements:

1. A complete and authentic description of every job to be evaluated must be made so that the evaluators can relate each detail duty requirement to the proper measuring factor.

2. A job evaluation committee representing labor, management, and arbitration must be set up. The arbitrator is usually an outside consultant acceptable to both labor and management. He directs the accumulation of the required information and activates the proceedings and conclusions of the committee.

The committee need not be large and may include only one labor member, one management member, and the consultant. Larger committees waste time in harmonizing divergent viewpoints, but are sometimes necessary if there is no labor organization in the plant. In any event, it is imperative to the success of any job evaluation program that labor be fully represented in the formulation of the plan and, if necessary, in its application.

After the job evaluation committee is organized, the arbitrator should have prepared and approved by the committee a standard list of occupations to be evaluated and should secure job descriptions for each of these occupations. The importance of good descriptions cannot be overstressed. A job evaluation is no better than the job description from which it is derived. Description is the only basis on which the various job factors and their degrees can be determined. The job descriptions may well err in the direction of too much detail, as it is much easier to throw out irrelevant information than it is to supply missing information.

To secure full interest in the program, every worker should be encouraged to participate in the drawing up of his job's description. Although questionnaires have some very practical disadvantages, they can in some cases supplement the other sources of information available for describing the job.

The job description enables the evaluator to determine the exact degree of the factor considered. That is to say, if the factor of experience has 120 points allotted to it, the job description will determine how many of those points should be allotted to experience for that particular job. In practice if the job description is correctly and completely made out, it is surprising how closely evaluators will agree on the allotment of factor points. When the job descriptions are ready, they in turn are reviewed and approved by the committee. They may be evaluated in full committee sessions, which may call in as ex officio advisors such shop stewards, foremen, and other labor–management spokesmen as are necessary to establish a competent and final scale position for each job.

When all the occupations have been acceptably evaluated, the work of the committee is finished, and the real problem comes into view. How much are these jobs worth in money?

APPLICATION

One of the purposes of a job evaluation program is to establish how much a given job is worth. This cannot be done until the relative position of the job is discovered, and, therefore, it becomes an eventual rather than a primary objective. Nonetheless, it is an objective and must have its proper place in the picture of labor–management relations.

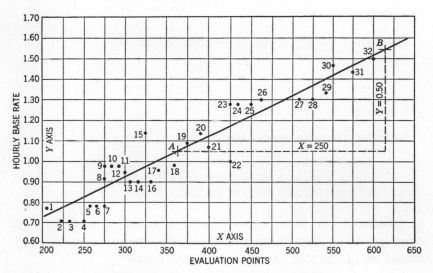

FIG. 57.   Job-Evaluation Scatter Chart

The matter of pricing jobs must necessarily be one of bargaining for the money value, to be assigned to the point spread between the lowest rated and the highest rated job. The consultant can determine what the average evaluation actually is.

This is done by means of a correlation or "scatter" chart (see Figure 57) with the horizontal scale divided off into the point range used. The vertical scale shows the actual hourly base rate paid for each job. Each job is plotted on this chart and a pattern of wage-point positions is established.

By careful mathematical analysis, the consultant finds the average evaluated base rate line running through these positions, the line usually running upwards across the chart.

The actual method of finding the average evaluated base rate line requires a rather detailed mathematical calculation. Otherwise, the final results of the analyses are challengeable. For this reason a careful explanation is given here of the use of a simplified form of the equation of "least squares." This will determine the correct location of the average evaluated base rate line to be drawn through the scatter of points plotted in Figure 57.

Calculation No. 1

Determine the slope (a) of the line by the equation

$$a = \frac{\Sigma xy}{\Sigma x^2}$$

Step 1

Reading from the chart (Figure 57),

> Job no. 1 has an X value of 200, and a Y value of 0.74
> Job no. 2 has an X value of 225, and a Y value of 0.70
> Job no. 3 has an X value of 235, and a Y value of 0.70, etc.

as tabulated and summarized under columns X and Y. The average of the base rates and evaluation points is thus determined and is plotted as point A on the chart.

Step 2

If the average values of X and Y are subtracted from each job value of X and Y, the algebraic x and y values of each point are found as shown under columns x and y. These x and y values represent the distance of each job point from point A.

Step 3

Calculation of the terms x^2 and xy, and their algebraic totals as shown under columns x^2 and xy.

Calculation 1 is then completed by solving for

$$a = \frac{\Sigma xy}{\Sigma x^2} = \frac{786.64}{388,438} = 0.002,$$

DATA FOR CALCULATION 1

Job No.	Step 1		Step 2		Step 3	
	X	Y	x	y	x^2	xy
1	200	0.74	−168	−0.30	28,224	+ 50.40
2	225	0.70	−143	−0.34	20,449	+ 48.62
3	230	0.70	−138	−0.34	19,044	+ 46.92
4	250	0.70	−118	−0.34	13,924	+ 40.12
5	260	0.78	−108	−0.26	11,664	+ 28.08
6	265	0.78	−103	−0.26	10,609	+ 26.78
7	275	0.78	− 93	−0.26	8,649	+ 24.18
8	275	0.90	− 93	−0.14	8,649	+ 13.02
9	275	0.96	− 93	−0.08	8,649	+ 7.44
10	285	0.96	− 83	−0.08	6,889	+ 6.64
11	295	0.96	− 73	−0.08	5,329	+ 5.84
12	300	0.92	− 68	−0.12	4,624	+ 8.16
13	310	0.90	− 58	−0.14	3,364	+ 8.12
14	320	0.90	− 48	−0.14	2,304	+ 6.72
15	325	1.14	− 43	+0.10	1,849	− 4.30
16	330	0.90	− 38	−0.14	1,444	+ 5.32
17	340	0.94	− 28	−0.10	784	+ 2.80
18	360	0.98	− 8	−0.06	64	+ 0.48
19	375	1.08	+ 7	+0.04	49	+ 0.28
20	390	1.12	+ 22	+0.08	484	+ 1.76
21	400	1.06	+ 32	+0.02	1,024	+ 0.64
22	425	1.00	+ 57	−0.04	3,249	− 2.28
23	425	1.26	+ 57	+0.22	3,249	+ 12.54
24	435	1.26	+ 67	+0.22	4,489	+ 14.74
25	450	1.26	+ 82	+0.22	6,724	+ 18.04
26	460	1.30	+ 92	+0.26	8,464	+ 23.92
27	510	1.30	+142	+0.26	20,164	+ 36.92
28	525	1.30	+157	+0.26	24,649	+ 40.82
29	540	1.34	+172	+0.30	29,584	+ 51.60
30	550	1.44	+182	+0.40	33,124	+ 72.80
31	575	1.44	+207	+0.40	42,849	+ 82.80
32	600	1.50	+232	+0.46	53,824	+106.72
Total	11,780	33.30	. .	. .	$\Sigma x^2 = 388,438$	$\Sigma xy = 786.64$
Avg.	368	1.04				

which is the slope of the best average line running through point A.

Calculation 2

The equation for a straight line is $a = y/x$ or $y = ax$. If a value of 250 is assumed for x and it is known that $a = 0.002$,

$$y = 0.002 \times 250 = 0.50.$$

Point B is found by measuring these x and y values from point A, and a straight line is then drawn from point B through point A to intercept the Y axis or any convenient ordinate close to it.

Although theoretically the line has some curvature between its lowest and highest points, in actual practice it is straightened out and establishes the actual evaluated base rate at each end of the line. For example: The evaluated base rate at the lowest evaluation of 200 points might be $0.70 an hour, and at the highest evaluation of 600 points it might be $1.50 an hour. If the line is a straight line, every evaluation point above 200 is worth ⅕¢ in the hourly rate. What it should be, if the actual evaluated rate line is not acceptable to labor, is something for labor and management to agree on, through accepted channels of bargaining. Each side must accept the following principles: that there be equal pay for equal work, that the highest rated jobs receive the highest pay, that the evaluated rates of pay be consistent with the rates of pay in the industry or community or both.

Job Classification

One other frequently used method of job evaluation is the classification method. Several or many classes of jobs are established, from the lowest to the highest defined occupation, and all jobs are then sorted into one of these classifications. This is really a variant of the factor comparison method. The wages paid form the basis for judging the class position of the job, after consideration has been given to its position relative to other jobs.

Although it has the virtue of extreme simplicity, it also has the serious fault of being dependent entirely on the unmeasured judgment of the person or persons making the specific assignment to a classification. It requires of that person or persons a thorough knowledge of the jobs so that all work factors will be considered, as well as a careful differentiation in the skill, effort, and responsibility required.

The classification method has a rather limited application in industry. It is usually the first method tried by a company when circumstances compel it to review the inequalities in its wage structure. The chief objection to its use for this purpose lies in the fact that it does not give a straight line relationship between the base rates and the various job classifications. When problems of wage inequalities arise, it becomes difficult to support the reasoning that resulted in the conclusion under fire.

However, this analysis does have a definite place in the problem of wage administration as a method of rate classification. If it is not confused with true job evaluation, it can be a useful tool in an emergency.

Position Evaluation

An extension of the principles of job evaluation into salaried positions of a supervisory or a clerical nature has also been developed within recent years. Although the technique is the same as that used in plant job evaluation, the factors used are quite different. As mentioned earlier in this chapter, they lay greater stress on the responsibility and mental requirements of the job than on other factors of skill or experience.

To illustrate the wide divergence in the factors used in job evaluation and position evaluation, they are compared in the following table:

JOB EVALUATION	POSITION EVALUATION
Responsibility for:	Responsibility for:
Injury to others.	Supervision.
Direction of others.	Procedures.
Delays.	Decisions.
Materials.	
Equipment.	
Total Points—240	*Total Points—400*

JOB EVALUATION—*Cont.*　　　POSITION EVALUATION—*Cont.*

Aptitudes:
　Manual skill.
　Mental skill.
　Accuracy.
　Dexterity.

Skill in:
　Independent action.
　Analysis and interpretation.
　Planning.
　Knowledge of grammatical
　　structure.
　Training.
　Manual effort.
　Mathematics.

Total Points—250

Total Points—275

Practical knowledge	80 points	Relationships:	
Mental effort	100 points	Internal.	
Experience	120 points	External.	
Working conditions	100 points	Verbal expression.	
Physical effort	60 points	Written expression.	
Fatigue	50 points	*Total Points—250*	

Working conditions—75 points

Grand Total—1000 points　　　Grand Total—1000 points

Although position evaluation has not been subjected to the same critical scrutiny as job evaluation and has not been as generally applied, nevertheless it is a sound and proved tool for management. It is just as applicable in the office as job evaluation is in the shop.

CHAPTER 36

SUPERVISORY
TRAINING

•

DEFINITION

Supervisory training consists of a scheduled program of instruction. Such programs teach the supervisor how to handle human relations and everyday technical problems relating to production personnel.

ORIGIN

The training of supervisors is not something which is new to industry, nor is it at all mysterious. Management has for years endeavored to impart to employees the knowledge and experience which its own executives so painfully acquired. In the early days the father trained the son in his trade, pointing out to him the right and wrong ways of doing things. This procedure was truly an effective one. It was not formalized; but it was continuous, and it was personal.

Supervisory training today is at the other end of the pendulum's swing. The man who started the average business has grown further and further away from his supervisors, not from desire, but because businesses do expand. Our functional specialization, along with the increasing complexities of operating a business, make it almost impossible to maintain that all-important close personal contact.

Along with the changes just described have come more rapid changes in management. The need arose to bring new capital into the business. Owner management, although far from extinct, has decreased through death, or absorption, or for numerous other reasons.

As a result supervisory training has been relegated to a staff function, usually under the personnel department. Too often it has deteriorated into a pseudopsychology course of little or no interest to the trainee and of even less benefit to him.

Supervisory training should never be considered as a packaged product which can be bought off the shelf. To be effective, it must be constantly adjusted to meet the continually changing needs of the company. Of equal importance, it must be continuous. Very poor results will be obtained if a supervisory training course, no matter how good, is carried on for only two months and then forgotten for a year, or two years, or five years.

Supervisory training is something like a wage incentive in that it can seldom be put into operation at the time a company wants it. A wage incentive is bound to fail if a company has a bad base rate structure, unsound production control, poor methods, or unqualified time study men. Equally, to be successful supervisory training requires preparatory effort.

PURPOSE

Before initiating a supervisory training program, management should give thought to the following:

1. *Why do we want to train our supervisors?* The apparently obvious answer is often not the correct one. If management thinks the supervisors need training because labor relations are weak, management should first find out why they are weak. Perhaps it is management that needs training.

If management thinks productivity of the workers is too low, it might be well to remember that labor is just as efficient as management plans for it and gives it the tools with which to work.

Consideration may indicate that the supervisory training program should be postponed until certain corrective measures have been taken.

2. *What supervisors do we want to train?* It is usual to want to start with the foremen, but this is seldom the right place to begin. Some of the following points will make this self-evident.

3. *What do we expect of the men we plan to train?* This is a most important question, and there are many tangible and intangible problems which arise in connection with it. Often it will be found that management does not have even an organization manual to outline the duties and responsibilities of the trainees. The very foundation of the training plan must then be initially prepared.

4. *What will we train them in?* This discussion can be expanded very widely, but will here only receive direction of the thought which must be given to it. If management decides to train supervisors in labor relations, it must first acquaint them thoroughly with those policies of the company which affect labor relations. Seldom are such policies written. Often they are inadequately defined, even in the minds of responsible management.

The policies must be defined; they must be analyzed and written down. If done with the co-operation of the supervisors, this action in itself becomes an excellent supervisory training program.

What supervisors are to be trained in must be carefully worked out. This points the way to the selection of the training material. As previously stated, such material cannot be bought as a package off the shelf.

5. *Who will do the training?* By the time management arrives at this consideration the importance of intrusting the training program to qualified personnel will have become evident. Seldom can a program be carried on by one individual. One man may be responsible for it, but many must enter into the active instruction and direction. It will be found, however, that Mr. President must start the ball rolling. He will have to initiate the activity with his immediate associates.

TRAINING PROGRAMS

When all the preceding points have been considered, then and only then can a training program be developed which will truly

meet the needs of the business. Points of emphasis will have
been indicated, and the best means for giving this emphasis will
have been decided on. The program may be further supplemented by learning more about the individuals to be trained. A
carefully worked out test plan will not only cover testing as discussed in Chapter 34 of this section, but will also include analysis
of merit ratings, if they exist, as well as interviews and questionnaires to determine the supervisors' needs.

There are a number of subjects, applicable to most companies,
which should be considered in developing the final training program. These will be commented on briefly to indicate the
thought behind them. They should be adjusted, however, to the
company's particular needs.

Supervisory Analysis

In any training program it is well to aid the trainee to know
himself better and to help him understand what kind of person
he really is. This is important if he is to deal expertly with
human relations problems. It can be done by testing the supervisor and counseling with him, but should be done only by a
thoroughly qualified individual. If there is any doubt at all as
to the counselor's ability, this step should be omitted.

Industrial Relations Problems of Supervisors

This subject should be handled in its initial stages by an individual whose training and experience permits him to interpret, in
everyday language, the fundamental human relations aids available to the supervisor. Common complexes can be discussed and
illustrated, and the techniques of dealing with each can be given.
The tools which are useful in dealing with personnel should be
presented in as convincing a form as possible and should be illustrated by actual cases from the company's own experience. After
the groundwork has been carefully laid, this subject can be broad-
ened into panel or question-and-answer meetings.

Organization

In order to secure proper co-ordination, co-operation, and control of men, the relationship between co-operating units should be defined. Along with this goes explanation of lines of authority and of the line and staff functions of the various parts of the organization. The supervisor cannot intelligently co-operate or understand the reasons why certain things are done unless this picture is clearly explained to him.

Personnel Policies and Procedures

This subject requires explanation of company policies and procedures in selection, placement, indoctrination, upgrading, training, and the like. It should cover wage payment plans, disciplinary procedures, handling of grievances, and all other related subjects. The discussion should not be limited to the company's activity alone but should discuss the methods used by other firms and the advantages and disadvantages of each. Disciplinary procedures and the handling of grievances should be dramatized by case studies drawn from actual company experience. This subject alone affords enough material for a long training program, and its importance cannot be too strongly stressed.

The Man and His Job

This subject deals with job evaluation, job classification, and other techniques used to define and rate the job, along with testing, merit rating, and other procedures used to learn about the man. This training, of course, has as its objective the placing of the square peg in the square hole and the round peg in the round hole.

Labor Laws

The laws which regulate labor should be analyzed, interpreted, and discussed and their relation to the company set forth. The discussion should cover Federal, state, and local regulations. It may often be enlivened by inviting qualified representatives of the regulating departments or agencies to speak at the meetings.

The Technical Phases

The supervisor should be considered as a plant manager in miniature, and the various controls relating to production, labor, quality, and expense should be carefully explained to and discussed with him. Methods of dealing with wastes, both in material and time, should be described and illustrated, along with the details of safety and good working conditions. This subject may be treated in terms directly applicable to the company, as well as in general. The company may be a job shop, for example, but it is most helpful to the supervisor to compare the various functions of the job shop type of operation with those of line production.

TRAINING METHODS

It has been previously explained that a supervisory program should be continuous. This means not only from month to month, and from year to year, but also from day to day. We may scoff at the informality of the old-fashioned way in which father taught son or tradesmen taught apprentices, but it was more effective than most present-day methods for only one reason. It continued from day to day, and the help given was by application, not theory.

The training program is helpful if conducted in an academic manner, but benefits can be doubled or tripled if the classroom approach is supplemented by immediate personal application of what has been taught. If the supervisor has acquired knowledge of industrial relations by listening and discussing, the seed of knowledge can be made to grow by having the trainer spend enough time at the supervisor's workplace, immediately thereafter, to assist him in applying this knowledge to his everyday bothersome problems.

This underlines the need for small training groups which, in any event, are desirable if maximum results are to be secured.

BENEFITS

The benefits to be derived from a soundly conceived and carefully applied supervisory training program are both tangible and intangible. Tangibly, direct savings are accomplished in the various operations. Intangibly, better employee and interdepartmental relations are secured; supervisors have a keener appreciation of the policies and desires of management; and the company grows and develops from within when a sound training program is followed.

I N D E X

405